Johnson, Sam Houston
My Brother Lyndon

DATE DUE

FEB 2 '78		
FEB 14 '78		
FEB 1 9 '79		
OCT 1 9 '79		
FEB 9 '83		
MAR 1 6 1983		
APR 20 '83		
MAR 21 '84		
MAR 21 84		
MAR 21 '84		
OCT 21 '87		
APR 20 '94		

My Brother Lyndon

My Brother Lyndon

by SAM HOUSTON JOHNSON

edited by Enrique Hank Lopez

COWLES BOOK COMPANY, INC.

NEW YORK

To

Josefa Johnson White,
my favorite of the family,
who had lots to do with any
success I may have achieved.

I want to thank Gilda Dahlberg, who introduced me to my editor and, with the help of
her son, Craig Dahlberg, did a tremendous
amount of research for the book.

I also wish to express my gratitude to
Holmes Alexander who gave me the inspira-
tion to write the book; and to Dr. and Mrs.
Glenn Wilson, whose research efforts were
enormously beneficial to me.

Acknowledgment

I want to thank my editor, Enrique Hank Lopez. Having graduated from Harvard Law School, which he attended on a scholarship after being elected to Phi Beta Kappa at Denver University, Hank has a keen analytical mind that helped me probe into every aspect of my close and extensive relationship with my brother Lyndon.

There were times when he acted like a relentless cross-examiner in a jury trial, but I readily forgave him when I realized that he simply wanted me to give a frank and revealing portrait of LBJ.

Since Hank learned politics the hard way (he was the Democratic candidate for Secretary of State of California in 1958, losing by less than 1 percent after receiving 2,500,000 votes), he had a professional awareness of the various phases of my brother's career. I also got the benefit of his broad literary experience as a frequent contributor to such national magazines as *Life*, *Harper's*, *Atlantic Monthly*, Horizon, and *American Heritage*.

Anyone who likes this book and finds enjoyment in it can give me full credit. Those who do not like the book can blame it on my editor.

Sam Houston Johnson

Contents

CHAPTER ONE

Dominoes after Midnight

About six weeks before he announced that he would not seek reelection, my brother Lyndon called my room about 2:00 A.M. and asked me to join him for a game of dominoes. When I got downstairs (my bedroom was on the third floor of the White House), he was hunched over the table, staring at a pile of dominoes in front of him.

He merely nodded when he saw me, and I could tell he had something heavy on his mind—like Vietnam, the student riots, or Bobby Kennedy. Whatever it was, he was worried and was probably hoping that a game of dominoes would distract him for awhile. Most of the time we played just for the hell of it, but sometimes he seemed too troubled to enjoy any kind of relaxation.

Back in the old days we used to play dominoes with some of his close friends on the Hill. His partner would be Jake Pickle or Homer Thornberry, while one of the girls (Lynda or Luci) would team up with me. Well, pretty soon I found out that Lyndon and Jake would pass signals to each other on the sly. Lyndon would lean back and say, "Wonder what ever happened to Judge Stokes?"

And Jake would look over his stack and answer, "Don't reckon I know, Lyndon. Ain't seen Stokes for a long time."

Obviously, "Judge Stokes" was just a code name for some particular domino—a double deuce or a three or something else. So Lyndon was really saying that he had deuces and Jake was telling him he didn't have any.

Knowing they were trying to pull a fast one, I would scramble their damned code. "Hell, I saw Judge Stokes just this morning," I told them. "Saw him two or three times before noon."

Now, that would really puzzle my brother. Because he realized we both knew that Judge Stokes was down in San Antonio, a thousand miles away. Therefore, he could only conjecture that I was aware of their secret signals, and that I might have more deuces than he had. Accordingly, he would hold back his deuce to keep me from going out. But since I really didn't have any deuces, he'd be trapped by his own trick.

Of course, a lot of his tricks I wouldn't (or couldn't) figure out, no matter how hard I tried. Lyndon has a theory about dominoes, a very complex system of moves and countermoves that will confuse even a smart man like Walt Rostow, who taught at M.I.T.

He especially likes to play against people with a big reputation for brains, and it's awful hard for a visitor to the ranch to get away from there without receiving the "Johnson treatment" at the domino table. It could be a distinguished head of state like De Gaulle or Prime Minister Wilson or a big businessman like Henry Ford II.

Just before he got out of the Presidential race, Lyndon had a game with Arthur Krim (head of United Artists Corporation), who was spending the weekend at the ranch to discuss campaign finances. Since he's mighty shrewd about anything dealing with numbers, Arthur caught on to the game right away; but Lyndon finally pulled some fancy maneuvers and won two hundred dollars from him before the night was over.

The next morning he took Arthur to church with him and

the family. When the collection plate came around, Lyndon pulled out the two hundred-dollar bills he had won the night before at dominoes.

"Here's the money I won from you, Arthur," he said. "It's going to a good cause."

Then, as Lyndon dropped the bills into the plate, Arthur smiled from ear to ear. "That's fine, Mr. President," he said. "Now I can declare it as a deduction from my income tax."

I wish I could say that my brother is as graceful a loser, but I can't. It's not the money that would bother him—he's always very generous in that respect—it's just that he hates to lose, period. I remember one particular game when Lyndon had only one domino left. Snake eyes, one on each side. Not knowing what he had, I put down a six-one that covered a blank-one at his end of the table.

"That's a stupid move," he said with some annoyance. "Why don't you cover this six over here with the double six in your hand? Hell, Sam, you ought to know you're supposed to play your big numbers at the end."

Well, I knew right there and then that I had blocked him off, that he'd been fixing to cover the one.

"Tell you what I'll do," he said, pretending to be generous with me. "I'll let you take it back so you can play your double six."

"No, Lyndon," I said, smiling to myself. "I'll just stay where I am."

"That's pretty damned stupid, Sam." He was riled up now. "Here I am, giving you a chance to play it right, and you're being stubborn."

He got so irritated that I almost laughed, but I managed to keep a straight face as he reached for another domino still mumbling about how dumb I was. After the next move, I finished the game and left him with that double one still in his hand.

"You wouldn't have beat me," he growled, "if you'd played right—the way you're supposed to, damn it!"

It was all for fun, of course, even when we got annoyed with each other. But on that particular night in February, 1968, he wasn't in the mood for any light banter. Mind you, it was way past midnight, and I could see he was very tired and deeply worried. He was having one of those sleepless nights that make an old man of anyone who becomes President, and he sorely needed a moment of diversion. So we laid out the dominoes and started our game. However, after a few moves I knew for sure his mind was somewhere else. I had just set down a double five and was waiting for him to make his move, but he just sat there—hunched over the table, absentmindedly fingering a double blank, and staring at some distant point far beyond the room. There was a look of loneliness and deep anguish in his eyes and his mouth was set tight.

"It's your move, Lyndon," I said, trying to distract him.

He didn't hear me. He just sat there, staring way off yonder. Finally, after a long weary silence, he slouched back in his chair and said, "That's just the trouble, Sam Houston—it's always my move. And, damn it, I sometimes can't tell whether I'm making the right move or not. Now take this Vietnam mess. How in the hell can anyone know for sure what's right and what's wrong, Sam? I got some of the finest brains in this country—people like Dean Rusk, Walt Rostow, and Dean Acheson—making some strong and convincing arguments for us to stay in there and not pull out. Then I've got some people like George Ball and Fulbright—also intelligent men whose motives I can't rightly distrust—who keep telling me we've got to de-escalate or run the risk of a total war. And, Sam, I've got to listen to both sides."

Well, he paused there awhile, still pinching that blank domino with his big tough fingers. His eyes looked sadder than I've ever seen them, and I couldn't help thinking about all those damn dirty hippies calling my brother a murderer.

"Sam Houston," he finally said. "I've just got to choose between my opposing experts. No way of avoiding it. But I sure as hell wish I could *really* know what's right."

Then pulling himself out of his chair, he wrapped his robe around him and started to leave, his loose slippers slapping a little on the carpet. I saw him to the door and watched him shuffle down the hall toward the elevator on his way to the Situation Room in the basement to get the three o'clock report from Saigon. He looked tired and lonely as he pushed the down button.

CHAPTER TWO

Tough, Tender Years

My brother and I have had much happier times playing dominoes. As a matter of fact, it was Lyndon who taught me the game when I was only four years old. I remember he was very gentle and patient with me—like any big brother would be. He even let me beat him that first time; and I want to tell you that was a sure sign of brotherly affection, because Lyndon never let anybody beat him at anything if he could help it—even then, when he was only ten years old.

He was always kind and protective toward me, and sometimes it caused him considerable discomfort and embarrassment. I have in mind my very first day in school. Just before noon I was up at the blackboard, trying to scribble my name, when I had a sudden urge to relieve my bladder. Not knowing what to do, I just stood there squirming like a worm, rubbing one leg against the other and pressing that chalk against the board till finally it broke. When it broke, I broke, and let out a warm stream that soaked through my short knee pants and puddled on the floor. I started to cry.

After awhile, the teacher asked one of my classmates to fetch Lyndon. He was upstairs in the sixth grade. First of all, he had to get some newspaper to clean up the mess I'd made on the floor, and he did it without the slightest show of annoyance. Then he led me out the door (I was still whimpering a little) and took me home, comforting me all the way and telling me it could happen to anyone. He also tried to explain all that business about putting up one or two fingers for permission to go to the outhouse, but I wasn't listening too much. I was too damned mortified.

When we got home my mother took me in her arms and let me cry a little more, finally convincing me that I hadn't ruined my life. She also told me about the one-and-two-finger signal that would automatically get me excused.

"You mean any time?" I asked. "Any time I put up my finger, the teacher will let me go?"

"Of course," she said. "She has to."

Well, that little lesson stuck in my mind right away, and later on I used it fairly frequently. Until, one day, it backfired on me. It happened late in May, at the height of the marble season. On this particular morning, just before school started, three of us (Joe Crider, Otto Flemming, and I) were in the middle of a game of marbles when the bell rang. Not wanting to give up during a winning streak, I told Joe and Otto to put up one finger as soon as class started. Then after awhile I would put up two fingers, so we could finish our game out yonder behind the outhouse.

But by the time I stuck up my fingers, after my buddies had left the room, Miss Richards had smelled a rat. She wouldn't let me go.

"I have to," I hollered, waving all four fingers. "My mama said you have to excuse me."

Now, that got her mad. "Listen here, Sam Houston," she said, pointing a ruler at me. "Your mother doesn't run this school. I don't care what she told you."

When I got home and told my folks what had happened, they were both terribly angry—but for different reasons. Mama was mostly worried that I could have wet my pants again. My daddy, on the other hand, resented the teacher's comment about my mother, especially since she had made it before all the kids in my class.

"Who in hell does she think she is?" he asked of no one in particular. "I'll have to take that girl down a peg or two."

By sheer coincidence he ran into Miss Richards at the post office the following afternoon. And when she said, "Hello, Mr. Sam," he simply ignored her—didn't even look her way. Knowing that he was a state legislator and the most powerful politician in Johnson City, she was disturbed by this silent treatment.

"Is something wrong, Mr. Sam?" she asked, standing directly in front of him.

"Yes, by God, there is. I don't like the way you handled that business with my boy yesterday."

"But Sam Houston was pulling a trick. He didn't really have to go. He just wanted to play. . . ."

"I'm not talking about that, Miss Richards. You were quite right in not letting him go. That *was* a trick, and I'm glad you caught him. But I don't hardly appreciate that wisecrack you made about his mama not running the school. Now, my wife never throws her weight around—but she damn well could! And you'd better remember that, young lady."

He was merely reminding her (not too obliquely) that mama was on the school board and the editor of her own newspaper. She was probably the best-educated woman in the whole county—majored in journalism at college and even taught elocution at the local high school. Her side of the family had intellectuals all the way back. It was her grandfather, a Baptist preacher, who founded Baylor University. He also baptized a child who was to become the greatest hero in Texas history, General Sam Houston. Most of her ancestors had been preachers or wives of preachers—except for her own father, who was a very prominent lawyer in Fredricksburg.

We had politicians in the Johnson branch of the family and, of course, my brother Lyndon carried that aptitude to its ulti-

mate conclusion. Though he never got beyond the state legislature, my daddy was considered one of the brightest politicians in Texas, an easygoing but very perceptive man who
taught us all the fundamentals of politicking on the local level.

I imagine I was closer to him than anyone in the family.
When I was four or five years old, I would get up with him
before sunrise so we could talk awhile and have breakfast
together. I would make the fire in our coal stove while he
shaved in the flickering light of a kerosene lamp hung over
the kitchen sink, where he propped the mirror on a little shelf.
With my eyes half on him and half on the fire, I'd watch
him carefully scrape off his heavy beard with an ivory-han-
dled straight razor as he bunched his tongue inside his cheeks
to stretch out the skin. Once in awhile I would roll my tongue
inside my own cheeks, imitating every move he made and
feeling awful proud that this giant of a man was my father.

Then we would sit down at the kitchen table and casually
eat the breakfast he had cooked—fried eggs, smoked ham, hom-
iny grits or huge servings of pan-fried potatoes, all of it freely
sprinkled with Tabasco sauce. (Even to this day I carry a bottle of Tabasco everywhere I go and pour gobs of it on my
food.) Sitting there in the half light of dawn, my feet not quite
reaching the floor, I would listen hours on end to daddy's
stories about the legislature in Austin, about colleagues named
Sam Rayburn, Wright Patman, and Jim Ferguson, that great
populist who later became governor. Naturally, I couldn't
really understand most of what he told me, but I could sense it
was all very important and sometimes very funny. My daddy
had a way of poking fun at even the most serious things, a life-
long habit that sometimes brought him more trouble than he
bargained for.

After awhile, when the sun was staring hard through the
windows, Lyndon and my sisters would come in with my
mother and we would all sit around the kitchen talking about
most anything. We were a family of great talkers with strong
opinions on just about any subject you could mention. There

was nothing neutral about us. But much as I appreciated the more general family conversations, I preferred those long early-morning sessions alone with my daddy—sort of talking man-to-man, even though I was only four or five years old.

I don't think Lyndon ever had that kind of relationship with daddy. As a matter of fact, there was a kind of tension between them, a sort of competition that frequently occurs between a father and the oldest son. Even in small unimportant matters, they seemed to be competing. Take this, for example:

When I was about three years old and Lyndon was nine, we used to sleep together in a bedroom off the kitchen next to daddy's room. (Mama stayed with the girls on the other side of the house.) Well, about midnight my daddy would yell, "Sam Houston! Come in here and get me warm."

And I would crawl out of bed and scramble into his room like a little puppy, snuggling my always-warm body against his. Pretty soon he'd fall asleep and start snoring, with me right next to him, holding mighty still and afraid to squirm even a little bit because it might awaken him.

Then I'd hear Lyndon calling me. "Sam Houston, come on back. I'm getting cold."

Back I'd go, moving away from daddy quiet as a burglar and snuggling up to my big brother. But that might not be the end of it. Later on, maybe at three or four in the morning, daddy might get cold again and would call me back to *his* bed. That's what you get when you've got a warm body: People seem to impose on you.

Aside from competing with him in little things around the house, Lyndon sometimes objected to certain aspects of my daddy's life style—drinking, for example. This was during the early stages of Prohibition, when most of the menfolk in our town used to get together for an afternoon beer at a saloon down on Main Street. (Once in awhile the bartender might have a little bootleg liquor under the counter for special customers, but he'd be taking a chance in a Baptist community like ours.) My daddy, being a state legislator, would frequently meet some of his political cronies at the saloon and spend a few hours there discussing the latest developments at the state capitol.

Well, that was what Lyndon objected to: Old Demon Rum. Since he was only twelve or thirteen years old, I guess he didn't realize that 3.2 Hoover beer (or was it Coolidge beer?) was about as intoxicating as soda pop. Or maybe it was just the smelly saloon that Lyndon couldn't stand. Whatever his reason, he once got together a couple of friends and they stood outside the saloon yelling for their daddies to get out.

"Come on home! Come on home!" they kept shouting, holding the swinging doors wide open so all the drinkers could see them.

At first my daddy—he told me about this much later—thought it was all a joke. So did his friends. He even offered Lyndon a quarter to leave the place, and that was a right good bribe in those days. But when Lyndon refused it, my daddy knew it was serious. No, sir, nobody could sway Lyndon when he had his back up. Well, after staying awhile to let his friends know he wasn't yielding to pressure from a mere kid, daddy came on home somewhat mortified and rather annoyed with my brother.

That was only one example of how stubborn and independent Lyndon could be. No one could boss him or even persuade him to do anything he didn't want to do. Even as a very small boy, he always resisted the authority of my grandmother, who lived at our home and took care of us while daddy was legislating in Austin and mama was working at her newspaper office. It was a battle of wills between grandma and Lyndon, marked by frustrated tears on her part and stiff-lipped silence on his.

More than once she told my folks and anyone else who would listen, "That boy is going to end up in the penitentiary —just mark my words!"

Having lived in the White House with Lyndon, with all

11

its terrible restrictions, I sometimes think grandma was dead right. More than she ever imagined. Anyone who's elected President *is* serving a stiff sentence in my opinion. His whole life is circumscribed, with no freedom or privacy whatsoever. I am not only referring to all the Secret Service men who continually surround you wherever you go, hardly ever letting you go off on a sudden whim. I am also referring to a kind of public imprisonment to which the President is subjected, his every word and gesture coming under the most severe scrutiny. Indeed, his whole family shares that cell without walls. Even I came to feel like an inmate on the third floor of the White House. My few visitors had to go through a security rigamarole—like gun molls visiting their husbands at Sing Sing. It was even worse when I stayed in the family quarters on the second floor—across the hall from Lyndon's room.

For quite understandable reasons, no one could have visitors on that floor—not even Lady Bird or the girls—without specific Presidential permission. The reasons were quite obvious: Lyndon might be having a very private and confidential meeting with the Russian ambassador or some head of state—or perhaps a private consultation with one of his outside advisers like Abe Fortas or Clark Clifford—and he wouldn't want any of *our* guests running into them in the corridor and thereafter leaking their little tidbit to the press. ("Guess who visited LBJ last night?")

I was damned happy to move up to the third floor, where the visiting procedures were a bit more relaxed. Even so, I couldn't resist joking about "my cell on the upper tier," and I would always give my own special signal when I was driven through the outer gates of the White House—raising my two wrists held close together as if I were handcuffed.

"Back to my cell," I'd tell the gatekeeper. "Back to my cell."

Well, that was the "penitentiary" my grandma never contemplated when she was predicting Lyndon's future back in 1920, when she thought of him as a hopelessly incorrigible delinquent who wouldn't obey anyone.

I, on the other hand, was far more submissive and obedient. To be perfectly frank, I wanted her approval and worked hard to earn it. My brother refused to do certain chores around the house, but I cheerfully did more than my share—chopping wood, milking the cow, sweeping the barn, toting water from the outside pump, and running errands. And come to think of it, I can't really blame Lyndon for passing up the chores. If I had a little eager-beaver brother to do them, I would do the same thing. Nor did I ever complain. I worked hard for grandma because I wanted her praise, her constant approval, and sometimes went overboard to get it. I have in mind a little trick I pulled with the milking.

Having gotten grandma's proud praise for getting quite a bit of milk from our cow (almost ruining her teats with too much pulling and probably starving her calf), I went a step further the next day. After draining that poor animal of every drop of milk she had, I stopped by the water pump and gave the pail a real filling. Right to the top. Well, it didn't take grandma a single minute to see what I'd done.

"Bend over, Sam Houston," she said with a mean scowl on her face. "I'm going to teach you a good Christian lesson right here and now."

I know Lyndon would have never bent over to take a whack on the rump. Not from her or anyone else. But I did. I just leaned over and let grandma have a good slap at the boniest part of my anatomy. Then, of course, she cried more than I did, hugging me close and begging me never to doctor any more milk again. She was kind even when she was punishing me, so I naturally tried to please her.

Someone once asked me what I wanted to be when I grew up and—realizing that grandma preferred girls because my brother had turned her against boys, and also knowing she was a strong Baptist—I quickly said, "I wanna be dandma's dirl and a Baptist preacher."

That, of course, became a family joke, and a few years later Lyndon used it to good effect when he delivered the valedictory address to his graduating class at Johnson City High School. I was about ten years old then and was sitting in the front row with my closest buddy, Clem Davis, whose father was a local preacher. Coming to the main theme of his speech —ambition—Lyndon said that everyone should have a special goal in life, a well-defined ambition. "Now, just take my brother, for example. He's sitting right there in the first row. Well, several years ago someone asked him what he hoped to be when he grew up, and he said, 'I wanna be dandma's dirl and a Baptist preacher.' Well, Sam Houston can't be a girl, but he might become a preacher."

Everybody laughed, of course, except me. I covered my face to hide my tears and ran out of the gym-auditorium before Lyndon finished talking. It took me a long time to get used to the ribbing I took from everyone in town, especially the kids my own age, but I was eventually able to see the humor of it and even laughed at myself when Lyndon started repeating the story during his first campaign for Congress.

In a quite different way, I used to embarrass Lyndon by certain things I did. He was particularly mortified by some of the outside jobs I had when I was about nine years old. Aside from shining shoes on Main Street and sweeping out the church, I landed a job behind the counter of Joe Crider's restaurant (best restaurant in Johnson City—in fact, the only one), which also dispensed a little bootleg whiskey on the side.

On my second day at work I saw Crider's brother, Otto, emptying a crate of Coca-Colas into the sink and then filling them with some brownish liquid from a pewter jug. Then, after carefully replacing the bottle caps and tamping them down with the heel of his big bruising hands, Otto put them on a high shelf above the big icebox—out of my reach.

Though I didn't know he had put whiskey in those bottles, I had a suspicion there was something better than Coke in them. So that afternoon, when one of Lyndon's schoolmates came in and asked for a Coke, I grabbed a chair, put a wooden box on top of it, and reached for one of the bottles on that high shelf.

"Hey, boy," Crider hollered, "what the hell you doin' up there? Get your cotton-pickin' hands off that liquor!"

It didn't take long for that story to get around town. "Hey, you hear about Sam Ealy's little boy peddling bootleg licker? That's what they say. Right over there at Joe Crider's place. Sam Houston Johnson—only nine years old—selling booze in Coke bottles." Wild talk like that, all over town.

In no time at all Lyndon got wind of it and nearly blew a gasket. His friend, that young customer I was about to serve, probably told him and added a few embellishments of his own. My daddy was pretty upset, too, but he was even more worried about what people would think about him letting his little boy work behind a lunch counter, like a poor orphan kid. So I had to quit my best job to spare Lyndon and my daddy any further embarrassment.

My income was drastically reduced when I left Crider's payroll—he paid me about a dollar a week, as I remember—but I managed to earn a few nickels here and there, running errands at the general store and shining boots for a few ranchers who came shopping on Saturday afternoons. Finally I saved up $11.20, free and clear of any outside debts. And that's when Lyndon approached me with a business deal.

"How about you and me goin' partners, Sam Houston? Get together and buy us a secondhand bicycle."

Well, I couldn't have been prouder. My favorite and only big brother—six years older than me—offering to be partners with me! Of course, I accepted. I couldn't have been more pleased. Without waiting another minute, I rushed into the house and got my bank (an old tobacco pouch) from under a loose floorboard in the pantry, and followed Lyndon down to the bicycle shop.

I don't remember what we paid for it, though there was a lot of haggling between the shopkeeper and Lyndon, but I imagine my savings covered most of the price. Whatever the cost, it was certainly a beautiful bike. Curved racing handle-bars, a chrome back fender, and a practically new red-and-white paint job on the frame. There was just one problem: It was too damned big for me. My toes could barely reach one pedal when it was in the up position, the other pedal being at least eight inches beyond my other foot. For Lyndon, who was a tall, gangling fifteen-year-old with legs like a grasshopper, the bike was a perfect size.

Apparently sensing my sudden doubts, my brother tried to perk up my spirits. "I'll let you have the first ride," he said. "You can be the senior partner."

With the bicycle propped against his body, he helped me onto the seat and gave me a shove down a dirt road with a slight incline. Unable to reach the fast-moving pedals as the bicycle picked up speed, I soon panicked and turned the han-dlebars with a desperate jerk that sent me sprawling into a nearby ditch.

Fortunately, the ground was soft so I wasn't hurt much—just a scratch on my elbow. Too stunned to cry at first, I lay there staring at the overturned bike. Then I let out a bellow like a lost calf, tears sprouting from my eyes like two gushers as Lyndon ran up to take care of me.

"Don't cry, Sam," he kept saying, his skinny arm around my even skinnier shoulders. "I'll teach you how to do it right."

Well, he never got a chance to—at least not on that bi-cycle. When my daddy came home that night and heard about my accident and about our partnership, he gave Lyndon a lecturing he never forgot. I had seldom seen him so angry.

"You give Sam Houston his money back," he finally said, in a low, threatening voice. "And don't you ever make a deal like that again."

Besides getting my money returned, I got a brand-new midget bicycle from daddy and my brother taught me how to ride it without putting my hands on the handlebars. But I wish to hell Lyndon hadn't taken our daddy's admonition so seriously, because I'd sure like to be his partner right now.

In spite of these occasional strains between daddy and Lyndon, there was a very decided sense of family loyalty between them, a solid standing-together against any outsiders whenever a conflict arose. I especially remember an incident that occurred when my brother was a senior in high school.

He was dating Carol Davis, the prettiest and the most popular girl in her class. As you would expect, there were several other people interested in her, one of whom was the basketball coach. To make matters just a bit more complicated, Carol's father didn't much care for Lyndon because he knew that his wife had once been engaged to our father. However, none of this bothered my brother in the slightest degree, even though the coach was a big husky fellow with a fairly good reputation in local athletic circles.

Lyndon was the brainy type who didn't have to prove himself with a show of muscle. In fact, he didn't have much muscle to show. Standing close to six feet tall and weighing less than a girl cheerleader, he damned well had to rely on his brains.

Now, that sets the stage for an October afternoon in 1924, when Lyndon got into a harmless schoolboy scuffle with his best friend, Luke Simpson. They had been squirting water at each other at an outdoor fountain and later started to wrestle in a friendly way, pushing and grabbing with no harm meant. Suddenly Coach Donley ran up and pounced on Lyndon, picking him up off his feet and slamming him to the ground. No warning, mind you—just a sudden attack that caught my brother off guard.

I didn't see all this because I was spending the recess in class, reviewing my geography lesson for an impending exam. But when Margy Wills came running in to tell me the coach was "trying to kill Lyndon," I ran outside and saw all these kids huddled around my brother.

My God, I was mad! I wanted to kill that coach. Yet all I could do was to sit down on the school steps and bawl like

17

I never had before. After awhile Lyndon put his arm around my shoulder and led me home; he shed not a single tear but merely set his mouth tight, never saying a word.

He finally broke his silence when we got home. It was a short, flat statement.

"I'm not going back to that school," he told mama. "I'm quitting."

Though I hadn't seen a thing, I gave her a tearful but lively account of what had happened, adding an imaginary kick to give it more substance.

"You don't have to exaggerate, Sam Houston," my brother broke in. "It was bad enough as it really was."

Mama, of course, reacted as any mother would. She hurried over to the telephone, cranked it several times and asked the operator to ring my father's number at the state legislature in Austin. Without even waiting to hear the end of what she started to say, he rushed out of the capital in his Chevvie and raced on home over the bumpy unpaved highway to Johnson City.

I was waiting on the porch when he drove up, and he seemed bigger than usual as he climbed out of the Chevvie—bigger and angrier than I had ever seen him. He was six-feet-three inches tall and rather husky, and everyone around town knew that he could be mighty rough when the occasion demanded.

Some years earlier, when he had been threatened by some Ku Kluxers, he had not hesitated to use a baseball bat to fend them off. Though naturally quick-tempered, he had trained himself to be more deliberate in times of stress, and on this occasion he took special pains to get all the facts before he acted. First of all, he talked to Lyndon and then to some of his friends, all of whom verified my brother's version.

"Now I'm going to hear Coach Donley's side of it," he told mama. "And he'd better have a damned good explanation."

The coach lived in a rented room near the school, but he wasn't there when daddy came around.

"Must be at the school playground," someone told him.

When daddy got near the school, three or four of us kids trailing behind him, Coach Donley apparently spotted him and took off like a scared rabbit. Jumped over the fence and disappeared. His landlady later had to mail him his belongings. Now, there was a Nervous Nelly if I've ever seen one.

With the coach gone, Lyndon was persuaded to return to school, though he was not entirely happy about it. He was undoubtedly grateful for daddy's intercession, yet he would have preferred to deal with the matter in his own way. Almost totally independent and self-reliant, he often seemed to resent outside help—especially from his parents. One of his recent biographers referred to Lyndon as a "spoiled mama's boy," and that is easily the most stupid of several stupid judgments in an otherwise interesting book.

I rather suspect that our biographer, Professor Goldman, is one of those mama's boys who, having suffered all their lives from excessive maternal attention, tend to view everyone else's problems in the same light. Lyndon may be uptight about certain things—none of us is free of emotional stress—but the professor is way off the track when he starts talking about LBJ having a mother hang-up.

I also suspect, reading between the lines of his tragic book, that he suffered the misfortune of being exposed to the "Johnson treatment" on one or two occasions. He might have run into Lyndon in a White House corridor, with the President looking straight at him and *through* him without giving the slightest sign of recognition, then brushing past him without acknowledging his stammered "Good morning, Mr. President."

Or perhaps, in one of the very few group conferences he attended in the Oval Room, Professor Goldman made what he considered an important or clever suggestion and got a different variation of the Johnson treatment. That's when Lyndon appears to be listening with a tight, quick-flickering half smile and a cool look in his eyes—probably thinking, "What-the-hell-is-this-ass-talking-about?"—then, with no response whatsoever, turns to someone else and says, "Okay, what's on your mind?"

To be ignored like that, especially if you've been accustomed to the rapt attention of Princeton undergraduates, is liable to curdle even the gentlest cream puff. Small wonder that the good professor poked around in his verbal grab bag for the most insulting label he could find ("mama's boy"), which he slapped on Lyndon with high glee.

Now if he wanted to call *me* a mama's boy, he might be closer to the truth. I was also daddy's boy, grandma's boy, and even sisters' boy. They all spoiled me and got very little discouragement from Sam Houston. In that respect, Lyndon and I were two different species: I liked to be pampered; he liked to rebel.

Just after he graduated from high school with honors, for example, he decided to take off for California although he knew mama and daddy wanted him to stay home and go to college. The California fever had struck several other boys, all older than Lyndon, and they had all pitched in to buy a used Model-T to drive out to the coast about midsummer.

Naturally, in a small town like Johnson City, the word spread pretty fast that the two Crider boys, Jeff Simpson, and Sam Johnson's older boy were going to Los Angeles. Even the most casual visitor, stopping at a local lunch counter for a cup of coffee, would know about the big safari before he got his first refill.

"Sure don't know what's got into these kids now days," the waitress would say apropos of nothing in particular. "Get a flea in their britches and off they go to California or Alaska or most anywheres."

"That so?"

"Oh yes, indeedy. Happening all the time." Then a long pensive stare out the window. "Now take that Johnson boy. Skinny little old thing—not more than fifteen years old, and he's fixing to go. That's him over there, working away on that broken-down flivver they're goin' to drive. Crazy damn kids. Ain't ever satisfied."

"That Sam Johnson's boy?" the visitor would ask, knowing about daddy who represented the whole county.

"Yep. That's him all right. And let me tell ya, Mr. Sam ain't too happy about this California business."

"No, I reckon not."

"You darn betcha he ain't. Why, he was in here yesterday —here's some more coffee—and he was telling me, sittin' right there where you are, that the minute he sees Lyndon gettin' into that car to take off, he's going to yank him out by his britches and drag him off home. That's just what he said, sitting where you are. Goin' to yank him right out in front of everybody."

"Means it, I guess."

"Oh, sure he does. Mr. Sam's got a real temper. Don't pay to mess with him."

When I heard conversations like that, even with daddy's language toned down a few decibels, I simply assumed that Lyndon would never be able to leave. Which just goes to show how little I knew about my big brother. Quite obviously, he had heard about daddy's widely announced threat. He was merely biding his time for the right moment. It came sooner than expected.

Having heard of a cheap farm for sale near the town of Blanco, my daddy (who occasionally dealt in real estate) rushed over to put in a bid or at least investigate that possibility. Well, the minute he took off, Lyndon ran into his room, pulled his already packed suitcase from under the bed, and quickly called his fellow travelers together. In less than ten minutes they stashed their bags inside the Model-T, filled the gas tank, and zoomed out of town at close to thirty miles an hour.

Evidently convinced that she couldn't stop him, or perhaps feeling it would be best for him to get away from home for awhile, Mama made no effort to make him stay. She did, however, phone Aunt Josefa in Fredricksburg to tell her that Lyndon had forgotten to take a pillow.

"If you can stop them as they come past your place, would you please give Lyndon one of your pillows and I'll give you one of mine?"

It's a good thing Aunt Josefa never got to stop them. Can you imagine my brother trying to live that one down?

Daddy came home about three hours later and immediately exploded in several different directions. I had never heard such rich, inventive language. But when he finally got himself together, he went into action. Cranking the phone as if it were an ice-cream machine, he called the sheriff of nearly every county between Johnson City and El Paso on the far western border of Texas, asking them to arrest his runaway son and send him back home. To no avail. Lyndon, apparently anticipating such a move, had persuaded his friends to travel by night and sleep by day, so they drove through all those previously alerted counties while the sheriffs were snoring away.

With Lyndon gone to California and daddy off to the state legislature in Austin most of the time, I became the part-time chauffeur of the family Chevvie at the age of ten. Neither my mother nor my sisters could drive. And once I got the feel for driving, of course, I wanted a car of my own and started saving money to buy a tin lizzie.

Two of my school buddies, Otto Schultz and Jim Hoag, agreed to go partners with me and, after scrimping along for more than a year, we bought the most beautiful beat-up car ever to survive the junkyard. Somehow, after days of tinkering under the hood and below the chassis, we got her running by fits and starts—sometimes going a full half mile before she conked out.

Though it wasn't much of a car, I soon found out that it served at least one useful purpose. One evening, when I asked daddy to let me use his Chevrolet, he turned me down stone cold.

I begged him nearly a half hour and he kept saying no; then I hit upon another strategy. I asked mama for the flashlight, which I'd hidden in a clothes hamper. So we went searching around the house, under the sofa pillows, behind the bureau, and every which place. Finally, my daddy got irritated and asked why I was so desperate to find the flashlight.

"Well, I'm going out in my car," I said. "And I can't see too good at night on accounta my lights ain't working too good. Don't work at all 'til the motor's running. So I have to use a flashlight—hold it outside with one hand—so I can see where I'm driving."

When I told him that, daddy made a noise that was half snort and half groan. Reaching in his pocket for the car keys, he threw them at me. "You win, Sam Houston. Take my damn car."

Though she was somewhat amused by my back-door strategy, mama took strong exception to daddy giving in that way. "You're spoiling that boy," she said. "You'd never allow Lyndon to pull a trick like that. You've been too easy on Sam Houston and too strict with Lyndon. No wonder he took off for California."

That was only one reason, of course. Probably the least important reason. I imagine Lyndon was principally motivated by a sense of adventure, just wanted to roam somewhere else. He had been gone several months, writing us short, not-too-informative letters whenever the spirit moved him, which wasn't too often. He and his friends had picked grapes for awhile but soon decided the work was too hard and the pay too low. They also got tired of eating warm grapes (the sun was blistering hot) for breakfast, lunch, and supper.

Eventually Lyndon hitchhiked into Los Angeles to visit Tom Martin, a prominent criminal lawyer related to my mother. Probably prompted by mama during a long phone conversation, Cousin Tom asked my brother to stay at his house and offered him a job as an errand boy in his law office. One of his duties was toting the boss' briefcase to the courthouse, where Lyndon would sit hours on end listening to some fascinating verbal tugs-of-war between the best trial lawyers in California. As a high-school debating champion, he couldn't have found a more satisfying job.

Two or three months after my brother's arrival, Cousin Tom had to try a much-publicized case involving three Filipinos accused of murder. Having decided it would be rather difficult to handle the case by himself, he phoned his father in Texas to come help him. By strange coincidence, this second lawyer (Clarence Martin) was also in touch with mama; and when she found out he was going to Los Angeles, she made him promise to bring Lyndon home after the trial. Though he was a bit reluctant to come back, Lyndon later told me that the trial, which he attended from beginning to end, was a great climax to his California adventure.

In retrospect, I've always wondered why that courtroom experience didn't fire Lyndon with a burning ambition to become a lawyer, why it didn't prompt him to enter college right away so he could study law eventually.

Mama and daddy tried to make him go the moment he got back, but he simply refused. No amount of arguing or threats could make him change his mind. Instead, he took a job on a highway construction gang.

Fortunately—for him and for the political development of this country—my brother was never cut out for hard manual labor. With the hot Texas sun blistering his skinny shoulders and that constant prairie wind blowing dirt into his nostrils and ears and his hands getting raw from handling a pick and shovel, Lyndon quickly decided that brainpower offered a better road to success in this world.

He came on home and told mama, "If you can get me into San Marcos (Southwest Texas State College), I'll go right away."

CHAPTER THREE

Education, Politics, and Marriage

It has been generally reported that Lyndon hitchhiked all the way to San Marcos to begin his studies at Southwest Texas State College, and that's undoubtedly true. But he didn't have to. I'm sure my daddy offered to drive him there in the family car—it's only about sixty miles from Johnson City—but that was my brother's way of declaring his sense of independence. For a writer searching for a dramatic rags-to-riches angle, that picture of Lyndon trudging along a dusty country road with a cardboard suitcase is understandably tempting; but it gives a false impression about our family's economic condition.

Though he was never a wealthy man, our daddy was always able to provide for his family, sometimes more lavishly than others but never bordering on poverty. Our home was certainly no mansion by any definition, yet it was probably the nicest house in town while we were growing up. (Incidentally, I was born in that house and Lyndon was born out at the ranch, which means that more tourists visit *my* birthplace than *his* because it's much more convenient to reach.)

Therefore, it wasn't poverty that caused Lyndon to thumb rides to San Marcos, it was more independence. Not wanting to rely on anyone. He never knew (perhaps still doesn't know) that within a few minutes of his departure daddy grabbed the phone and called the president of the college.

"Dr. Evans, this is Sam Ealy Johnson talking. From down here in Johnson City."

"Yessir, Mr. Sam. What can I do for you?"

"Well, I've got my boy Lyndon headed your way—plans to matriculate in the next day or so, probably tomorrow."

"Oh, yes, Mr. Sam. I know all about him. Your wife called me a couple days ago. Look forward to having him."

"Well, I just wanted to let you know that we want to be sure he gets anything he needs. And if there's any expense involved, please bill me directly."

All that was unnecessary, of course, because Lyndon was determined to make it on his own. In fact, a few days later he got a job in the college president's office and thus never had any need for financial assistance from home. Perhaps more important than the money he earned, my brother had a first-hand exposure to an administrative process, getting a close look at how the president of an organization runs things, and how decisions are made.

Years later, when he was the youngest National Youth Administration director in the country, and doing a fine job, someone asked him where he had learned his administrative skills, and Lyndon told him he had gotten his initial on-the-job learning back at San Marcos.

Aside from his job in the president's office and an accelerated academic schedule, he immediately got involved in campus politics. In those days the varsity athletes ran everything, completely dominating all extracurricular affairs with a hard, heavy hand. For a tall, skinny student like Lyndon, who had no more athletic skill than a girl cheerleader, this state of affairs was naturally intolerable. He had to change it.

First of all, he came to some quick statistical conclusions

(his penchant for nose-counting comes from daddy): Less than 10 percent of the men students were varsity athletes, and the female students—most of whom seemed drawn to brawn—were also in a minority. Therefore, most of the non-athletic students secretly resented and probably hated the Saturday heroes, no matter how much they apparently enjoyed the games. Quite obviously, since every practical politician knows that hate and fear offer more forceful tools for organizing than love and respect, Lyndon had a rather fertile field at San Marcos.

Using his great persuasive powers as a born debater, he started organizing his effort in a gradual step-by-step fashion, buttonholing the skinny, four-eyed president of the biology club and then the chubby editor of the yearbook, quietly pressing the theme that "brains are as important as muscle."

Somewhere down the line he glued his separate forces together and called them the White Stars—as opposed to the Black Stars, the name of the varsity athletic group.

As you might expect, the huge swaggering "jocks" merely scoffed at the timid bunch of nearsighted challengers. And the more they sneered, the harder Lyndon's people worked, personally contacting every student on campus and making sure he voted.

Nobody except my brother thought the White Stars would win on that first go-around. Most of them just wanted to crack the wall a bit, get a little exposure for the next time. But Lyndon had sized up the situation like an old pro. He had that gut knowledge about the little man's resentment of the big man. His slate won by a comfortable margin, and the White Stars increased their percentage throughout Lyndon's career at Southwest Texas State.

I heard several installments of his campaign against the Black Stars during my periodic weekend visits to San Marcos, always listening with wide-eyed admiration as my brother outlined his strategy for the coming week. Even now, I can still visualize him restlessly moving back and forth in his room

above a garage just off campus, sometimes lounging on his
bed and then moving to a rickety wooden chair near the
window, his eyes gleaming with anticipation and his deep voice
tense with emotion.

Thinking back on those wonderful conversations (mono-
logues, really) that ran through the long Saturday afternoons
and Sunday mornings—skinny little brother marveling at
big skinny brother as if he were some kind of campus hero,
an intellectual All-American—I clearly see that political
strategems have always been my brother's natural vocation
and favorite pastime.

His politicking was always fascinating to me, but I have
often wondered how it affected the girls he dated in college.
How often would they tune him off with a glassy-eyed "uh-
huh" just as he got to the climax of some new ploy against
the Black Stars? Pretty often, I'd imagine.

As a matter of fact, both Lyndon and I had a similar problem in that respect. Perhaps overproud of my own debating
and oratorical skills when I finally got to college, I used to
tell my dates to name any subject and I'd immediately give
a half-hour speech on that subject. Some of them were wild,
silly-ass speeches that got nowhere, yet always given in a
serious booming voice like an old Baptist preacher, with all
kinds of fancy oratorical gestures. I imagine some of my girl
friends flinched when I asked them to "give me any old subject," but I enjoyed myself so much I don't think I paid much
attention to how they reacted.

Though I can't really pinpoint it, I'm quite sure I learned
this gambit from Lyndon. He undoubtedly made speeches to
his dates. Talking was plain recreation for us Johnsons, almost
a compulsion. But my speechifying to girls finally came to an
abrupt end on the night I was courting a pretty local girl during my senior year. In the middle of what I considered a
brilliant harangue on woman suffrage, she cut me short.

"Damn it, Sam Houston, shut your mouth! A rumble seat
is no place for oratory."

She wouldn't have said that to my brother. No girl, no matter how pretty or popular, would have dared to put him down under any circumstances. He wouldn't accept even an indirect put-down by the girl he was informally engaged to marry just after his graduation from San Marcos. She was one of the prettiest girls on campus and the daughter of the richest man in town, who also happened to be a prominent member of the Ku Klux Klan. Since our daddy was a liberal populist and agrarian reformer in the Jim Ferguson tradition, her daddy reacted quite negatively when she told him of her plans to marry Lyndon.

"I won't let you," he said. "I won't have my daughter marrying into that no-account Johnson family. I've known that bunch all my life, one generation after another of shiftless dirt farmers and grubby politicians. Always sticking together and leeching onto one another so the minute one starts to make it, the others drag him down. None of them will ever amount to a damn."

He probably said a lot more nasty things about the Johnsons; but that's the part she (poor naïve girl) later reported to Lyndon, no doubt intending to marry him despite her father's objections. Well, she never got a chance to express her own feelings. Lyndon never let her.

"To hell with your daddy," he said. "I wouldn't marry you or anyone in your whole damned family. But he's right about us Johnsons sticking together—we always have and always will, and we sure don't need to mix with your family to get along. We'll make it our own way. And you can tell your daddy that someday I'll be President of this country. You watch and see."

It was she who later told us about her damn-fool decision "to be frank" about her daddy's reaction and about Lyndon's blunt response. After my brother left Texas to work in Congressman Kleberg's Washington office, she sometimes visited our family in Johnson City, knowing that my folks liked her despite the stupid remarks of her reactionary father. Whenever she found out that Lyndon was home she would "just happen by," evidently hoping he would take her back. He, on the other hand, was cool and polite, completely controlling any residue of emotion that might still be lingering inside him. And the moment she'd leave, he would turn to mama with a certain impatience.

"Why do you let her come?" he would snap. "I don't want anything to do with that family. Besides they're a bunch of damned Kukluxers."

My daddy would have said "Kukluxsonofabitch." I had heard him use that phrase way back in my childhood, during those early-morning breakfast chats when I was only four or five years old. "Kukluxsonofabitch." I never realized that "sonofabitch" was a separate word, standing all by itself, until I got to high school. Even so, I found it difficult to say without that "Kuklux" prefix.

Of course, my daddy had good reason to tie those words together into a rumbling angry oath. The Ku Klux Klan had threatened to kill him on numerous occasions after he had made a widely publicized speech on racial tolerance before the state legislature. His words were quoted in newspapers all over the state, mostly in articles and editorials that condemned his stand, and almost immediately he started receiving anonymous phone calls and unsigned letters that threatened his entire family.

Then, one night, when we had a visit from his brothers George and Tom, my daddy got another one of those anonymous calls.

"Now, listen here, you kukluxsonofabitch," he shouted into the receiver, "if you and your goddamned gang think you're man enough to shoot me, you come on ahead. My brothers and I will be waiting for you out on the front porch. Just come on ahead, you yellow bastards."

Without hardly saying a word, the three men motioned the women into the cellar and got some shotguns from the hall closet. My uncles stationed themselves at either end of the wide porch and my father stood on the middle stoop, his eyes scanning the darkness as if to spot a rattlesnake. They stood guard for several hours, occasionally whispering remarks about the yellow-bellied Klan and telling us kids to keep out of sight.

They waited there until dawn, and the Kukluxsonofabitches never showed up. But after that my daddy carried a gun wherever he went, even as he sat in the House of Representatives at Austin. He never had to use it, though. They never came near him.

Considering our family's long-standing feud with the Klan, I guess it was providential for Lyndon not to marry that girl, after all; he would have had in-law trouble all his life. Her reactionary daddy and my populist brother would have argued till doom's day, neither side giving an inch, though it's quite possible Lyndon would eventually wear him down.

Aside from his innate debating skill, Lyndon has always been able to chip away at an opponent in a curious, relentless way—hardly letting him rest—until he finally gives up from sheer fatigue. Some people call it persuasion or bargaining. I think it's something more than that, something that can't be described in ordinary terms. You might call it person-to-person filibustering, with a heavy reliance on psychic stamina, which Lyndon has in vast quantities. (When I read about those all-night bargaining sessions between student rebels and college administrators, I feel pretty damned sorry for the administrators for letting themselves get hooked into that trap. They don't have even half the psychic energy of those angry kids.)

Lyndon may have been a born debater and persuader, but he also drew on other sources to sharpen his skills, paying special attention to the biographies of famous orators and political statesmen like Henry Clay, John C. Calhoun, Daniel Webster, and others less famous in a national sense. In this latter group was a man named Joe Bailey, who once represented Texas in the U.S. Senate. Just after I matriculated at San Marcos, my brother gave me a book on the life of Joe

31

Bailey, indicating certain episodes that caught his fancy. One of the passages he underlined in dark ink told about a speech the senator made at Nashville, Tennessee, in support of his party's Presidential nominee.

The crowd was apparently infiltrated by hecklers who wanted to embarrass him. At one point in his talk, when he was quietly attacking the opposing party with subtle sarcasm, the hecklers started shouting "Louder! Louder!"

Not knowing at first that they were merely heckling him, Bailey pitched his voice a little higher, but they still kept shouting "Louder! Louder!" Then he realized what their game was and suddenly shifted to a rumbling sonorous voice, like a circuit preacher in full flair.

"When we have all died," he said, "and passed over yonder to our great reward—when we get to the pearly gates and Gabriel blows his horn—there will always be some damned jackass hollering 'Louder, Gabriel, louder!' "

That was one of our favorite stories, and I used it quite frequently several years later while campaigning for Lyndon in his first congressional race. I would plant three or four hecklers in the audience with specific instructions to shout "Louder! Louder!" on a prearranged cue. Then, of course, I'd pull that Joe Bailey retort about Gabriel. It always got a big laugh and plenty of applause; and I'll have to confess that I let them think it was my own original spontaneous gimmick. Never gave the senator an ounce of credit. Though I can't recall any particular instance, I imagine my brother tried that same stunt at least once or twice.

While still on the subject of Joe Bailey, I'm reminded of another story that concerns our mama and daddy. This goes back to 1916, when Bailey ran for governor against a conservative named Pat Neff, who generally got strong support from the Baptists.

As the political leader of his district, daddy campaigned long and hard for Bailey, traveling all over the country to buttonhole every man he knew. He had always been a proponent of methodical precinct-by-precinct coverage by his volunteer staff, urging them to press the doorbell of every voter in every precinct.

"You've got to be a nose-counter in this business," he used to say, and he took particular pride in being able to predict the exact vote in his home district of Johnson City.

The Bailey-Neff election was the sole exception, a disturbing exception that caused daddy great concern. His pre-election forecast was in error by a margin of one vote!

"Someone double-crossed me," he complained in a hurt voice. "Some sneaky, two-faced louse lied to me. I covered this district myself, always have,. and I personally talked to every voter on the list—didn't miss a damned one. And, by God, I really counted noses, counted every one for us and every one against us. Wrote them down on my tally sheet like I always do. But someone lied to me—no doubt about that—someone told me a bald-faced lie."

Unable to bear his anguish (which had become comically exaggerated), mama finally put a stop to it. "That's sheer nonsense, Sam," she said. "No one lied to you. And you *didn't* talk to everyone. You never asked *me* how I was going to vote. You took it for granted that I'd vote for your man. Well, I might as well tell you that I voted for Neff."

Daddy was flabbergasted. "You didn't!" he sputtered. "You couldn't have voted for that pinched-face reactionary fraud."

"Well, he's not pinched-faced—nor a fraud, either. He's a good decent Baptist, and that's why I voted for him. You won't catch me voting against my own people."

That was enough for daddy. He knew there was no point arguing any further. Certainly not when religion got in the picture.

With a long line of preachers in her family background, including the one who baptized Sam Houston, mama was naturally quite loyal to the Baptist church. My father, on the other hand, didn't practice much of anything. Though not exactly an atheist or agnostic, he never seemed to give much thought to a formal religion. Still, he was deeply committed to certain ideas that you might consider religious. He was certainly a believer in the dignity of all human beings regardless of race or creed, and some of that rubbed off on all of us.

When I was a teen-ager in Johnson City, my best friend was a Syrian named George Serur, whose father had a small store down on Main Street. One afternoon a tight-mouthed old lady took me aside and said, "Don't play with that boy. Don't you know any better? Why, he's nothing but an Arab or maybe a Jew."

I shook her hand off my arm and told her off. "Who cares if he's an Arab or a Jew or a Mexican or anything else?" I said. "He's my friend—my best friend."

When I told my daddy about it later on, probably that same night, he seemed right proud about what I'd said.

Though George never went to college with me, preferring to help his daddy with an expanding business, we still remained close friends. In fact, he would sometimes help me put on some big-shot airs with my girl friends. I would give Greta Schultz a note addressed to George at the store: "Give this girl a pair of silk stockings on my account," signed with a fancy "SHJ," and George might give her two pairs and tell her how important I was.

When I was leaving San Marcos to attend law school, he gave me a farewell banquet with bootleg whiskey smuggled from across the border. That's when I made a slightly boozey speech explaining why I was going to become a lawyer.

"Tell you why I'm going to law school," I said, winking at a friend named Jim Riley. "I'm going to learn how to defend old Jim, because if he keeps doing what he's always been doing, he damned sure is gonna need a lawyer."

Getting back to the original point—my daddy's proud reaction when I told the old lady that I didn't care if George was an Arab or a Jew or a Mexican—I personally feel such attitudes are a form of religion, which you can acquire without having to attend church every Sunday. Daddy didn't go to church very often, practically never, nor did my brother and I until many years later.

Sometimes, in a half-humorous mood, my sister Becky will tell people that "Lyndon never set foot in a church till he got to be President."

She's joking, of course. We both know he started going to church fairly often even before he was elected to the Senate. It was Lady Bird, more than anyone else, who encouraged his church-going, mostly to Episcopalian services. When he was Vice-President, he attended church regularly. Later, his every-Sunday attendance was widely publicized when he became President.

There were a number of cynics who openly accused him of "courting the church vote" by going from one denomination to another—Episcopalian, Baptist, Methodist, Catholic, Quaker, everything but a Jewish synagogue. They were dead wrong. I am personally convinced that the Presidency, with all its terrible and awesome burdens, made him feel a desperate need for greater spiritual comfort. In going from one church to another, I think he was unconsciously searching for some special type of solace, a kind of spiritual ease that no President can hope to have.

I, too, have felt that special need. During the long months I spent in a body cast, following surgery that left me with one leg five inches shorter than the other, a close friend introduced me to the Reverend Francis B. Sayre, Jr., grandson of Woodrow Wilson and distinguished Dean of the Episcopal Washington Cathedral. He came to talk with me day after day at a time when my spirits were at low tide, never once pitying me but somehow conveying an enormous sense of compassion. Gradually, he pulled me out of despair, mostly by showing me that there was still much to laugh about in this world, even when you're suffering intense physical pain. I owe no man a greater debt.

It's rather ironic that this same man, the Reverend Francis

B. Sayre, Jr., some years later made a public statement about the 1964 campaign that undoubtedly distressed my brother.* Coming from the lips of someone who had befriended me, the statement was even more distressing to me. I felt especially sorry for Lyndon because I knew of his high regard for the clergy.

When Luci converted to Catholicism before her marriage to Pat Nugent, no doubt irritating some of her kinfolk back home, my brother took a special interest in her new religion and frequently went to church with her. Though it's pretty late in life for him to change, I've heard Lady Bird speculating that he might someday convert to Catholicism. That wouldn't surprise me the least bit, but I am sure some members of the Johnson clan will find it hard to take. Aunt Jessie, for example.

Not long ago I tape-recorded an interview with her for the family section of the Johnson Memorial Library. Commenting upon her neighbor's criticism of Lyndon, she said, "There's one old woman down here who even said Lyndon was nothing but a Catholic—that he was trying to be like those Kennedys. Well, I wasn't going to let anyone call *him* a Catholic, not on your life. I let her have it right there and then. I told her Lyndon was no more Catholic than she was—and, let me tell you, she's right big in the local Baptist church. But I wasn't going to let her say that about Lyndon."

If my brother *does* become a Catholic somewhere down the line, I don't want to be around Aunt Jessie when she hears about it.

While on the subject of conversion, I am reminded of the

* *Editor's Note:* Speaking of Goldwater and Johnson, the minister said in part: ". . . We behold both parties completely dominated by a single man —the one, a man of dangerous ignorance and devastating uncertainty; the other, a man whose public house is splendid in its every appearance, but whose private lack of ethic must inevitably introduce termites at the very foundation. . . . We stare fascinated at the forces that have produced such a sterile choice for us; frustration and a federation of hostilities in one party; and in the other, behind a goodly façade, only a cynical manipulation of power."

36

Episcopalian minister from Austin, Texas, who wrote Lyndon a letter saying that he had heard he was thinking of becoming an Episcopalian and was therefore inviting him to join his congregation. "It would mean so much to me personally if you would become a member of my church," or words to that effect.

My brother was really annoyed when he read that letter. "I don't give a damn what it means to *him*," he snapped. "I'm only interested in what it means to *me*. We're not dealing with some damn social event!"

Whatever he decides—whether to remain a Protestant or become a Catholic—you can rest assured that he will have the complete understanding and support of Lady Bird. She's probably been the most important influence in his life.

They first met in 1934 at Eugenia Lasseter's home in Austin. Gene, who had gone to school with Lady Bird in St. Mary's Episcopal School for Girls in Dallas and later at the University of Texas, had previously suggested that Lady Bird might call my brother while on a sight-seeing tour in Washington. He was then secretary to Congressman Kleberg.

Probably feeling that no well-bred Southern miss should ever phone a total stranger, Lady Bird decided against it. But when Lyndon later walked into that social gathering in Austin, his tall lanky frame and curly black hair seemed to attract her. She was also immediately aware of his determined forceful personality. And when my brother spotted that lovely girl with the pale olive skin and beautiful dark hair, he lost no time getting acquainted with her.

Although he was escorting another girl, he somehow managed to get a moment of privacy with Lady Bird and asked her to have breakfast with him at the Hotel Driskill, where he generally stayed on his periodic trips to the home base. She didn't say yes or no, sort of left it hanging in mid-air. But the next day she "happened" to have an early-morning appointment near the hotel and she saw Lyndon sitting at a window table as she walked past the Driskill. On what some women choose to call "a sudden whim," she went inside and accepted a second, more-persuasive invitation to breakfast.

Afterward they took a long ride in the country, and Lyndon told her all sorts of things that she found unusually frank for someone on a first date—about how much insurance he carried, his net take-home pay as a congressman's secretary, his long-range ambitions, his experiences as a teacher of Mexican children who could barely speak English, and about his whole family. But it wasn't mere idle chatter. He wanted her to know his complete background and his full capabilities, because he had already decided to ask Lady Bird to marry him. And that's exactly what he did—he asked her to marry him on their very first date.

Taking her baffled silence as a possible yes, Lyndon went into high gear. With only a week's vacation from his Washington office, he felt a need to move fast and decisively. First of all, he brought her home to Johnson City and introduced her to a family that immediately liked the shy, soft-spoken girl from Karnack, Texas. My mother, who had an intuition in such matters, was particularly impressed with Lady Bird's highly cultured background. (Both she and my mother had majored in journalism, which, of course, gave them a certain natural tie.) From that very first meeting, we all knew that Lady Bird was a well-bred girl from an exceptional family.

Her daddy, Thomas Jefferson Taylor, had come from Alabama to open a general store in Karnack, quickly accumulating some parcels of good land in the surrounding area. Then he went back home to Autanga County to marry Minnie Lee Patillo, the very lovely daughter of a Confederate officer who had several large plantations. When he died without leaving a will, his lands were divided in a very strange way.

As Lady Bird recalls the story—it would make a great scene in a movie—someone wrote slips of paper relating to each tract of land, put the slips into sealed envelopes, and scattered them on the floor. Then Uncle John Patillo—wearing a heavy blindfold—crawled around the floor, picking up the envelopes and handing them out to the heirs in alphabetical order. Minnie Lee's envelope yielded a handsome inheritance, which was wisely invested by her husband in new lands around Karnack.

Lady Bird, whose real name is Claudia Alta Taylor (her Negro nursemaid tagged her with that nickname when she told someone, "Lawd, that child's purty as a ladybird.") remembers her mother as a soft elegant woman who sometimes seemed strangely out of place in that far-off bayou country with its backwoods atmosphere.

She went off to Chicago almost every year for the opera season and would come home with piles of books to read on the wide veranda, meanwhile listening to the records of Enrico Caruso, with Lady Bird and her two brothers sitting nearby. But aside from her cultural interests, Mrs. Taylor was an advocate of women's voting rights and of the integration of whites and blacks, even to the point of inviting certain blacks into her home for long conversations that no doubt disturbed her more orthodox husband.

When Lady Bird was nearly six years old, her mother died. Realizing his children needed a woman's care and affection, Mr. Taylor persuaded his spinster sister-in-law, Effie Patillo, to move into their home as a kind of second mother. It was Aunt Effie, an extremely gentle woman, who reared Lady Bird during her most formative years.

None of this personal history was revealed in her first visit with the Johnson family. Lady Bird was much too shy and reserved to discuss such matters on first acquaintance. But her shyness gradually gave way to curiosity as Lyndon continued his romantic blitz.

From Johnson City he drove her at a breakneck speed (he has always liked to mash the gas pedal to the floorboard when no troopers are around), burning the asphalt all the way, to the fabulous King Ranch owned by the Kleberg family near Corpus Christi. The ranch, a real showplace, stretches through four counties. As you might expect, the congressman said some nice things about Lyndon and his "brilliant future" in politics; and his mother drew Lady Bird aside and openly advised her to marry my brother right soon.

Pressing his advantage still further, Lyndon took her to San Antonio to several other friends of varying affluence and influence. Among them was Daniel Quill, an up-and-coming young politico who worked in the county clerk's office. Quill, of course, wanted to entertain his long-time buddy and his possible fiancé, but he was short of funds at that particular moment. Never at a loss for new strategies, he finally resolved his dilemma by taking them to a fancy gambling house that served lavish free meals to its prospective losers. The three of them, inwardly amused by Quill's sly ploy, ate some very fine steaks in the downstairs dining room and then walked out without ever visiting the gambling tables upstairs. Lyndon later told me those steaks tasted as good as stolen watermelon.

Still uncommitted though obviously affected by my brother's whirlwind drive, Lady Bird invited him down to Karnack to meet her father and Aunt Effie. Sometime during that brief get-together, while Lyndon was absorbed in charming her aunt, Lady Bird asked her daddy how he felt about her sudden suitor.

"You've been bringing home a lot of boys up till now," he told her. "This time you've brought home a man."

Yet, in spite of her father's positive reaction, she was still a bit reluctant to dive into marriage on such short notice. So when Lyndon pressed her to "say *yes* right now," as they were barreling along the highway back to Austin, she told him she'd have to wait awhile before making any firm commitment. More determined than ever, my brother resumed his campaign the minute he got back to Washington.

Pausing now and then in the furious work schedule he habitually forced on himself—he's always had energy to burn —Lyndon kept up a steady barrage of phone calls and letters to Karnack. Many years later, in one of the family albums,

I saw a photo my brother sent her at that time. The inscription scrawled across the bottom was: "For Bird, a lovely girl with ideals, principles, intelligence, and refinement, from her sincere admirer, Lyndon."

Though he himself hardly ever read a novel or poetry or any kind of fancy literature, preferring to give his attention to only those things directly related to his work, Lyndon admired Lady Bird's capacity to enjoy writers like Fitzgerald, Hemingway, Dreiser, Edna St. Vincent Millay, and some Russian authors he had never even heard of. He was also impressed by her appreciation of certain music and art that most men don't find too appealing. In that respect, Lyndon was pretty much like her daddy and his own daddy. I guess that's generally true all over this country. Most men are too damned busy earning a living, wearing their brains out to keep up with all the trade magazines and books that cover their own particular profession.

Take a tax lawyer, for example. I doubt that he's going to sit down and read a novel after a long, hard day of reviewing the Internal Revenue Code and a pile of difficult tax cases. He'll want to relax with television or something else that will let him unload his mind. Women, on the other hand, have a lot more time for heavy literature and symphony music and a greater inclination for culture of all types—classical ballet, pop art, foreign movies, plays, and concerts.

That's why Lyndon used to say that culture was the business of womenfolk, and he was pleased that Lady Bird had a natural refinement. She was all that he desired in a wife, and he certainly didn't want to lose her.

Less than two months later he came back to Texas, bound and determined to marry her. They took another long drive on a country road, and Lyndon renewed his previous arguments for an immediate marriage and tossed in a few fresh ideas, she meanwhile suggesting that they wait awhile, that they should get better acquainted.

"If you say no," he finally told her, "it just proves you

don't love me enough to dare to marry me. We either get married right away or we never will."

Thinking there was a possibility of losing him, she finally said yes.

Sometime later she told us, with a certain pride in her soft voice, that my brother let out a Texas yip you could hear in the next county.

Rushing to the nearest phone, he called Dan Quill in San Antonio and asked him to make all the arrangements. In view of the normal legal obstacles to instant marriages—health certificates, prior written applications, and the like—Lyndon picked the right man to cut all the red tape. Dan worked in the county clerk's office. Consequently, all the necessary documents were ready when the happy couple roared to San Antonio a few hours later. They were married that same evening, November 17, 1934, at St. Mark's Episcopal Church.

In the harum-scarum rush to get away to their honeymoon in Monterey, Mexico, they forgot to get their marriage certificate. Twenty years later Dan accidentally came across it among some old files in the county courthouse. In a properly sentimental ceremony, full of nostalgic remembrance, he delivered it to them on one of Lyndon's trips back home. Lyndon subsequently named Dan Quill postmaster of San Antonio.

CHAPTER FOUR

The Gamble with Roosevelt

As I have previously indicated, Lyndon became secretary to Congressman Richard Kleberg before his marriage to Lady Bird. Congressional secretaries, by the way, are not mere office workers or stenographers; they occupy a role comparable to that of a chief administrative aide to a senator. Lyndon got the job shortly after Kleberg's election in 1931.

My father had campaigned hard for Dick and gotten good results in Blanco County, so two or three days after the votes were counted he got together with Lyndon and me and said, "I'm pretty sure I can get one of you boys a job in Kleberg's office. Now, Lyndon's already finished college, while you're just starting, Sam—so it oughta be Lyndon."

Though he liked his work as a schoolteacher and coach of a champion debate team in a Houston high school, my brother readily agreed to move to Washington if the right kind of job were available. With that decided, daddy started the ball rolling. First of all, he talked with a local state senator, Willy Hopkins, to get an endorsement from him. Hopkins, however, seemed somewhat hesitant or at least noncommittal. So daddy went straight to Roy Miller, who had served as the chief campaign manager. No problem there.

"Why, sure, Mr. Sam," he said. "We'd be right glad to see your boy. Heard some good things about him."

Meanwhile Lyndon had talked with Senator Hopkins, and I imagine he therefore assumed the senator got him the job. Well, to be perfectly frank about it, I doubt that it was Hopkins or my daddy or even Roy Miller who got Lyndon started in Washington. He sold himself to Kleberg on that very first interview and was offered the top job right off the bat. You've got to have something more than political pull to make that kind of impression when you are only twenty-three years old.

Kleberg's gut reaction to Lyndon proved right from the very outset. In no time at all he took charge of that office and became a sort of congressman *de facto*, with his boss absent a great deal of time on a number of extracurricular matters. Easily the richest man in Congress, Dick had a flair for social life and was only too happy to have a diligent resourceful assistant "tending the store."

Busy as he was with the mixed bag of duties that befall a congressional secretary, Lyndon found time to favor certain other aspects of Capitol Hill. He especially liked to hear Huey Long's controversial speeches in the Senate and soon arranged for one of the pages to call him whenever the Louisiana senator took the floor.

It's always been unfashionable to say nice things about Huey, particularly in areas outside the South, but my brother never hesitates to tell people that he listened to every word that man said, "and I never heard him make a speech that I didn't think was calculated to do some good for some people who needed some speeches made for them."

Both Lyndon and I have always felt that Huey Long was greatly misunderstood by people who overreacted to his Southern style, who never realized that he was years ahead of his time in pleading the case of the common man. I'm afraid that any politicians from the Deep South or Southwest (including my brother) are frequently damned by Northern liberals from the moment they open their mouths. They might be saying and thinking the same damned thing as some Harvard-educated congressman from the East, but they'll never get credit for it. It's all-out snobbism against an accent, a mode of expression, a way of dressing, a way of eating—against a whole manner of living. I have even heard my brother's family ridiculed because they didn't have a fancy French chef in the White House kitchen, as if eating snails in garlic sauce will make you more civilized and human than eating plain meat and potatoes.

Now some of the same critics are making snide remarks about Nixon liking ketchup. I am certainly no partisan of his, but I'm damned sure that eating ketchup won't affect his attitude on Vietnam. The minute some people hear you're from Texas or Alabama or Mississippi, a whole rash of ugly assumptions are made about you—assumptions that become hard-ass conclusions that are never subject to rational proof or disproof. For these very same reasons, Huey Long was never given credit for the good things he advocated years before they were enacted.

I guess my brother expressed the case for Huey as well as anyone when he later said: "He thought that every man had a right to a job, and that was before the Full Employment Act. He thought that every boy and girl ought to have all the education they could take, and that was before the G.I. Bill of Rights. He thought that the old folks ought to have social security and old-age pensions. I remember when he scared the dickens out of Mr. Roosevelt and went on nationwide radio talking for old folks' pensions. And out of that probably came our social-security system. . . . He hated poverty with all his soul and spoke against it until his voice was hoarse."

Huey Long's political creed wasn't totally new to Lyndon; he had been exposed to that kind of thinking from early childhood. Our daddy had been a staunch supporter of that wonderful rambunctious liberal, James E. Ferguson, about the most popular governor in Texas history. He first came on the scene in 1914, suddenly announcing his candidacy with a bold provocative statement that made all the headlines and a few history books later on:

> Whereas, I, James E. Ferguson, am as well qualified to be Governor of Texas as any damn man in it; and Whereas, I am against Prohibition and always will be; and, Whereas, I am in favor of a square deal for tenant farmers; Therefore Be It Resolved that I will be elected.

Thus, at the age of forty-three, having been a wealthy lawyer and the owner of a bank and a big ranch—Ferguson literally became a traitor to his class in taking up for the forgotten poor. Campaigning in a very personal manner and talking to people in a language they could understand, he concentrated on the impoverished country districts, where his promise to limit the landlord's share of crops immediately won him the backing of ragged, starving tenant farmers. His anti-Prohibition stand earned him a more general support because drinking corn likker cuts across all classes of people, rich and poor.

I imagine a few Baptist males, having first agreed with their wives' mean-faced opposition to whiskey and gin, slipped in a vote for "Old Jim" in the welcome privacy of the voting booth. There must have been a whole army of secret drinkers double-crossing their Baptist womenfolk, giving Ferguson an upset victory over a better-financed opponent who had been endorsed by the entrenched party machine.

With the legislative support of people like Sam Rayburn, Wright Patman, and my own father, Ferguson managed to follow through on some of his promises to help the poor. But during his second term he was accused of certain financial hanky-panky with his own bank, and a reactionary Texas legislature impeached him and also banned him from ever holding public office. (Clarence W. Martin, a neighbor and political associate of my daddy, served as chief counsel for the governor.) However, his constituency of forgotten men wouldn't accept that verdict. In a special election they followed Old Jim's advice and voted in his wife, Miriam Amanda ("Ma") Ferguson, electing her again in 1932. To no one's surprise, Ma allowed her husband to give her a hand now and then—like every hour on the hour—providing him with an office next door so it wouldn't be too inconvenient.

Whatever his detractors may say or write about him, Jim Ferguson gave the poor a better shake in Texas and thus influenced a lot of young people like my brother Lyndon.

His much more conservative boss, Congressman Kleberg, would have probably disagreed with Lyndon's populist views, but he wasn't around the office often to hear them. (Later on, when my brother became a congressman himself, their opposing philosophies became readily apparent in their voting records. More about that in a future chapter.)

In any event, Kleberg allowed him a fairly free hand and even encouraged some of Lyndon's outside activities. He was, in fact, quite pleased when Lyndon got himself elected speaker of what was known as the Little Congress. This was a group composed of congressional secretaries and administrative aides to the senators.

Within a short time of his arrival, Lyndon walked into a meeting (his second one, as I recall) and surprised everyone by announcing his candidacy for speaker. They were even more surprised when he won. Had they known him better, had they ever observed his innate ability to organize his forces in a quiet, deliberate manner—always "pressing the flesh" in a methodical approach to all prospective voters—had they really known his political instincts, no one would have been surprised. Yet there he was, a freshman congressional secretary scarcely twenty-three years old, becoming speaker of the Little Congress without any prior noticeable signs of support.

Any serious student of history—if he were able to probe and understand the inner workings of that "second layer" of Congress, where congressional aides exercise prerogatives that aren't in the book—will soon realize that a great deal of Lyndon's subsequent success as a legislative genius dates back to 1931-32, when he was speaker of that Little Congress.

Though the Little Congress, had no official functions, being mostly a social club, it gave my live-wire brother an opportunity to meet and become intimate friends with congressional secretaries from all over the country. And in the course of their leisurely socializing, he learned an awful lot about their bosses, about their strengths and weaknesses, their pet legislative projects, their ties with other congressmen, and their real political inclinations as opposed to their public views.

He knew firsthand about Congressman So-and-so's troubles with a labor union back in Denver and how he had barely squeezed through with only 312 votes in the last election; about Senator Smith's worries with an up-and-coming governor who would challenge him in the next election; that Congressman Jones drank too much but never failed to show up for a vote on farm subsidies. As time went on, Lyndon was personally introduced to numerous congressmen after popping into an outer office to chat with some fellow member of the Little Congress. ("Come on in and meet my boss." "Sure—I'd be glad to.")

Fascinated with anything that concerned Congress and the people who make it run, he absorbed all that information because he had (still has) the kind of mental computer that never rejects any data, however irrelevant it may seem at the moment of input. And, in the final analysis, I guess nothing is ever totally irrelevant.

Aside from this continuous, perhaps compulsive, compilation of his own personal Who's Who, Lyndon was also becoming part of a vast network of political alliances between rising young politicos (all congressional secretaries fit that category, without exception) who would someday become congressmen themselves—or senatorial aides or lobbyists or government executives. These are the people who know where all the buttons are . . . and how to press them.

My own experiences with the Little Congress, when I later replaced Lyndon as Kleberg's secretary, were of a different order. Whereas my brother was mainly concerned with the serious aspects of the Little Congress, I was drawn to its social possibilities—particularly the periodic visits to New York by the board members. There they would be wined and dined by local politicians and businessmen, given the keys to the city, and interviewed on the radio. With that prospect in mind, I was easily persuaded by like-minded friends to run for speaker in 1938.

They chose me, let me be frank, because I had a reputation as a pretty good party-giver—plenty of booze and lovely girls. Even as a mere secretary, I was making more money than Congressman LBJ because I had an additional stipend as a public-relations man for the King Ranch. Consequently, I could afford a nice apartment, handsome clothes, and a resourceful valet to keep them spiffy. I would like to think it was my natural charm that drew congressional colleagues to my apartment, but I suspect it was the free liquor.

At any rate, some of them thought I would be just the man to organize a Little Congress fun-trip to New York, so they decided to run me for speaker. Confident that I had poured enough free liquor into enough people to get me elected by a comfortable margin, I put on a so-so campaign. Moreover, my opponent was a senatorial aide named Charlie Beemis, and I figured the congressional secretaries outnumbered the senate crowd by four-to-one. Well, I hadn't counted on how many enemies Sam Houston Johnson had made by being a show-off with his nice apartment and valet. I imagine a lot of the people who drank my liquor resented the hell out of me for being able to afford it. Anyway, they voted against me in sufficient numbers to elect Beemis.

Ordinarily, I would have followed my daddy's advice on

such occasions: "Take your licking and shut up." But my party-loving backers wouldn't let me; they had Broadway on their minds. So did I. Therefore we decided to meet the problem rear-on (or whatever is the opposite of head-on).

We got hold of the Little Congress charter and by-laws and devised an amendment that would give power over all social functions to a special five-man committee, thus stripping the speaker of this long-established prerogative. Then we shoved it into the agenda of the next meeting, treating it as a most trivial, innocuous matter that was indifferently approved by voice vote. With equal ease, our people got three positions on that five-man committee which, in turn, elected me chairman.

I don't really like to brag—except when the occasion presents itself—but I reckon the trip I organized to New York was one of the social highlights of that decade. Johnny Johnson, who worked for a Georgia congressman, was assigned to get us free railroad tickets from a lobbyist representing the Pennsylvania Railroad; Allen Emmett, a smooth talker from Tennessee, got all the liquor we needed from a well-known distiller; Ross Lazzari got show tickets through his congressman's New York office; and I arranged for some "complimentary suites" at a fancy Manhattan hotel. Mayor La Guardia, in a friendly little ceremony at City Hall, handed us a big wooden key that we symbolically tried in every keyhole we could find.

When I told Lyndon all we had done, he just shook his head like all big brothers do. "Sam Houston, you're a goddamned nut . . . but I guess you're having fun."

There you have two different attitudes about the Little Congress: Lyndon as a solemn, hard-working speaker and his little brother as a laughing goof-off social chairman.

I don't mean that he was always serious, because everyone knows that he's done his share of drinking and joking around; no one can tell a story with more gutty flavor when he's in the mood. I simply mean that Lyndon had never let pleasure interfere with his work. From the moment he entered Dick Kleberg's office, he started making his mark on Capitol Hill. No one could have been more satisfied than his boss, but he finally had to leave for personal reasons. Having sided with Kleberg in some family disagreement that needn't be discussed here, Lyndon later felt estranged from Mrs. Kleberg and thus decided to leave his job.

He came home to Johnson City and suggested that I take his place. "I've already told the boss that if Sam Houston can't get along with her, nobody can!"

A few days later he was named state director of the National Youth Administration (NYA), the youngest administrator (twenty-seven years old) in the whole country. He was also the most energetic. In the very first year he helped eighteen thousand Texas boys return to school for high-school diplomas and helped create government or private jobs for another twelve thousand youngsters. This was 1935, in the midst of the Depression, and the spectre of poverty all around him spurred him to work twelve to fourteen hours a day.

Once in awhile, when he got back to Washington to confer with Aubrey Williams and other NYA officials, we would go out to eat at some fancy place I had chosen on my ample income. Then, right smack in the middle of a fine steak dinner, he would ruin my appetite and make me feel guilty with a long recitation of statistics concerning the ill-housed and ill-fed people in his jurisdiction. When he got wound up that way, Lyndon would make you think his people in Texas were suffering more than any other people in this country.

He didn't only *talk* about the problem, he did his damndest to solve it. What's more, he expected all those who worked for him to do the same—not only expected, but *demanded* that they pour all their energy into the job. Right from the start, he got a reputation for being a tough man to work for.

Soon after Lyndon became administrator, while he was

still looking for someone to handle publicity, Maury Maverick recommended a friend of his, whom I'll call Roger Welton so as not embarrass his family.

"Now, Roger's got a drinking problem," Maverick told my brother. "But it's generally a weekend habit that shouldn't affect his work. And he's an awful damned good writer."

"Well, I don't mind a man drinking a little," said Lyndon, "as long as he does his job. Send him on over."

Just to make sure Welton understood his general attitude toward all his staff, Lyndon had a brief chat with him on the morning he reported for duty. "I frankly don't give a damn what a man does off the job. If he wants to drink, that's his business. But I do want to make myself clear on this point," he said, looking directly at the older man across the desk. "If your drinking should ever, in any way, affect the performance of your work, you'll automatically lose the job."

Saying he respected Lyndon's frankness, Welton accepted that condition and dived into his work with the kind of driving fervor my brother liked. And everything seemed to be going smoothly—Welton working hard from Monday through Friday, then drinking just as hard on the weekend—until one particular weekend late in October.

Lyndon had asked his staff to show up for a special Saturday morning meeting at headquarters. Through some misunderstanding (probably because he was out of town when the announcement was made) Welton failed to show up. As a matter of fact, he had already hit the bottle when one of the staff called his home to tell him about the meeting. Knowing he shouldn't show up drunk, Welton said he wouldn't be coming in.

Early Monday morning he walked into Lyndon's office and said, "I'm sorry about missing that Saturday meeting, chief. I had already started drinking when Jenny called."

"Well, I'm a lot more sorry than you are," said my brother. "I really am sorry, Roger, but you know what our deal was. If ever your drinking interfered with your work, you would automatically be fired. That's how it's gotta be, Roger, and I'm terribly sorry 'cause you've done a good job."

When Lyndon told our folks about it, probably on his next visit to Johnson City, daddy hit the roof. My God, he was mad at my brother. "How in the hell could you do such a thing?" he asked, rising from the kitchen table where they'd been having coffee. "You don't do yourself any goddamned credit by being so holier-than-thou. If he was doing his job well, that's all that matters, for Christsakes."

My sisters told me it was a lot stronger than that, but Lyndon stuck to his guns and stubbornly pointed out that Welton had agreed to those terms.

There is, of course, a more pleasant sequel to this story. Some years later Lyndon hired Roger Welton to work in his Senate office, setting forth the same condition but in somewhat different language. This time, when the inevitable happened and Welton failed to show up because he was drunk, my brother called him in the next morning and said, "Well, it's happened again, Roger, and you remember we agreed that if your drinking interfered with your work, I would have to take you off the payroll. That's what I'm going to do. I'm taking your name off the payroll and substituting your wife's name. You do the work, she gets the paycheck. I need you and want you to help me, but I know you ain't going to change your habits. So this way I can honestly say that I don't have any problem drinkers on my payroll."

Welton stayed on for a long time; and when he died from a liver condition, Lyndon let his wife stay on the payroll as a bona fide staff worker.

Lyndon's rising career as an NYA administrator came to an abrupt end in 1937. Congressman Joseph Buchanan, whose district covered Austin and the surrounding area, suddenly died, and a special election was called to fill the vacancy. There were several prominent men who immediately became contenders for that seat: C. M. Avery, his campaign manager and staff director; Burton L. Harris, a lawyer; Robert Sheldon, a well-known local politician, and several others.

Thinking it might be risky to go against a large field in a winner-take-all election where the top men could win without getting a majority, Avery let the word get around that Buchanan's widow ought to run unopposed for the unexpired term. He, of course, figured that his chances would be much better in a regular primary election the following year. Not wanting to offend Mrs. Buchanan, everybody sat back waiting for her to make a decision.

Faced with this impasse but still anxious to run, Lyndon went down to Johnson City to talk it over with daddy.

"Don't go waiting on her," he told Lyndon. "That's just some damned stallin' tactic by Avery. He just wants an easier shot later on. You go on ahead and announce right away. The minute Mrs. Buchanan knows she's got opposition, she won't get in. Hell, Lyndon, she's too old to campaign."

That's all my brother needed to hear. He probably had the same gut-reaction all along but wanted confirmation from an old pro he could trust. That same evening he rode back to Austin and officially announced his intention to run. And within forty-eight hours nine other candidates, including Avery, tossed their hats into the ring. True to my daddy's prediction, Buchanan's widow declined to make the race.

With the aid of an initial campaign contribution of ten thousand dollars from Lady Bird (she asked her father to take it from her inheritance), Lyndon launched his first campaign for public office at the age of twenty-nine. He started stomping that district from one corner to another, shaking every hand he could reach, letting people see that he had more get-up-and-go than all the other candidates combined.

I offered to take a leave of absence from my job as executive secretary to Congressman Kleberg to join the campaign, but he asked me to stay there to guard against certain pressures that might come out of the Democratic National Committee, which probably opposed Lyndon for reasons I'll

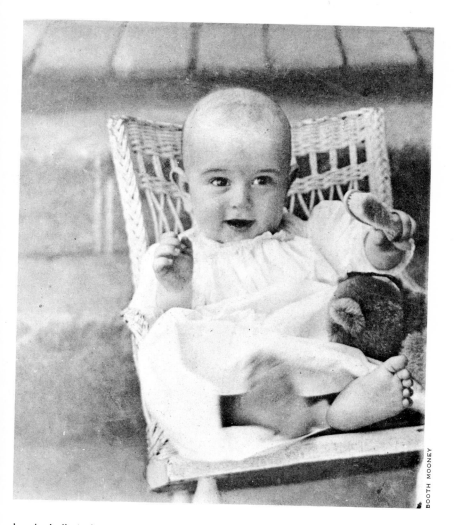

Lyndon's first picture. He was six months old at the time.

An early picture of Rebekah Baines Johnson, our mother, taken when she was publisher and editor of the Johnson City *News*.

An early picture of our father, Sam Ealy Johnson.

The birthplace of Lyndon B. Johnson.

Josefa, a little friend, Luci, and the author (with cap); behind them, Rebekah and Lyndon.

The Johnson brothers and sisters at their home in Johnson City, Texas.
From left to right, Lyndon, Rebekah, Luci, the author, and Josefa.

Lyndon with two of his classmates at Southwest Texas State College in San Marcos.

BOOTH MOONEY

President Franklin D. Roosevelt congratulates Lyndon a few days after his election to Congress. Governor James V. Allred of Texas looks on.

Lady Bird astride her favorite horse at the LBJ ranch.

explain later. We called each other nearly every night to discuss this or that strategy, mulling over some issue that might have popped up that very day. And once in awhile he would use me as a kind of long-distance straight man.

"Are you sure Sam Rayburn said that?" he would say apropos of nothing I had said. "You actually heard him tell Wright Patman that Avery would be a weak sister?"

Since I had said nothing of the sort, I realized he was just pretending for the benefit of someone listening to his end of the conversation, perhaps some local politician who was wavering between Lyndon and Avery. The next time he might come up with: "When did Jim Farley tell Kleberg that Avery was begging for outside help?"

Well, I'd simply let him create a dialogue out of thin air, knowing it was intended for someone he was trying to influence on his end of the line. We had used this ploy before, having learned it no doubt from daddy.

Near the end of the campaign I used the same technique to quash some pro-Avery activity by certain government officials. Having heard that Dale Miller, a high-ranking executive in the Treasury Department, was secretly supporting the other side, I waited for Miller's father to make one of his frequent visits to our office. This was Roy Miller, a close friend of Kleberg's and a prominent lobbyist on the hill. The minute Roy came in I picked up the phone and called Lyndon, motioning Roy to sit down while I finished the call.

Then, after listening to some preliminary chat from my brother, I said loud and clear for Roy's benefit: "Don't you do it, Lyndon—that would be a little too drastic."

"What in the goddamn hell are you talking about?" said Lyndon, who had been telling me about an outdoor barbecue rally in Blanco County.

"I know that Dale Miller is helping Avery on the sly," I continued. "But there's no need for you to complain to his boss about it. . . Bitching to Morgenthau would sure as hell get Miller fired, but that's too drastic."

Suddenly realizing that I probably had Roy Miller in my office, Lyndon chuckled and said, "Pour it on, Sam Houston, pour it on. I'm on to you."

It wasn't necessary for me to say much more. Roy Miller broke in and urged me to keep Lyndon calm. "I'll handle this myself," he said. "I'll get my boy to lay off. He oughta know better, he's liable to get himself 'Hatched.'" *

Before leaving my office, Roy tossed me a three-hundred-dollar check for Lyndon's campaign fund. But it somehow never got to him. At this late (and legally safe) date, I must honestly confess that I used that check to pay myself a campaign consultant's fee. Had my brother known that way back then, he would have tanned my hide . . . or something worse. His funds were pretty skimpy and he could have used that three hundred dollars.

With far less money than most of his opponents, Lyndon had to find an issue that would set him apart and get him the kind of publicity he couldn't pay for. Fortunately, he had the issue right at hand and—equally important—the courage to grab hold of it. President Roosevelt had just proposed what instantly became known as "the bill to pack the Supreme Court." Angered at the Nine Old Men, who had avoided some of his New Deal legislation, FDR wanted to expand the Court's membership to fifteen so he could name some liberal justices. It was easily the most controversial and most universally damned proposal he had ever made. Most Democratic congressmen and other politicians were strongly opposed to it but they didn't want to openly buck an immensely popular President, so they chose to keep mum.

Lyndon, however, favored the plan and decided to make it the main issue of his campaign. "I'm not 70 percent for Roosevelt, nor 90 percent. I'm for FDR 100 percent!" he announced.

This drew headlines all over Texas, and a lot of editorials blasted him. Then the national press services picked up the

---

* He was referring to the Hatch Act, which prohibits all federal government employees from engaging in political activity.

story. Pretty soon radio commentators like Lowell Thomas and Walter Winchell started saying that this special congressional election—the only one taking place at that time—would be a test of public sentiment on FDR's plan to pack the Supreme Court. The President, of course, was well aware that a young man named Lyndon Johnson was taking a big gamble on his pet project.

With the whole Congress in a turmoil over the Supreme Court, I couldn't resist pulling a joke that nearly backfired on me. Disguising my voice, I phoned Congressman Morgan Sanders, a hot-tempered, irascible old man who had barely squeezed through his last election with a slim margin of seven hundred votes. I knew he was straddling the fence on the packing plan.

"Mr. Congressman," I said, knowing he liked that "Mister" business. "This is Ralph Benson of the *Washington Herald,* and I'm wondering if you can let me interview you on the telephone."

"Why sure, Mr. Benson. Be happy to."

"Well, my newspaper is anxious to know your views on Roosevelt's plan to pack the Court."

"Now I want to be perfectly frank with you," said Sanders, a slight quiver in his voice. "I think that's a very important piece of legislation. Yessirree—it's a mighty important piece of legislation. And you can quote me on that, young fella."

"Yes, I realize that, sir—but how do you feel about it? For or against?"

"Well, I certainly intend to study it quite closely."

"I'm assuming all that, Congressman Sanders, but I still want to know if you favor the bill."

"Well, now . . . ," he hedged still further. "There's bound to be some amendments."

"Dammit," I said with a pretense of anger. "Quit your damned pussyfooting. Just tell me yes or no. Do you support the President?"

He gasped for a moment, then exploded. "Listen here, you

goddamned sonofabitch, you can't badger me around!"

"Can I quote you on that?"

"You're goddamned right you can, you smart-aleck bastard. You can quote me any damn way you please!" he slammed the receiver as he said it.

With no intention of carrying the gag any further, I later told Roy Miller about it, and he instantly thought of a follow-up. "Let's you and me have lunch with Dick Kleberg and Jake Perkins over at the House dining room," he said with devils in his eyes. "We'll sit right next to Congressman Sanders' table and rag him a little."

An hour later, with Sanders sitting within easy hearing range, Roy went into his act. "Say, Jake, didya hear about Congressman Sanders' tough stand on the Supreme Court packing bill?"

"Now, don't tell me he went and took a position on it."

"He sure as hell did," answered Roy. "Seems like he gave an awful blunt statement to some reporter from the *Washington Herald*."

Just beyond Kleberg's right shoulder, I could see Sanders leaning back in his chair to eavesdrop on the conversation.

"Takes a lotta courage to come out that way," said Perkins. "That kinda statement can be political suicide, especially in tight districts like his. But you sure gotta admire his courage."

"No question about that," I said. "But it is liable to beat him in the next election."

"Well, I sure do admire his——"

Unable to tolerate any more, Sanders scrambled out of his chair and charged over to our table. "What the hell are you talking about?" he yelled in a hoarse crescendo. "I didn't make no statement. That goddamned, smart-aleck reporter's putting words in my mouth."

When we told him that everybody on the Hill had heard about it and that the *Herald* was planning to feature the hot interview in the next day or so, Sanders turned to Miller and

said, "You've got to help me outa this, Roy. I've helped you
—now you've gotta help me by killing that damned story."

Winking at me, Roy started to say how hard it would be
to suppress the *Herald*, but Sanders was awfully insistent.
"You've just got to do it," he pleaded as he turned to leave.

Well, Roy was naturally pleased at the prospect of chalking
up some points without having to do a damned thing, and he
thanked me for setting up the gag. But that wasn't the end
of it.

As the story got around the Capitol, even Sam Rayburn
and Vice-President Garner got wind of it and teasingly called
Sanders to praise him for his suicidal courage. Then somehow
Sanders found out that it was all a practical joke. Accordingly,
when I called him again at Roy Miller's request—still pretending I was a *Herald* reporter—to tell him I wouldn't use
the story, Congressman Sanders literally yanked me through
the telephone wires.

"Goddamn you, Sam Houston," he yelled. "You get your
skinny ass over here right now! I know it was you that started
this."

Knowing his bad temper and also realizing that he always
had a loaded pistol in the top right-hand drawer of his desk,
I understandably hesitated to go over there, but finally did.
Fortunately for me, he had cooled off a bit by the time
I got there.

"Okay, Sam Houston," he said. "I'll let you off this time,
goddamnit. But first of all, you're gonna help me get even
with Roy Miller 'cause *he* probably put you up to it."

"I'll be glad to help you, sir," I said, glancing uneasily at
the gun drawer of his desk. "As a matter of fact, I got us
an idea right now."

So we huddled for ten or fifteen minutes and polished the
countermove against Roy Miller. Knowing that Roy (a top
lobbyist) generally joined some of the leading congressmen
for an afternoon sip of bourbon in Sam Rayburn's office, Con-

gressman Sanders grabbed his gun and headed for Rayburn's suite. As he came through the door, he pretended to stagger like a wild drunkard and started waving that pistol over his head.

"Where's that goddamned reporter who misquoted me?" he hollered. "I'm going to blow out his lousy brains."

Everybody scrambled for cover, of course, dropping to the floor or jumping behind Mr. Sam's desk. Still yelling up a storm and lurching around the room with his gun held high, Sanders let them lie there awhile and then suddenly started to laugh. He nearly split a gut laughing at all those scared-ass congressmen.

If you'll bear in mind that this soon-famous gag was originally based on Sanders' fear of taking an outright position on FDR's plan to pack the Supreme Court, you can better appreciate my brother's bold decision to back him all the way.

Driving harder than ever, saying again and again that he totally supported Roosevelt, my brother came down to the wire at a furious pace. Then just a few days before the election he was stricken with an acute attack of appendicitis. Advised to submit to immediate surgery, he first called the press to his hospital room and told them that he was herewith asking his opponents to name two impartial doctors to confirm or dispute his own dictor's diagnosis.

"I don't want people to think I'm merely grandstanding for sympathy—that I'm not really in need of surgery."

He was still recuperating when the votes were counted, giving him an upset victory over a field of several better-known veteran politicians. He got twice as many votes as his nearest rival.

President Roosevelt was fishing in the Gulf of Mexico not far from Galveston when he heard the results, and he happily invited Lyndon to come down for a visit on his boat. Still aching from his operation, my brother nevertheless had a very pleasant stay that eventually resulted in a long and fruitful friendship. Thus when Roosevelt took the train back to Washington, he asked my brother to accompany him part of the way.

As Lyndon started to leave the Presidential pullman car at Texarkana, FDR warmly shook his hand and said, "If you ever have any trouble getting things for your district, just come straight to the White House and talk to Tommy Corcoran or Sam Rosenman. I'll tell them to take good care of you."

By cultivating his elders in Congress and making strategic use of his special pipeline to FDR, Lyndon got more than his share of federally financed projects for his Tenth District. Federal Housing Project Number One was built in Austin, Texas; the Rural Electrification Administration (REA) created the Pedernales River Electric Cooperative, providing cheap electricity for Blanco County, Johnson City, and the area where Lyndon's ranch is presently located. It's one of the largest rural electric cooperatives in the country, and it was my brother who personally persuaded Roosevelt to waive a population-density regulation (from 3 persons per square mile to 1.6 per square mile) so as to bring that parched, impoverished area within the scope of the REA.

The farmers of the district received soil-bank and conservation payments, peanut and cotton allotments, and other federal aid. The Tenth District got perhaps more than its share of schools, hospitals, and recreation areas mainly financed by Uncle Sam. Austin alone eventually built four hospitals by means of funds provided by the Hill-Burton Act. And our barren hill country got "Roosevelt willows" to replace the ugly nettle and thistle that were eating away the soil.

Damned few—if any—freshman congressmen could point to a list of accomplishments comparable to Lyndon's. He learned early and fast about how the machinery of government worked and what kind of wheels needed certain kinds of grease to get them moving. Much of it was accomplished through personal contact, but a lot of it was the result of an intimate, detailed knowledge of governmental structure and bureaucratic regulations. That's what the later New Frontiersmen—that fancy-talking bunch of young amateurs who helplessly tried to get things moving for President Kennedy —never knew. They didn't understand a damned thing about the government. (We'll have more about them later on.)

My brother, on the other hand, had an intuitive "feel" for government operations, and he was also willing to work hard as hell to learn a lot more from anyone who could teach him —Rayburn, Wright Patman, Huey Long, "Tommy the Cork," Jim Rowe, Sam Rosenman, and many others. Roosevelt, of course, was his chief mentor and he was an avid and loyal student of the FDR technique. Moreover, he completely supported Roosevelt's philosophy of government. Consequently when the President decided in 1940 to run for an unprecedented third term, Lyndon stuck with him against the wishes of Sam Rayburn and Vice-President John Nance Garner.

They were, in fact, pretty goddamned mad at my brother. Everyone knew that Garner wanted to be President and all his fellow Texans (except LBJ) naturally supported him. And there were a lot of other prominent Democrats outside of Texas who violently opposed a third term—including the national chairman, Jim Farley, who also wanted to move into the White House.

Needless to say, Lyndon's maverick stand in FDR's favor cemented their friendship all the more, while Sam Rayburn's stock came down a bit. Subsequently, when Speaker Bankhead died and Rayburn wanted to replace him, Roosevelt let it be known that he was not in favor of Mr. Sam. Realizing that Lyndon was closer than ever to the White House, a group of Rayburn backers asked him to intercede in Sam's behalf. The next day my brother had a long chat with FDR and finally persuaded him to back Sam Rayburn for the speaker's post.

Still rankling from Sam's opposition to his third term, Roosevelt told Lyndon, "I'll go along with this for your sake, Lyndon. But I want you to keep a close eye on Rayburn. I'm still not sure I can trust him all the way."

People still insist it was Sam Rayburn who made Lyndon Johnson. But in view of what I personally observed way back then, I think it was the other way around. I know that my brother, in all loyalty to Mr. Sam, will publicly disagree with me—but I think my views on this matter would have been borne out by Franklin Roosevelt himself. Lyndon was the most influential man in Congress.

It was during his early years in the House of Representatives that Lyndon asked me to move in with him and Lady Bird, letting me have the spare room in their relatively modest house at 1910 Kalorama Road. I lived in their various homes (including the White House) for many years—before, between, and after my two marriages, both of which ended in divorce.

I guess Lyndon wanted me close by so that he could keep a big-brotherly eye on all my extracurricular activities. It was obvious that he had never approved of my fancy apartment or my having a valet at the age of twenty-three. And since he still wore baggy, ready-made suits from Sears Roebuck, my custom-made clothes also offended his sense of prudent frugality.

Both he and Lady Bird have always had an inordinately high respect for tight budgets—not stingy, mind you, but certainly never wasteful. Time and again, when I had fallen asleep reading, Lyndon would come into my room and shake my shoulder to wake me up. And when I'd finally opened my bleary eyes, he would snap off my light with the same one-sentence lecture every time: "Goddamn it, Sam Houston, are you working for me or the lousy power company?" Then he would stomp out of the room with some grumbling complaint about waste.

I just can't remember how many times he's done that, but he has never stopped doing it. Seven or eight times, when I was staying on the family floor of the White House, he came into my room and pulled the same act: Shake me awake, deliver that same damned lecture, and snap off my light. That's one of the reasons I preferred to live on the third floor. He still might come up to put off my light, but it would be a little harder on him. So help me, if everybody followed Lyndon's example, the power companies would go broke.

Aside from my wasteful subsidies to the heirs of Thomas Edison, my brother also worried about my occasional carousing and night-lifing and would frequently wait for me to come home (sometimes way after midnight) so he could chew me out for drinking too much. He drank himself and fairly regularly, but always managed to remain in complete control of himself.

In all the years I've known him, I have seen my brother drunk only once. There have probably been other times, but only once when I was present. The reason may be that he's wanted to be an example for his little brother Sam. Even on the occasion I saw him drunk, he couldn't resist being the big brother.

He had been out at the Burning Tree Country Club all afternoon with Senator Smathers. They had planned to play golf but adjourned to the bar for a few drinks when it started raining. Well, the rain never stopped and Lyndon finally absorbed more Scotch then he generally did. When he got home after dark—his clothes soaked through to the skin and his hair plastered down with rain that was still pouring—he came into my room (I'd gone to sleep early), snapped my light on, and shook my shoulder.

"Wake up, Sam Houston," he said in a thick voice. "Wake up and look at me!"

Lady Bird, who had followed him into the room, tried to calm him. "Come on, honey. Leave Sam alone. Come on to bed."

"Just leave me alone, Bird," he slurred. "I want Sam Houston to look at me. Yes, by God, I want you to take a damned good look at me, Sam Houston. Open your eyes and look at me. 'Cause I'm drunk, and I want you to see how you look to me, Sam Houston, when you come home drunk."

"Okay, Lyndon," I said, turning my back. "I've seen you."

"No you don't," he persisted, turning me around again. "I want you to look good and hard, so you'll know what I see, Sam Houston."

Well, Lady Bird finally managed to get him out of my room and I went back to sleep, wondering if I really did look that awful when I tied one on.

That incident happened many years after we had moved from the house on Kalorama Street. As I said before, it was an unpretentious place that reflected Lyndon's modest income as a congressman with no personal wealth. There were several things that never got repaired or improved for lack of money, and I particularly remember the creaky ninth step on the front stairway leading to the upstairs bedrooms. Lyndon left it that way—not because he couldn't afford ten dollars to fix it, but because that damned noisy step always gave me away when I came home late and not entirely sober.

Several times I offered to pay a handyman from my own pocket, but he wouldn't let me. Consequently, I sometimes used the noiseless backstairs, coming through the basement bedroom occupied by our wonderful cook and housekeeper, Zephyr Wright. If ever I saw her light on, indicating that she was entertaining one of her friends, I would tap on her door and she would wave me through her room with that knowing grin that all of us sinners share in common. She was my constant ally and frequently allowed me to hide my bottle of gin in her closet. (And I might add that she was a damned intelligent ally, having graduated in home economics from Wiley College in Marshall, Texas.) Naturally, whenever I could, I would do *her* a favor.

One Thursday morning, as she was preparing to leave the

house for her day off, Zephyr motioned me into the kitchen for a little chat. "Mr. Sam," she said. "I've got me a problem and need your help."

"Why sure, Zephyr, anything you say."

"Well, it's like this, Mr. Sam. I've been secretly married to this soldier man for about a year now, and I've been getting his 'lotment check from the army."

That surprised me, of course, but I was glad to hear it and told her so.

"Now my problem is this, Mr. Sam," she continued, "that 'lotment check is due in the mail today on accounta this being the last day in the month, and I don't want Miss Lady Bird to see it. She liable to cut my wages if she hears 'bout my 'lotment. So I'm wondering if you could maybe pick up the mail yourself when the postman come and hide that envelope for me."

"Of course, I will, Zephyr. Be glad to oblige."

Neither Lady Bird nor Lyndon ever found out about that secret marriage or the allotment checks. As a matter of fact, when Zephyr told them, several years later, that she was getting married (to the same man who was already her husband), Lyndon gave her a big reception and a beautiful bridal dress from Nieman-Marcus, the finest department store in Dallas.

The Kennedys had a fancy French chef who prepared all kinds of unpronounceable dishes, but I'm sure the White House has never had a better cook—nor a more independent one—than Zephyr Wright. When she cooked her special roast with Pedernales River chili sauce or fried chicken with spoon bread, you started wishing you had two stomachs.

Once in awhile, however, some of Lyndon's guests would try to improve a little on her chili sauce. During a Christmas vacation party down at the ranch, the guests (Sam Rayburn, Wright Patman, Jake Perkins, Homer Thornberry, and several others) kept going back and forth to the kitchen to pour themselves another drink. And each time one of them passed by the stove he would pick up the bottle of Tabasco sauce and shake some into Zephyr's simmering pot of chili sauce, boozily ignoring her warnings. We almost had to call the fire department when they sat down to eat.

"I kept telling those fools," Zephyr told Lady Bird. "But they wouldn't pay me no mind. Now let them burn."

That was one of the few times she wasn't in complete control of her kitchen. I've even heard her tell President LBJ that "I've waited long enough to keep that meal hot for you —now you'll just have to eat it cold."

Aside from her fine cooking, Zephyr was an awfully tidy housekeeper and quite good at ironing shirts. During his early days in the Senate, when he started to get more and more finicky about his clothes, Lyndon would pay her extra to iron all his shirts.

"How much do you charge him for doing those shirts?" I once asked her.

"That all depends, Mr. Sam," she said. "I varies from time to time."

"You don't have a set price?"

"Well, I kinda do and kinda don't," she answered with a faint smile. "It works like this, Mr. Sam. I sets a price of twenty cents a shirt, but I don't collect each time. I lets the account ride along till it's something like maybe $6.20— then some evening when I see he's had a drink and feeling kinda good, I ups and tells him could I collect my money for the shirts. Well, he generally ain't got the right exact change, so he give me a ten-dollar bill and tells me to keep the change. And that's why I can't rightly tell you, Mr. Sam, how much I charges him for each shirt."

Knowing Lyndon, I'm sure he was on to her game from the very start; but he was so fond of Zephyr, she could get away with almost anything.

The rest of his employees were treated with less *noblesse oblige*. He has always demanded hard work and total loyalty from his staff, expecting them to work the same extra hours that he does. "An eight-hour man ain't worth a damn to me," he often said, and meant every word of it. As a consequence of this attitude, some of his staff members were apt to develop into nervous humorless drones, plodding along with a wary eye on the boss—afraid to displease him, certainly afraid to criticize him. Small wonder that he has often been surrounded by scared-assed sycophants who have deliberately failed to express their doubts about policies they have privately disagreed with, wanting only to hang onto their jobs.

In the kind of solemn atmosphere these people created, I occasionally felt compelled to lighten the mood in Lyndon's office. While still working for Congressman Kleberg, I once called one of my brother's staff members, imitating Lyndon's voice. "Say, Bill, I need some reports brought over here to the House chamber right away," I said. "I want you to go over to the Agriculture Department and get me the annual reports on crop subsidies for the past ten years. So hustle on over, y' hear."

An hour later a page boy laid the heavy stack of reports on Lyndon's small desk in the chamber. "What in the devil are these?" asked Lyndon.

"One of your staff members brought them over and told me to put them on your desk," the boy said. "He's out in the hall."

With the page boy trailing him up the aisle, Lyndon rushed into the corridor and nabbed Bill near the phone booth. "Who in the hell told you to bring those damn reports over here?"

"You did, sir. You called me an hour ago."

"I didn't call you," he said, suddenly realizing it was me. "It was that damned Sam Houston. I'll take care of him later."

That's exactly what he did. As we were sitting down to supper that evening, he gave me a real LBJ tongue-lashing. "Goddammit, Sam Houston, you stay away from my staff, y' hear. Next time you pull one of your damn-fool smart-aleck tricks, I'm going to . . . ."

There's no need to repeat his unprintable threats. If it hadn't been for Zephyr's fine cooking, that chewing-out would have ruined my appetite. As it turned out, I had only one serving of dessert.

Yet, in spite of such momentary setbacks, I couldn't resist making an occasional fake phone call to lighten the mood around Capitol Hill. Certain people are tailor-made for that sort of monkey business. I particularly remember a fellow I'll call Cecil Bowers, who worked for a congressman we shall conveniently name Joe Hill so as to completely mask their true identities. Though he was fresh on the Hill, with no previous exposure to government, Cecil immediately started telling us more-experienced congressional secretaries how to do our jobs. There was nothing he didn't know more about than anyone else; and, as so often happens with full-blown egotists, he had absolutely no sense of humor, especially about himself.

So one afternoon, after I had made sure Congressman Hill was back in Texas, I asked my secretary to call his office and pretend it was the White House calling Mr. Hill. And just as I expected, Cecil Bowers took the call.

"Hello, Congressman," I said, somehow faking a Northern accent and a deep important voice. "This is Steve Early* over at the White House."

"Yessir, Mr. Early," said Cecil with an eager tremor in his voice. "But this ain't Congressman Hill, sir—this here is Cecil Bowers, his chief assistant. Joe just went back to Texas this morning, and I'm in charge here, sir."

"Well, now, that's too bad," I said. "I know the President will be disappointed. He has just decided to give a little dinner for some of the congressmen who've supported him most, and we naturally hoped Congressman Hill could be here."

"Oh, that sure is a shame, sir," said Cecil. "I know Joe would like to come. He sure would. You know, him and me are like brothers—went to college together, so I know

* Press secretary to President Roosevelt.

exactly how he'll feel when he hears about this. Yessirree."

"Well, now," I said. "If you're that close to each other, with you knowing all about him and his philosophy of government——"

"Oh, I sure do, sir. Me and Joe are——'

"Perhaps you can come in his place," I said, interrupting his interruption. "You can represent him, as it were."

"You mean that? You really mean it?"

"Of course, Mr.—ah. I'm sorry I didn't get your full name, young man."

"Bowers, sir. Cecil Bowers. c-e-c-i-l b-o-w-e-r-s. Cecil Bowers, sir. The congressman's head man."

"Very well, Mr. Bowers," I said. "You're to be at the East Gate of the White House at exactly 7:00 P.M. No later, sir."

"Oh, I'll be there, all right."

"And Mr. Bowers," I added in an offhand manner. "You realize it'll be a formal dinner. White tie and tails. The usual thing."

That night, shortly before seven, two of my colleagues and I sat in a car across the street from the East Gate when Cecil Bowers arrived in the niftiest tails he could rent. He argued fifteen minutes with a very stubborn guard and finally walked off in one helluva sniff. He seemed a lot less arrogant after that.

CHAPTER FIVE

Most Powerful Man in Washington

In the spring of 1941 my brother decided to run for the unexpired term of Senator Morris Sheppard, who had died on April 9. Having first conferred with President Roosevelt, he made his announcement from the steps of the White House a few minutes before a Presidential press conference.

When asked about Lyndon's candidacy, FDR grinned from ear to ear, his eyes clearly reflecting his approval. "First of all," he said, "it is up to the people of Texas to elect the man they want as their senator; second, everybody knows that I cannot enter a primary election; and third, to be truthful, all I can say is Lyndon Johnson is a very old, old friend of mine."

To the press (and everyone else) that was a pretty clear indication of Roosevelt's preference; but such an endorsement proved to be a rather unmixed blessing in Texas, where the New Deal was beginning to arouse considerable opposition.

Martin Dies* and Governor W. Lee ("Pappy") O'Daniel, both extremely conservative, hit hard on the theme of too much spending, too much government, and too many Commies in Washington. Lyndon, supported by thousands of young people who remembered his NYA efforts, hit just as hard on his plea for a "compassionate government." He also argued against an increasing isolationism in the face of a Nazi threat in Europe.

It was a close election, with Lyndon leading by 5,000 votes after 96 percent of the ballots had been counted on the second day after the polls closed. Then, for reasons I have always suspected, a few remote outlying counties came in with tallies strongly supporting "Pappy" O'Daniel. He won by a margin of 1,311 votes out of a total of nearly 600,000. Some people theorized that Lyndon's anti-Hitler warnings had alienated the German votes; but all those *hold-back* votes led me to think "we were took" and I urged Lyndon to demand a recount. Knowing such measures are seldom, if ever, successful, he merely shrugged.

"You can't win 'em all, Sam," he said. "There's always another ball game."

He had to wait seven more years for that next ball game, the famous senatorial election in 1948. During that long interim, Franklin Roosevelt died (1945), leaving Lyndon in a very depressed mood. "He was like a second daddy to me," he told one reporter. "I am absolutely crushed."

However, when one of his secretaries came into the office daubing her eyes with an already wet handkerchief and half-sobbing, "What shall we do—who will take his place?"—Lyndon put his arm around her and said, "Why, honey, there's Mr. Truman."

He knew things had to go on, no matter how saddened he might feel, but we all knew that Roosevelt's death had deeply affected him. He lost some of his drive, periodically

* Former congressman and controversial chairman of the House Un-American Activities Committee.

pausing in the middle of his still-crowded work day to stare out the window with a troubled look in his eyes. He might spend a half hour that way. Then he would suddenly busy himself with paper work and long phone calls to fellow congressmen about some pending legislation, driving himself and his staff as never before. Still, despite his fevered activity on Capitol Hill, there was a certain dissatisfaction brewing inside of him, and he occasionally talked about returning to Texas to get into a line of work that would yield a better income (and more security) than his congressional job. Lady Bird had invested most of her inheritance in a radio station, and they were both anxious to expand into television.

As the 1948 primary drew near, he was still contemplating a new, nonpolitical career. Thus, in May of that year he went back to Austin to announce that he would not run for the Senate. But on the very last day for filing, just a few hours before the deadline, a group of young liberals who had worked with him in the NYA, finally persuaded him to make the race.

"Damn it, Lyndon," one of them said. "You got us into government and convinced us it was the most useful kind of work a man can do—so don't go leaving us high and dry when we need you, when the state of Texas needs you."

At thirty-nine years of age, with thousands of former NYAers supporting him, Lyndon launched the most crucial campaign of his career. His principal opponent was the conservative, popular Governor Coke Stevenson, whose administration had just been favorably rated by 71 percent of the people interviewed in a statewide poll of public opinion. The other main contender was a Houston lawyer named George Peddy. To everyone's surprise, "Pappy" O'Daniel had decided not to run for reelection.

Once again, as in his first congressional race, Lyndon became seriously ill during the campaign—only this time it was at the beginning instead of the end. Having come down with a kidney infection, he was flown to the Mayo Clinic in Minnesota by his good friend, Jacqueline Cochran, and he returned to Texas two weeks later with a different kind of infection —the flying bug. Taking to the air in a helicopter equipped with huge loudspeakers, he zoomed and flitted over the whole damned state, dropping into little pump-water towns where nobody had ever seen one of those crazy flying machines.

One old man in Kickapoo (just north of Pointblank) kept staring at Lyndon as he talked about farm prices, never hearing a word. Finally, he turned to his wife and said, "If he can keep that damn thing from chopping his head off, he might make a good senator."

Midway through the campaign Lyndon and I had a rather sharp disagreement regarding the Taft-Hartley bill, which was due to be voted upon in the fall term. We were having supper with mama at our home in Johnson City when the matter came up.

"I'm preparing a press release for you on Taft-Hartley," I said. "Should be ready by tomorrow."

"What am I saying?" he asked.

"You're attacking it, of course."

"Like hell I am," he said, with a certain bite in his voice. "I'm not attacking anything. As a matter of fact, I'm voting *for* Taft-Hartley."

"You can't do that," I said, hardly believing what my ears had plainly heard. "Damn it, Lyndon, that's an anti-labor law. The unions will crucify you!"

"Have you read the bill, Sam Houston?" he asked, motioning to mama for the sugar bowl and winking at her with outright smugness.

"No, I haven't," I admitted. "But I *do* know that labor is dead against it."

"Well, you'd better read it before you go off half-cocked and start calling it antilabor," he said. "I've read every word of that bill—several times—and it isn't what labor says it is. It's a good law, and I'm voting for it."

"I don't give a damn about that," I argued, pointing my

fork at him. "You'll lose three hundred thousand votes if you support it. You can't afford to, Lyndon. They'll go over to Coke Stevenson."

"The working people know better than that," he said. "They know he's antilabor, always has been."

Lyndon was right about Coke Stevenson's conservative attitude on organized labor, but he was wrong in assuming the unions would prefer him to Coke. The minute he announced his position on the Taft-Hartley bill, the unions went all-out against him. And in that first primary election Lyndon suffered the full impact of their anger, while Stevenson reaped the benefits, receiving 477,077 votes to Lyndon's 405,617. The other nine candidates got 320,000 votes.

The only thing that saved him in the run-off election was an article that appeared in the late Drew Pearson's column, "The Washington Merry-Go-Round." Later on I found out that Jack Anderson (Pearson's colleague) actually wrote the piece I have in mind. It arose from a confrontation that occurred when Coke went to Washington after his victory in the first primary election "to look over the offices he was sure to occupy" after the Democratic run-off against Lyndon, which would be tantamount to election in Texas. Fully confident that he would easily win, he held a press conference that proved fatal.

Jack Anderson, knowing that Coke had gotten strong labor-union endorsements despite his antilabor record, immediately asked him how he stood on the Taft-Hartley bill.

Coke hedged all over the place, mouthing vague platitudes, but Anderson wouldn't let him go. He kept badgering him for a direct answer, and finally Coke desperately and foolishly said that *he didn't have his notes with him* and therefore couldn't answer the question.

Anderson's subsequent column (appearing under the highly regarded Drew Pearson by-line) was a devastating attack on Coke Stevenson's wishy-washy evasiveness, and we had it reprinted and distributed all over Texas. I can think of no other single factor that contributed more to Lyndon's election than Anderson's article.

Taking full advantage of this sudden break, Lyndon launched an attack that gained full momentum each day. "If my opponent has promised to repeal the law," he said, "the people have a right to know. If he has not made such a promise, the people have a right to know. And I think the laboring men should ask their leaders to tell them openly why they wanted the union to break a fifty-year precedent of nonendorsement in order to endorse a faltering candidate who did not have the courage to sign or veto the state's vicious antilabor law when he was Governor."

Helicoptering from here to there, he kept jabbing at Coke with that steady accusatory question: "How does he stand on Taft-Hartley? Why won't he tell you?" In view of his AFL endorsement Coke had to remain silent—like that mythical man who is asked, "When are you going to stop beating your wife?"

What followed was one of the toughest, most controversial campaigns in Texas history, with all of us working day and night to reach every possible voter. At times Lyndon looked as if he would cave in from exhaustion, and Lady Bird worked almost as hard.

On the day before the election, she joined my mother and two sisters (Becky and Lucia) in a final effort to canvass the Austin area by telephone. They tore apart a phone book, took a section apiece, then wore their index fingers to the bone dialing one number after another. It could well have been that single finishing chore that turned the tide for my brother.

We also made damned sure—remembering the strange last minute flip-flop in 1941—that all the polling places were closely watched so as to prevent any hanky-panky in the final count. A few soreheads later accused us of "watching too damned close," broadly hinting that we voted a few dead people here and there. That's sheer nonsense. We just wanted to be sure that our opponents wouldn't use a graveyard vote. "Ma" Ferguson had kindly warned us about certain counties with a high corpse count.

Had we been less vigilant we might have lost. Lyndon won by only 87 votes (494,191 votes to 494,104), probably the narrowest landslide in any Senate election, at least in this century. Those figures alone clearly indicate that neither Coke's nor Lyndon's people tampered with the vote. If you're going to steal an election, you sure don't fool around with a piddling margin of 87 votes.

With charges and countercharges coming from all angles, the Democratic State Executive Committee met at the Hotel Commodore Perry in Austin to officially certify the results. When the initial tally was announced—28 to 28—I suddenly noticed that one of our supporters was absent (let's call him Jim Smith). Remembering that I had seen him headed for the upstairs men's room, wobbling a bit from one drink too many, I rushed into the lavatory section and found him soaking his head in a washbasin.

"For Christsakes, Jim," I hollered. "Get back in that committee room. We need your damned vote."

A couple of minutes later Jim slowly walked into the room and cast the deciding vote for Lyndon. Thereafter, practically everyone on our side took credit for rounding up old Jim, and my brother made good use of their willingness to do so. Wherever he went, he would take someone aside (thirty or forty people eventually) and whisper, "Hey, Walter, I understand it was you that got Jim Smith outa that bathroom."

Feigning just a shade of modesty, Walter or Joe or Roger would say, "Well, it weren't much, Lyndon—but that damned Jim's sure tough to handle when he's had a snort. Yessiree."

All those people liked to be bragged on, and Lyndon was just the man to do it. Bragging on people has always been one of his most effective political techniques. It's kind of a Southern trait. And, of course, he's never discouraged people from bragging on him.

Later that night Lyndon called mama and told her all about it. "I wish daddy had been here," he said. "He would have been proud of Sam Houston. He won it for me."

Mama told me about their conversation the next day.

Lyndon had asked me to join him for a celebration party that night, but I reluctantly declined. I was too tired to celebrate; besides, I wasn't drinking at that time. I had temporarily given up the sauce.

The following morning I decided to take a brief vacation in Monterey, Mexico (with a friend, of course), but when I got off the plane in San Antonio I saw some newspaper headlines announcing that Coke Stevenson was challenging the election in both the state and federal courts. So it was back to Austin for me. When I got there all our people were in a big fret—everyone except Lyndon. He was cooler than a cucumber.

"We'll have to get Abe on this," he said. "Ain't a smarter lawyer in the country."

He was referring, of course, to Abe Fortas. They had known each other from the early New Deal days, when Fortas was the legal wizard of the Department of Interior. Besides knowing all the ins-and-outs of the federal bureaucracy, he was also a brilliant appellate lawyer—just the kind of man who could take this problem all the way to the Supreme Court, if necessary, or to tie Coke Stevenson's lawyers into knots at the district-court level. And that's exactly what he did. Within a few days he had the case thrown out of court, putting Lyndon back on the ballot for the general election in November.

Erroneously assuming that Lyndon had been hurt by all the hullabaloo caused by his eighty-seven-vote victory, the Republicans made a greater effort than usual in the fall election campaign. Their well-heeled candidate was a Houston oil millionaire, Jack Porter, who had once been a Democrat. Knowing he had it won (Texas being traditionally Democratic), my brother didn't bother to campaign anymore and still managed to win by a two-to-one margin.

There has always been a lot of cynical speculation about that 1948 election, some columnists referring to "Landslide Lyndon" and dropping hints of back-door machinations. More than a few eager-beaver reporters, sniffing around for a Pulitzer Prize, have dug through all the details of that over-publicized election without ever finding any concrete evidence of wrongdoing by our people. Had there been any, you can bet your last penny the press would have headlined it in huge letters.

I might add, incidentally, that the news media was never as curious about the Illinois (Cook County) vote for John F. Kennedy in 1960, although the Republicans raised a stink about heavy voting from long-abandoned empty lots. Like all human beings, newspapermen have their favorites and un-favorites, and I doubt that Lyndon could be placed in the first category.

Now that we have broached the subject of ethics, I wonder how many people (politicians, businessmen, reporters, lawyers, TV repairmen, auto salesmen, doctors, mechanics, entertainers, bellboys, professors, et al.) can look in the mirror and seriously say, "There is a completely moral human being."

How can a business executive, who cheats on his expense account to buy himself a hundred-dollar call girl get so sanctimonious about Adam Clayton Powell? And how about the auto mechanic who pays catalog prices for used parts, then triples his customer's bill?

Of course, the politicians themselves are the most sanctimonious hypocrites when one of their colleagues gets into trouble. They get on the floor of the House or the Senate and let their voices quiver with holier-than-thou horror and shock, then rush out to the airport to catch a plane to Europe to investigate student morals in Paris at government expense.

Everyone in Washington knows that most of those congressional junkets are simply free vacations, one of the fringe benefits of being a congressman.

Even those politicians (federal or local) who play it straight and narrow in financial matters have different kinds of skeletons in their closets. There isn't a single man in Congress—or any other officeholder—who hasn't stepped on someone climbing up the ladder, who hasn't double-crossed a friend, who hasn't fudged on his campaign promises, who hasn't committed some act that nibbles at his conscience in the middle of the night.

There were a lot of dismayed columnists who jumped on Bobby Kennedy for suddenly announcing his candidacy for President right after McCarthy's victory in New Hampshire, calling him ruthless and opportunistic for robbing poor old Gene of his hour of triumph. I don't know why they were so surprised; Bobby was completely in character—a cool, ambitious politician who moved when he had to, and to hell with ethical considerations. Ambition and egotism are the twin names of the game; without them, no man enters public life. And successful ambitious men, no matter what field they are in, are seldom deterred by mere scruple.

It may be that the electoral process—especially when an officeholder has to offer himself for public approval every two or four or six years—accentuates the need for driving ambition and blows up the ego to ridiculous proportions. The pretense of modesty in a politician is pure sham. Truly modest people don't grab at strangers' hands in supermarkets, nor do they worry about their best profile before a TV camera. I can't think of a less modest bunch of men than the U.S. House of Representatives—except, of course, the U.S. Senate.

When he joined the Senate in 1948, my brother was unusually sensitive about his colleagues' high opinions of themselves and was mighty damn careful not to bruise anyone's ego. He quickly accepted the club rule that new senators should be seen and not heard. But, since most of the incumbent senators were tired old men, Lyndon also realized that a conscientious hard-working freshman could make his mark in the Senate. With his photographic memory for names and all sorts of detailed information about governmental operations, he soon became the youngest old-timer on Capitol Hill. Before the year was over, quite a few older senators had asked Lyndon's advice on how to push through a particular law favoring their states.

Several old friends with whom he had served in the House of Representatives were now in the Senate, and he quickly became friends with senior members like Richard Russell of Georgia, Ernest McFarland of Arizona, Dennis Chavez of New Mexico, Virgil Chapman of Kentucky, and Edwin C. Johnson of Colorado.

As a new member of the powerful Armed Services Committee, headed by the scholarly Georgian, Lyndon developed an especially warm friendship with Dick Russell. (I had known Dick for many years. Before moving into Lyndon's house, I had a suite across the hall from Dick at the Hamilton Hotel. He always avoided the public bar downstairs but didn't mind having a drink at my place, sometimes in the cheerful company of a couple of my lady friends.)

In July 1950—after Lyndon had uncovered a lot of waste and corruption in our military preparation for the Korean War —Senator Russell appointed him chairman of the Preparedness Investigating Subcommittee of the Senate Armed Services Committee. Almost overnight the subcommittee became headline news, with Lyndon relentlessly quizzing witness after witness about price gouging by tin producers, waste of manpower due to the "hoarding of men" by the air force, surplus scandals, and whatnot.

One afternoon, just after he had made a devastating cross-examination of a munitions manufacturer, Lyndon looked at me with a sad, weary expression in his eyes. "You want to know something, Sam Houston," he said. "I don't especially like this role. I wasn't cut out to be a prosecutor. It makes me feel like a damned heel badgering people that way—but someone's got to do it."

The badgering paid off. In the army he found supply sergeants issuing golf clubs; expert pilots acting as post-exchange officers; illegal slot machines at an air base; trained tank mechanics assigned to reserve units that had no tanks; empty barracks at one army base while at another base hundreds of soldiers lived in packing crates and mule sheds.

In his home state of Texas, his investigators learned that a farmer had bought $1,200,000 worth of surplus airplane parts for $6.89 and then sold them back to the government for $63,000. The military brass got so worried about the subcommittee that the air force suddenly cancelled a $1,650,000 order for white dress gloves when Lyndon started checking their clothing requirements.

Eventually, the subcommittee (whose total operating expenses were $275,000) saved the U.S. government more than five billion dollars.

As a result of his investigators' fine record and his great skill as a legislative strategist who knew how, where, and when to push the right buttons, he was elected majority whip in 1951 by a unanimous vote of his Democratic colleagues. No one had ever risen to that position in so short a time.

Senator Ernest McFarland was majority leader, and he relied heavily on Lyndon's tactical know-how. He was a frequent visitor at the Johnson home, dropping by for a highball and long strategy talks on Senate business. One evening, as my brother was explaining how to speed a pending bill through a stubborn committee, McFarland leaned back in his chair and said, "Damn it, Lyndon, you ought to have my job—you know a helluva lot more about it than I do."

But Lyndon shrugged aside the suggestion. "I'm happy where I am, Ernie, just helping you."

Ironically enough, McFarland's half wish came true about a year later. He was defeated by Barry Goldwater in the

Eisenhower landslide of 1952, which also gave the Republicans control of the Senate.

Since Lyndon was still in his first term, just four years in the Senate, very few people expected him to become minority leader. Senator Russell, who had much more seniority and strong Southern support, was the obvious choice. But for reasons I've never figured out, Dick seemed reluctant to take over. Perhaps he expected to be drafted for the position, playing it shy so as to strengthen his hand later on—a tactic that I've always considered pretty damned foolish. Nobody ever gets drafted unless he arranges it himself.

That's exactly what we started doing for Lyndon—arranging a draft. I got together with Bobby Baker and worked out a kind of "me-second" plan that later helped John Kennedy before the 1960 convention. Knowing it wouldn't look right for *me* to call people, we decided to let Bobby phone or personally contact all the Southern senators with this kind of pitch:

"Senator, this is Bobby Baker calling. It's about this minority-leader situation, sir."

"Why sure, son," the senator would say. "I imagine you're thinking about Lyndon."

"Not exactly, sir," Bobby would say. "Senator Johnson really thinks Dick Russell ought to take it, sir. But we understand he doesn't want it. He's pretty busy with the Armed Services Committee, and with this war going on, I can see why he doesn't want to leave."

"No, I guess not. That's a pretty big handful."

"Well, that's just the point, Senator," said Bobby, moving in. "If Senator Russell won't take it, looks like Hubert Humphrey or one of them Northerners will get it."

"Huh, we can't have that, Bobby!"

"That's what some of us have been thinking, sir. If it can't be Russell, we sure ought to get someone like Lyndon. Draft him, if necessary. That Humphrey thing kinda scares me."

Remembering Hubert's performance as a Young Turk at the 1948 convention, that's all those Southerners had to hear. They started falling in with LBJ and urging him to take it. And that's when Lyndon began acting a bit coy. He knew that a minority leader might have to oppose Ike's administration from time to time—that Ike was especially popular in Texas, that he (Lyndon) and Sam Rayburn had just antagonized some powerful Texans by supporting Adlai a few months earlier, that they had threatened to "get him" in 1954, that he had barely been elected by eighty-seven votes, and that a popular governor, Allen Shivers, was planning to oppose him in about sixteen months. So why put himself in a possible anti-Ike position?

Knowing Lyndon's doubts, I had an off-the-record talk with the Washington correspondent of the *Dallas News*, the most powerful newspaper in the state.

"Understand, now," I told him. "This minority-leader race has narrowed down to Lyndon and Hubert Humphrey, and you know how Hubert stands on oil depletion."

That, of course, struck close to home.

"But my brother doesn't want it," I continued. "He's got too damned many other things to think about. With old Shivers coming at him next year, he's gonna have to spend a lotta time back home, mending those fences that got tore up when he opposed Ike."

Well, I went on in that vein for about an hour, periodically wondering aloud about what Hubert would do to the oil people if he got to be leader. The results were better than I planned. When the *Dallas News* came out the next morning, headlining the threat of Hubert Humphrey in large type, there was stack-up traffic on the long-distance wires between Dallas-Houston and Lyndon's office.

First of all, Amon Carter called.

Then Sid Richardson.

Then George Brown.

On and on, one call after another from powerful Texans

who had read the *Dallas News* article. They were urging Lyndon to run for minority leader "to keep that damned pinko outa there." And I watched my brother fencing with each one, expressing his need to spend a lot of time in Texas during the coming year to prepare for a primary fight against Allen Shivers. Each one, he later told me, gave him the same assurance.

"Don't you worry about Allen. He ain't gonna run against you. We'll take care of that."

Then Shivers himself—obviously at their prompting—phoned to assure Lyndon that he was quite content to go on living at the governor's mansion in Austin. "I've always planned to renew my lease," he said. "So don't go worrying about me."

With the Shivers threat apparently eliminated, Lyndon let it be known he was available for minority leader. And a couple days before the caucus of Democratic senators, the newly elected junior senator from Massachusetts (John F. Kennedy, who had beaten an overconfident Republican incumbent, Henry Cabot Lodge, Jr.) came by the office to tell my brother that he intended to vote for him. Kennedy was wearing a loose sweater and casual slacks, his hair slightly disheveled, making him look much too young for the Senate. "Seems like a nice kid," Lyndon said after Kennedy had left. "Probably has a good future ahead of him."

The so-called Humphrey threat, which Bobby Baker and I had "worried" about, had never really amounted to a puddle of warm spit. Hubert naturally tried to make it seem more important than it was, even to the point of personally conferring with Lyndon about certain committee assignments in exchange for his support. But Lyndon had no need to bargain with anyone; he had all the votes he needed. Nevertheless, the following morning Hubert phoned my brother about a half hour before the caucus, once again pressing for a few concessions.

Rising to his feet with the phone clenched in his right hand (when Lyndon stands up for a phone conversation, that's a sure sign he's mad), he snapped at the mouthpiece: "Goddamm-it, Hubert, I wasted enough time with you yesterday. So you can take your lousy eight votes and do what you please."

A few minutes later he was escorted into the caucus room by all the big guns in the Senate and got elected unanimously. No one else was nominated. Thus, at forty-four, he was the youngest man ever to be named floor leader of the Senate by either major party and the only one so designated during his first term.

So far so good—but we still had the possible problem of Allen Shivers in the coming election. His private promise not to run was certainly not binding. We knew he could change his mind any damned time he pleased. Consequently, I decided to give his promise a public airing.

Having first ascertained that Governor Shivers would be in Washington on February 13, 1953, I got some close friends to arrange a luncheon meeting of the Texas Congressional Delegation that would coincide with Shivers' visit. Quite obviously, he would be expected to come. Then we asked Sam Rayburn to attend so that he could award a testimonial plaque to Lyndon. However, when Mr. Rayburn heard that Shivers would be there, he backed off.

"No, sir," he snapped, "I wouldn't be in the same room with that sonofabitch—much less the same table."

Finally, at the very last minute, we confided our devious strategy to Congressman Wright Patman and asked him to persuade Mr. Sam. Then, knowing these luncheons were strictly off-the-record affairs with no official press, we asked each congressman to invite a reporter from Texas as his private guest. Against this stage setting, Sam Rayburn got up to deliver the bronze plaque to Lyndon with a flow of eloquent praise, reminding everyone that he had served with Lyndon's daddy in the state legislature and had known my brother when he was a ten-year-old hanging around the steps of the state capital. It was a warm personal speech.

Then Allen Shivers, completely unaware that half the guests

were newsmen (including a representative from *Time* magazine), decided to outdo Rayburn in his praise of Lyndon. "The state of Texas has never had a finer senator," he said. "And I personally hope he'll stay here a long time."

Well, the very next day every newspaper in Texas printed that statement—along with a picture of Shivers embracing my brother.

When Lyndon read them, he walked over to my desk and said, "You take this plaque they gave me, Sam Houston. You're the one who won it."

That night a friend of mine called me from Texas to tell me that he'd had a drink with John McConkite, the governor's chief aide. "Goddamn it," he complained to my friend. "Allen should have known better than to get boxed in like that in Lyndon's own backyard. He'll never be able to squeeze out of this one."

He never tried. He ran for reelection instead. But we did have an opponent in that 1954 primary, a young millionaire who hired the same public-relations firm that helped Smathers defeat Senator Claude Pepper in Florida. Having heard they were planning to publish a scandal sheet with a lot of muck about our family, Lyndon asked me to fly out to Texas to warn them against such tactics.

That was fairly easy. And while I was in Dallas, I also arranged to draw the wealthy candidate into a public question-and-answer session in which he fumblingly alienated several sectors of the voting population—all of which we tape-recorded for future use. Among other things, he denounced Truman for favoring Negroes and made some strong remarks against organized labor. His was such an inept performance that Lyndon never bothered to campaign a single day.

He even got annoyed with me for spending $125 for the tape recordings. "Damn it, Sam Houston, I wish you hadn't done that. I wanted to beat that boy without spending a single penny. Now I've got to report that $125 you spent."

He won by a huge margin, then easily defeated a token

Republican foe in the general election. Had it not been for a curious turnabout on Lyndon's part, he could have run un-opposed. Here's the background on that:

Shortly before the Republican state convention for the nomination of state-wide candidates, Lyndon arranged for me to fly back to Dallas in the private plane of one of the fat cats in the Republican party. Let's call him George Brant.

"Sam's got a wild hair up his nose and wants to visit some woman he met in Houston," Lyndon told Brant. "Could you give him a lift?"

Now, Brant didn't for one minute believe that line. You don't become a millionaire by being a fool. Consequently, within a half hour after the takeoff he stared right through me and said, "Okay, Sam, tell me what you and Lyndon are stewing about. It's got to be political, I know that."

"It ain't me that's stewing," I said. "It's Lyndon. He thinks you're going to run a tough opponent against him, with a big expensive campaign."

"Could be," said Brant.

"Well, he thinks that's kind of ungrateful of the Republican party. After all he's been doing to help Ike get his program across, sometimes alienating his own people, Lyndon naturally feels that Ike's party should lay off and not make him waste a lot of time campaigning. He knows he'll win, anyway, but he doesn't want to leave Washington with so much Senate business to take care of."

"He may have a point there," said Brant, looking only half-convinced. "But we've got to have candidates to build up the party."

"I personally hope you *do* have a candidate against Lyndon," I said. "Everyone knows he doesn't like opposition, but this year I hope he does have an opponent. Because if you do put up someone, he'll just have to campaign, and he's sure to beat hell out of anyone you can get. And that's exactly what I want: to have Lyndon beat your man so bad the Republicans will get rid of their stupid notion that Ike's victory in Texas has made this a Republican state."

With that kind of argument, I could see George Brant changing his mind right there and then. "We're not gonna give Lyndon that chance," he said. "Us Republicans ain't that stupid."

Sure enough, as soon as we got to Austin in his private plane—having first let off a couple of Democratic congressmen in Dallas—Brant started buttonholing the top delegates to the convention and persuading them not to run anyone against Lyndon.

"He'll just slaughter us," he kept telling them, "and make the whole party seem weaker."

They had, by the way, already picked their state-wide candidates, with Jack Porter slated to oppose my brother. But George Brant didn't let that bother him. He went ahead and finally convinced his party leaders that they should pull Porter out of the race and leave Lyndon a clear field.

That same night I phoned Lyndon and gave him the good news. "You're in free," I said. "I got George Brant to call 'em off."

"Wonderful, Sam Houston," he said. "That's wonderful. But how in the hell did you do it?"

So then I told him about my long talk with George and how he reacted when I said Lyndon *should* have opposition just so he could prove that Texas was still heavily Democratic. Then that strange turnabout happened. Lyndon himself bought my phony argument and immediately decided that he really should have opposition.

"By God, Sam Houston, you're right. I've got to have an opponent."

"See here, Lyndon——" I started to protest.

"You get ahold of George right away," he said. "And tell him to get Porter back in the race."

Well, that was a lot harder than what I'd done before.

However, George finally bought my counterargument that Lyndon shouldn't be given preferential treatment—that if Shivers had Republican opposition, so should Lyndon. Everyone knew Shivers would win, and he'd surely resent those Republicans who had played favorites between him and Lyndon. So back in the race came Mr. Porter. He scarcely made a ripple in the fall election.

Incidentally, a few weeks before the election Senator Joe McCarthy came by the office to let Lyndon know that he would be going out to Houston the next day to give a "major speech" on foreign policy at a meeting of rich conservative Texans.

"Tell me what you want me to do, Lyndon," he said, with a knowing glint in his eyes. "I can speak *for* you or *against* you—whatever you say."

"You do what you please," said my brother. "Doesn't make a bit of difference to me."

When McCarthy had left, Lyndon turned to me with a slight frown on his face. "He's a sonofabitch, all right, but sort of charming in his crazy weasel way. But what I can't understand is why Ike doesn't blast him for the things he's been saying about General Marshall. There ought to be some loyalty there. After all, it was Marshall who gave Ike his big chance in Europe. And now he just sits by and lets McCarthy smear his old friend as a 'Communist dupe' without a word of protest. He's even endorsed Joe for reelection. How do you figure that one, Sam Houston?"

I used to see McCarthy quite frequently in the bar of the Carroll Arms Hotel, across the street from the Senate. He would be taking one drink after another with two or three friends, gulping them down in quick order, never quite losing his equilibrium but getting more talkative and boisterous with each new drink. He wouldn't go into a stupor or mumble or anything like that—he just got more animated.

After he was censured by the Senate, however, the liquor really got to him. That's when he seemed wild and unintelligible, sometimes stumbling to the men's room to vomit. He even appeared drunk on the floor of the Senate, often staggering down the aisle, mumbling apologies to fellow senators who simply ignored him, turning their backs on him as he approached. His spirit had died long before the undertaker came.

Without the major Eisenhower name at the top of their ticket, the Republicans stumbled a bit in the 1954 elections, giving the Democrats control of the Senate. Thus, at the age of forty-six, Lyndon Johnson was the youngest man ever to serve as Senate Majority Leader. He also became the country's greatest practitioner of consensus politics, persuading men of widely divergent temperaments to work together, somehow convincing a reactionary like Senator Byrd to see eye to eye with a rambunctious liberal like Senator Wayne Morse on some specific piece of legislation.

"There's got to be some common meeting ground for everyone," he kept saying.

Arguing, pleading, flattering, compromising, reminding Senator X of some past favor, and hinting a future favor to Senator Y, he masterminded through the various committees and on to the Senate chamber a steady flow of legislation, always mindful of proper timing.

There was, of course, a strong personal element in his technique. He knew the personal likes and dislikes, the strengths and weaknesses of every man in the Senate, as well as the special needs and demands of their particular states, carefully weighing all these factors in his dealings with each individual.

Once, when Senator Kennedy told him that he would support Lyndon on a particular bill "even if it means going against the interests of my state," my brother shook his head. "I would never let you do that, Jack. Your first duty is to represent your people. I never ask a man to vote for me when it means going against his constituents."

When Kennedy had left, Lyndon turned to me and said,

"Who in the hell is he kidding? That damned bill has nothing to do with his Massachusetts constituents. But he's sure learn-how to spread the bull, Sam."

And though he may have been disappointed, Lyndon never said a word of criticism (at least not to anyone on his staff) when Senator Kennedy refused to vote in favor of the censure of Joe McCarthy. He probably realized that Kennedy had to contend with certain family pressures.*

Yet, in spite of his readiness to understand the weaknesses and foibles of his Senate colleagues, Lyndon was a bit more demanding with members of his personal staff. They had to work long extra hours, often neglecting their home lives, and suffering the constant threat of "being fired" for some slight infraction. I put quotation marks around "being fired" because he didn't really fire people; that was just his way (admittedly unpleasant) of showing his displeasure with some-body's work.

Whenever he put on the "You're fired" act, I would have to tell the person that Lyndon didn't really mean it—to take the rest of the afternoon off and come back tomorrow. After awhile I got to be known as "general counsel for the fre-quently fired employees of Lyndon Johnson," and I've always said that anyone who worked for my brother for at least a month deserved the Purple Heart.

He was still a pretty good boss, however. What better evi-dence is there than the long tenure of many of his employees, people who loyally stayed with him for years and years? I guess they knew Lyndon could be more compassionate than most employers, that he really cared for them as human beings.

Quite frequently, when he had scolded someone and later realized he was wrong, he would shower that person with kindness and great generosity. He might send a secretary on a short extra vacation to Florida, or give an administrative aide extra money for his children's dental work. Some of his

* His father had been a supporter of McCarthy.

staff members openly wished they would get the next bawling-out, thinking he might give them something special because that was his way of apologizing. I doubt that he has ever been able—even as a small boy—to make a straightforward direct apology.

About the closest he's ever come to apologizing (at least to my personal knowledge) was an incident that occurred some years ago. He had asked me to bring home some documents he needed for a trip he was making with President Truman, and I, in turn, asked my secretary to take them from the files and put them in my briefcase. Halfway home (I was giving her a lift to her apartment), she told me she had forgotten them. Not wanting me to drive back in the heavy traffic on that hot, muggy day, she offered to go for them in a taxi and bring them to me at a cocktail lounge nearby. While she was picking them up, Lyndon saw the file and grumbled about Sam Houston's forgetfulness. She told me about it when she handed me the documents. As things turned out, Lyndon got home just before I did, and he confronted me in the driveway.

"Goddammit, Sam," he said. "Why can't you do anything right? I told you to get those papers . . . ."

He went on and on like that, never letting me get in a word of explanation, until Aunt Effie put her head out the window and said, "Sam, honey, could y'all come and help me fix the bathroom faucet?"

Well, there was nothing wrong with the faucet; she just wanted to help me out of that noisy predicament. She also fixed me a highball from the bottle I had stashed away in her closet.

"Don't you mind Lyndon," she said. "I know it's awful bad manners for a grown man to act that way in public, but this heat gets him, I think."

Later on, when he hollered up the stairs for me to come down to supper, I put on a pout of my own. I never answered him. I stayed up in my room and read an old *Esquire* till I was ready to go to bed, Aunt Effie having meanwhile brought me a tray of summer salad and cold watermelon.

I was still in my silent pout the next morning when we drove to work. Finally, as we were speeding through Rock Creek Park, he turned and said, "About those papers yesterday, let's forget about it, Sam Houston."

"Okay," I said, knowing that he was trying to apologize but was painfully unable to say, "I'm sorry." If there is anything tragic about my brother, I would guess it's his profound inability to say those simple words.

This particular trait, when combined with a quick temper and instant generosity, made him a puzzling person to work for. His more sensitive staff people found it especially difficult. One of them, a hard-working man whose wife deeply resented Lyndon because her husband was seldom home for supper, developed a bleeding ulcer and a twitch in his left eye. (Let's call him Miller Bryant.) On two or three occasions I hinted that he should find another job, knowing that he was a highly employable public-relations man. But he never took the hint. He had a curious loyalty to my brother.

"The chief treats me fine," he would say. "And nobody works any harder than he does."

Then, one afternoon just after Lyndon became majority leader, a very prominent Texas industrialist (call him Clem Foley) came into my office and asked me to become his representative in Washington at a very handsome salary. "Lobbyist," some people call it. Well, in view of Lyndon's position and his probable intention to run for President some day, I knew I couldn't possibly accept such a politically vulnerable job. But I knew who could.

Pointing through the open door at Miller Bryant, I said, "There's your man. Good friend of Lyndon's, damned fine worker, and plenty of know-how about Congress. But don't let him know who recommended him. And you'd better check with Lyndon before you offer the job."

An hour later my brother buzzed me to come into his

office. "That damned Miller's been looking for another job," he said. "Clem Foley just told me he wants to hire him."

Knowing Lyndon never likes anyone to quit on him, I told him it was *my* idea. "This job's liable to bust up his home," I said. "You ought to let him take Foley's offer. He needs a break."

Shortly after that, Miller phoned me from a pay booth and told me Foley had offered him twenty thousand dollars per year, almost three times his present salary.

"You better take it," I said. "But you'd better get Lyndon's okay first. You won't be worth a damn as Foley's representative if the majority leader's annoyed with you."

"What if he says no, Sam?"

"That's the chance you've got to take, Miller. But I don't think he'll turn you down. He likes you."

Lyndon had gone home early that day to pack for a trip out west, so I advised Miller to call him right away and I got his permission to listen in.

"How much is he offering you?" asked Lyndon after Miller had told him about the job offer.

"Twenty thousand a year," said Miller.

"That's not enough," said Lyndon. "Tell that old bastard he's got to give you twenty-five thousand dollars plus another five thousand for expenses—otherwise I won't let you go."

And he hung up without another word.

"What should I do now?" asked Miller. "What if Foley says *no*, Sam Houston?"

"That's another chance you'll have to take," I said. "But I don't think you'll have much trouble. Foley's got lots of money."

A few minutes later, his fingers trembling as he dialed the number, Miller called Foley and repeated Lyndon's exact words—leaving out the "bastard."

"Why, sure," said Foley in a booming voice. "I think that's a right fair figure. When can you start?"

My brother grinned from ear to ear when I told him about

the conversation. "I should have said thirty plus five," he said.

Incidentally, Miller is still working for Foley at three times his starting salary, an ample adjustment for inflation.

Lyndon had been a lot less sympathetic when a different millionaire offered *me* a job several years earlier. "I don't think you should take it," he said. "You stay outa those jobs, Sam. There's nothing illegal about them—they're just political dynamite later on."

I had this advice in mind in 1956 when a New Jersey manufacturer asked me to represent him in Washington. Good salary, nice fringe benefits. We met at his company's swank apartment house near Dupont Circle.

"All right," I said. "I'll be happy to take your offer—but on one condition."

"What's that?"

"On the express condition that I'll never be asked to contact anyone on Capitol Hill," I said. "Because if my brother ever catches me talking to any congressman or senator about your business, he'll get my ass in jail—and yours, too."

Needless to say, that manufacturer never spoke to me again.

Unable to take the kind of job I was obviously most qualified for (my career had always been tied to the federal government, except for brief stints as the Mexican representative of the Texas Transport Company and an executive position with a Texas insurance company), I had found myself somehow confined to my brother's office. Fortunately, I was a bit more relaxed than most other staff members. I simply wasn't cut out to be a humorless drone.

With his new duties as majority leader, Lyndon drove himself and his staff to a point of near-exhaustion. Tired, nervous, and always wary of pulling some boner that might annoy the boss, his various assistants and secretaries put on a show of somber dedication whenever he was around. It was during this solemn period that Juanita Roberts decided to spruce up Lyndon's office with a couple of plants, never dreaming they would offend him.

"Get those damn things outa here," he told her when he spotted them. "I'm not running a greenhouse."

She came out to the secretarial office, tears welling in her eyes, and hastily put the plants on the windowsill near the water cooler. Unable to resist the obvious temptation, I later phoned the director of the U.S. Botanical Gardens.

"I'm calling for the Senate Majority Leader," I said. "And I'm wondering if you could bring us some big plants to pretty up our offices."

"Why, yes, sir—we sure can. What kind would you like, sir?"

"Well, the senator likes 'em big and leafy," I said, winking at Marie Wilson, one of our lovely secretaries. "How about some rubber plants and large ferns? Maybe a dozen or so."

Two hours later, while Lyndon was down at the Senate floor, a small cadre of men from the Botanical Gardens delivered thirteen huge plants, which I asked them to place along every wall of Lyndon's rather large office. It looked like a jungle suite. On the fern closest to his desk I put a large card that read: "To LBJ from one of his greatest admirers."

Then we all sat back and waited for the inevitable explosion. No matter how hard I try, I just can't find the words to describe his reaction when he finally got back to his office. I do know that "explosion" is too mild a word.

Lyndon continued to drive himself at a furious pace—ten, twelve, fourteen hours a day. Small wonder that early in July, 1955, he suffered a severe heart attack and was immediately hospitalized. Lady Bird was by his side constantly and mama flew out from Johnson City to visit him whenever his doctors permitted. I also spent a lot of time at the hospital, playing dominoes with him and trying to keep his mind off the affairs on Capitol Hill.

When he started beating me at dominoes and crowing about it, I knew he was on the mend. I also noticed that he seemed more reflective and that he was beginning to read things he had never read before. This was rather unusual because I doubt that Lyndon had read more than five or six books—of any kind—from cover to cover since graduating from college twenty-five years earlier. His reading had been confined to newspapers, magazines, and closely printed government reports and pending legislation.

After six months of well-controlled convalescence, he returned to Washington from the ranch and resumed his duties as majority leader. Anyone who feared that he hadn't fully recovered from his heart attack should have seen him in action when he got back to the office. It was during this period that Senator Russell appraised Lyndon's leadership in the following words:

> He doesn't have the best mind on the Democratic side of the Senate; he isn't the best orator; he isn't the best parliamentarian. But he's the best combination of all those qualities.

He could have added that Lyndon was also the most energetic man in Washington, heart attack or no heart attack, and some of that energy seemed to pour into the rest of us. Even I was infected with overwork, until I was cut down by an accident that severely injured my right leg in the autumn of 1957. For reasons I've never fully understood, my fractured leg didn't mend very well and the consequent pain was excruciating.

After awhile, Lyndon insisted that I consult Dr. Robert Robertson, a specialist at Johns Hopkins Medical Center, who told me it was osteomyelitis and recommended immediate surgery. Just to make sure, my brother sent my X rays to the Mayo Clinic, which confirmed the diagnosis. The Mayo doctors also assured us—bearing in mind Lyndon's insistence, "My brother's got to have the best doctoring money can buy"— that Dr. Robertson was among the finest orthopedic surgeons in the world.

After eight grueling hours of surgery, during which a section of bone was removed from my hip to replace the eroded bone in my leg, I wound up with a right leg five inches shorter than the left one. My troubles were compounded by the fact that I was placed in a body cast that stretched from my neck down to my toes.

When Lyndon came into my room and saw me lying there like a mummy, he choked up. He couldn't say anything except "Sam Houston," and tears welled up in his eyes. I finally had to make some crack about the return of King Tut to cheer him up, but I guess it wasn't very funny—even to me.

Thereafter he came to visit me almost every day in the hospital and at the apartment where I was living with my second wife—spending several hours discussing all kinds of things, obviously trying to keep my spirits up. But sometimes that body cast got him awfully depressed, and *I* would have to cheer *him* with some bit of nonsense. Finally, about a month after I got home, we both decided that the best mental therapy would be for me to start working again.

"Why don't you prepare a daily memo for me," he said. "You've got all this time to read the newspapers and magazines and to watch the TV newscasts and public-interest programs like *Meet the Nation* and all that. So why don't you just give me your views on them and let me know what I oughta do on anything that comes up in the Senate."

He couldn't have made a more welcome suggestion. The next morning, and every morning for the next eleven months, I would start dictating a memo to my wife at five in the morning. By eight thirty, she would have it typed and ready to be picked up by a special messenger from Lyndon's office. Then at ten o'clock he would call me to discuss the memo, often asking me to elaborate on some suggestion I'd made. One of the things we talked about a great deal was the space program. Just before my operation—not more than two or three days after the Russians had launched Sputnik I—Lyndon had come to the hospital on his way home from a visit to the White House.

"I can't understand Ike's way of thinking," he said. "There

I was, telling him we ought to start our own space program to counterbalance the Russians, and he keeps talking about his two little old Polaris missiles. Hell, that's like comparing a peashooter to a howitzer."

Shortly after that, he met with Dick Russell and Styles Bridges (the most powerful Republican in the Senate) and they agreed that Lyndon should launch an investigation by his Preparedness Investigating Subcommittee. To act as special counsel, Lyndon called on his old friend, New York lawyer Edwin Weisl. As his assistant counsel, Mr. Weisl brought along with him from his law firm a bright young attorney named Cyrus Vance, who later became Lyndon's undersecretary of defense and top international troubleshooter.

Testimony from prominent scientists such as Dr. Vannevar Bush, Dr. Wernher von Braun, Dr. Edward Teller, and top military leaders such as General James Gavin, General Bernard Schriever, and others, convinced my brother that we were woefully behind in the space race. Not long after that Lyndon created a blue-ribbon Special Committee on Space (which later became the permanent Committee on Aeronautical and Space Sciences) and became its chairman.

Using the legislative drafting skill of his Policy Committee Counsel, Gerald Siegel, my brother was able to write a bill that was unanimously accepted by the Special Committee. (Incidentally, Lyndon loved to do things with unanimous support. Of the hundreds of reports written by the various committees and subcommittees of which he was chairman, not one single negative vote was ever cast and not one single "minority" report was ever filed. I think that must be some sort of a record.)

After the usual compromises with the House, this became the Space Act of 1958, which created the National Aeronautics and Space Administration and laid the foundation for all the fantastic space shots we see today. Later, it was my brother who convinced President Kennedy that we should send men to the moon.

I have always felt that Lyndon has never been given enough credit for his part in getting us going in space. It really should have been Lyndon's name they left on that plaque on the moon. When Bill Moyers suggested that one of the Apollo 11 modules should be named after John F. Kennedy, I knew he was simply siding with the Kennedys against the man who started him in his career.

Fortunately, during that early period, Lyndon was also able to draw upon the expertise of my good friend, Dr. Glenn Wilson, who had been buried away in some minor job on his staff.

"From now on," he told the assembled staff, glancing at a résumé of Glenn's academic background, "no one will be permitted to call this man 'Glenn' or even 'Mr. Wilson.' In the future he'll be addressed as he ought to be—*Doctor* Wilson, my new personal adviser on space matters." (Despite his occasional cracks about intellectuals, Lyndon has a considerable respect for academic attainment.) Incidentally, I was the one who told him about Glenn, and he quickly followed my suggestion.

There was one other suggestion he didn't take. One afternoon he came by the apartment as I was watching a rerun of the McClellan Committee hearings on the Huntley-Brinkley newscast. In this particular segment Bobby Kennedy, as committee counsel, was badgering Jimmy Hoffa in a nasty, sarcastic manner that some people later called "ruthless." There was something holier-than-thou in his expression, a moral snobbery that tough prosecutors almost always have. It's the kind of black-and-white puritanical thinking that never permits the possibility of a possible gray. And I wondered how a son of Joseph P. Kennedy could consider himself all that holy. I'm happy to say that Hoffa snapped back at him, that he didn't cringe the way Dave Beck did.

There was something else I noticed on that newscast: Senator John Kennedy was sitting close to his little brother and would occasionally pass him a note. It was obvious he didn't object at all to Bobby's bully-boy tactics, yet he himself remained serenely out of it, letting his brother do the less-savory work.

"There's your main opposition in 1960," I said to Lyndon, referring to the Democratic Presidential nomination. "These hearings are the opening gun. He's letting Bobby scare the hell out of labor, so they won't dare oppose him. Hoffa and Beck have supported Republicans up to now, so he's not worried about them. But you know damn well the Democrat labor leaders are getting the message."

"You're too cynical about the Kennedys," said Lyndon. "Bobby's kinda tough, but Jack looks all right."

"That's just the point, Lyndon. He's getting the benefit of his little brother's prosecuting without soiling himself. He's running for President right now."

"Oh, I don't know about that," he said. "He might want to be Vice-President—but that's about all."

CHAPTER SIX

Miserable Three Years

John F. Kennedy had already bagged the 1960 Democratic nomination for President at least a month before the convention. With a highly financed new-style machine that was operated with brutal efficiency by brother Bobby, he swept through primary after primary while Lyndon sat in Washington, still hoping his old alliances in the House and Senate would grab the prize for him in a tight convention.

He thought, for example, that Senator Tom Dodd would line up the Connecticut delegation. So did Tom. Neither of them knew that John Bailey, the state chairman, had put together a slate favoring Kennedy.

Several other senators and congressmen had given my brother the same innocent assurances: "Don't you worry about the people in my state, Lyndon—I'll have 'em for you when the time comes."

Bolstered by such ill-founded promises, Lyndon stayed away from the primary races, never entered a single one. He knew, as does everyone, that it's possible to win all the open primaries and still lose the nomination because most of the delegates are chosen in closed state conventions, usually under the tight control of party bosses.

Obviously, Jack and Bobby Kennedy knew the same damned thing. They weren't banking solely on those primary elections; they had their people all over the country, button-holing the party brass and thousands of delegates and potential delegates to those private conventions. But they also knew that a solid string of victories in those states that held open primaries would undoubtedly affect the attitudes of delegates to the closed conventions. After all, *electability* has to be a most important consideration in picking a candidate. So the Kennedys spent millions to prove JFK was electable.

Poor old Hubert Humphrey tried to stop that powerful juggernaut in West Virginia, apparently thinking that his tattered empty-pocket sincerity would be more appealing to the impoverished miners and hungry farmers than the sleek, obvious wealth of his opponent. He couldn't have been more mistaken.

Democratic voters have always been fond of millionaire candidates like Franklin Roosevelt, Adlai Stevenson, and Jack Kennedy. As a matter of fact, every one of the candidates at the 1960 Democratic convention *except Humphrey* was a millionaire—Kennedy, Johnson, Stevenson, Symington, Chandler. The party of the poor has always been hospitable to the very rich. Consequently, Humphrey's poor-boy effort in West Virginia was doomed to fail. And just to make sure he stayed poor, the Kennedy people reportedly cut off the small trickle of funds he was getting from New York by placing strategic calls to a few Eastern friends.

More than ever before, the 1960 campaign emphasized the crucial importance of big money in politics. Television had become the most effective (sometimes the only) contact between the voters and the candidates, on local as well as national elections; and that's a medium that gobbles up money like a dollar slot machine in Vegas.

Inevitably, this need for bigger and bigger money will taint the political process. When a candidate has to raise hundreds of thousands of dollars, sometimes many thousands from a single fat cat, can anyone seriously believe those big contributors are merely interested in good government?

There isn't a single mayor, councilman, state legislator, governor, congressman, President, or any other elected official in this country who hasn't gotten a contribution from some fat cat expecting a government contract somewhere down the line. Some of these large contributions may not be solicited —perhaps even turned down by a rare office-seeker—but I find it hard to imagine Joe Smith giving a ten-thousand-dollar check to Congressman X's campaign without expecting something in return.

There are, in fact, certain perennial candidates who make money from elections they have never dreamed of winning. They announce their candidacy with a great hullabaloo, collect campaign funds in a big hurry, then conveniently withdraw long before Election Day, without having to spend more than a fraction of those contributions. It may happen now and then, but I never personally heard of any would-be candidate returning that money.

Another favorite gimmick is the off-season testimonial dinner, where thousands of friends of Senator Blow pay one hundred dollars each for a five-dollar cold-veal and dried-peas dinner. The $75,000 "take" is presumably saved for the senator's next campaign about three years from now, but, of course, the bookkeeping on that kind of operation is pretty relaxed. There is nothing more relaxed than the accounting procedures of political candidates. Thousands of dollars come and go without even a petty-cash voucher.

From all I heard, Humphrey's campaign in West Virginia was a genuine petty-cash affair, with no huge contributions for TV, radio, or newspaper ads. Kennedy ground him under. He was so far ahead when the convention rolled around that I never gave a thought to accompanying Lyndon to Los Angeles. I couldn't have gone, anyway, having injured my bad leg at the ranch just a few days before it began.

In my crippled condition, I would have had to remain fairly stationary, and that's no way to enjoy a nominating convention. You've got to get around from one state caucus to another, hustling from this hotel to the next one, always on the go from morning till night. So I stayed at home and watched it all on television, knowing Lyndon would feed me all the scuttlebutt when he got back to Texas. Moreover, I didn't want to be around to see him get whipped by the Kennedys.

I suppose Lyndon felt he had an outside chance, especially when that big Stevenson demonstration broke loose and seemed to threaten Kennedy's first-ballot blitz. I had heard Rayburn tell Lyndon that JFK would be in trouble if he failed to make it on the first go-around. "Some of his people will switch to you rather than Adlai if they see Kennedy slipping."

He was referring, of course, to the big-city bosses who had Adlai pegged as a loser. For awhile there, as thousands of people poured into the balconies with extra tickets from Paul Butler*, I began to think my brother might make it, after all.

"This looks like another Willkie deal," Walter Winchell told a roving TV legman.

The Kennedys knew better. They had carefully counted noses beforehand and were sure they could hold fast. One of their people—perhaps it was Larry O'Brien—told a network commentator they had X number of votes on the first ballot, and he wasn't far off.

Like any other Presidential nominee, Kennedy could choose anyone he wished as a running mate. Lyndon certainly didn't expect to be chosen. He had rubbed a sensitive nerve when he reminded certain liberals that Kennedy had not voted to censure Senator Joe McCarthy, and the Kennedys weren't known as easy forgivers—certainly not Bobby. Neither is Lyndon, for that matter. Few politicians are. Yet, despite his

* National chairman and ardent Stevenson supporter.

brother's strong objections (which were well known), John Kennedy obviously realized he needed Lyndon Johnson. As a Catholic attempting to overcome an historical bias against people of his faith, he particularly needed someone to boost him in the Bible Belt of the South and Southwest.

When he was first approached, my brother was naturally reluctant. Why should he give up being majority leader to accept the frustrating do-nothing job of Vice-President? Sam Rayburn certainly didn't think he should. Nor did any of the powerful Southern senators like Dick Russell.

Finally, John Kennedy personally called on Rayburn to persuade my brother to accept, basing his appeal on the quite logical ground that "Lyndon would be the most qualified man for the Presidency if anything should happen to me."

Lyndon was still reluctant. He wanted to be damned sure, he later told me back at the ranch, that Kennedy really wanted him over the long haul and not just for the fall election. Then, much to the dismay of Brother Bobby, certain labor bosses like Walter Reuther, and a few Southern congressmen who preferred Lyndon in the Senate, my brother accepted the nomination.

Cynic that I am, I thought he now had two choices: to campaign hard for Kennedy's election or to take it easy and slip back into his powerful post as majority leader. (He was, you may remember, also running for reelection as senator under a new Texas law that permitted a dual candidacy.) Choosing the first alternative, he campaigned harder than ever before, particularly concentrating on the South and some of the border states.

The final results clearly show that Kennedy knew what he was doing when he insisted on having Lyndon as his running mate. Without the electoral votes of Texas and two or three Southern states, JFK would never have become President. In those particular states it was Johnson carrying Kennedy. In Texas, for example, Lyndon coasted to an easy victory margin of five hundred thousand votes in the Senate race, while the Kennedy-Johnson ticket barely squeaked through with a margin of about fifty thousand votes—convincing evidence that Bobby's brother wouldn't have made it without *my* brother.

Lyndon no doubt expected some show of gratitude from the Kennedys and their covey of New Frontiersmen. Instead, they made his stay in the Vice-Presidency the most miserable three years of his life. He wasn't the number-two man in that administration; he was the lowest man on the totem pole. Though he has never said this to anyone (perhaps because his pride would never let him admit it), I know him well enough to know he felt humiliated time and time again, that he was openly snubbed by second-echelon White House staffers who snickered at him behind his back and called him "Uncle Cornpone."

Some of their smart-aleck jokes extended to my sister-in-law. Supposedly civilized New Frontiersmen had a great time repeating Jacqueline Kennedy's remark that "Lady Bird would crawl down Pennsylvania Avenue on broken glass for Lyndon." However, I imagine Lady Bird would do just that for my brother. So, might I add, would Eleanor Roosevelt, Bess Truman, and Mamie Eisenhower for their men. Still, I'm not too surprised that Mrs. Onassis would look down her elegant nose at that kind of wifely loyalty.

Judging from news reports and comments from some of my old friends in the Congress, the New Frontier crowd took over with a bang. An army of so-called "beautiful beautiful people"—many of them fancy Ivy Leaguers and others desperately pretending to be—invaded the official and social life of Washington, hoping to change things overnight.

They no doubt exercised a considerable influence on the *social* side of the Capitol, but their influence on the *governmental* side was considerably less. Hundreds of professors and foundation executives drafted ambitious programs for legislation aimed at "getting this country to move again," but none of them knew much about tedious and sometimes painful procedures involved in the legislative process—knowledge that comes only from experience.

The Kennedys had easy access to the greatest legislative strategist of this century—Lyndon Johnson—but they refused to use him. Instead, there was a swarm of young, conceited New Frontiersmen running around Capitol Hill trying to tell elderly congressmen "this is the way it's got to be" and to impress on Senator X or Congressman Y that they were speaking for the White House.

"I told that young smart-ass to get the hell out of my office," one senior congressman told a friend of mine. "No Harvard punk is going to tell me how to run my committee!"

On one of my few visits to Washington during those famous "one thousand days" (I had stayed away because I didn't want to be a firsthand witness to my brother's day-to-day humiliation), I had a couple of drinks at the Carroll Arms Hotel with Senator Dennis Chavez of New Mexico. The Punta del Este conference had just been held in Montevideo, and the Latin American countries had been told that six hundred million dollars would be made available by the U.S. for the Alliance for Progress.

"The President will have a tough time getting it," Chavez told me. "His people, particularly that Dick Goodwin, antagonized most of the Senators and Congressmen who were on the U.S. delegation. He started throwing his weight around as if he were the President himself and telling a couple of senior senators what they could or couldn't say to the press, that kinda crap."

He kept scowling at his glass and drumming the table with his thin bony fingers as he spoke in a whispery gravel voice. "These young know-it-alls are going to have to learn that you can't push the Senate around, and I don't give a damn whom they represent."

"Are they all that way?" I asked.

"Almost," he said. "Except for a couple of people like Larry O'Brien. He seems okay. But, hell, he doesn't hold a candle to the man who *ought* to be handling Congress. And you know whom I'm talking about—your brother Lyndon. Here they've got the best legislative strategist in history, a man who really knows how things are done on the Hill, how to push bills through the toughest committees without making a lot of enemies—and they send him off on some stupid mission to Timbuctoo. I can't understand this administration, wasting a talent like that. They must think Lyndon will steal their show."

Now Senator Chavez wasn't the only one who felt my brother was being wasted. Several other senators and representatives told me the same thing. And there were quite a few columnists, like Walter Lippmann and Arthur Krock, who kept wondering why Kennedy didn't use Lyndon to guide his proposals through the House and Senate. The New Frontier programs were stalled in various committees of both houses, where they were being "sat on" by powerful committee chairmen who had previously responded to the "Johnson treatment" that Mary McGrory described in one of her early columns.

Lyndon, as would later be proved, could have broken that log jam for the Kennedys—but, for reasons no one has ever satisfactorily explained, they chose to use their own ineffectual techniques.

John Kennedy should have known better. He had personally seen my brother in action as majority leader, pushing some of Eisenhower's proposals through a sometimes stubborn Congress, personally pressuring old allies whom he had assigned to the most important committees. Many of them were Southerners or Texans who had been opposed to Kennedy and who would have bolted to Nixon if Lyndon hadn't talked to them. They finally went along because they thought Lyndon would have a strong voice in the new administration, so they were understandably angry when they saw him being snubbed and insulted like a poor brother-in-law.

Having had the good sense to pick Lyndon as his running mate, and obviously concerned about the Southern vote in the general election, Kennedy should have realized it was even more important to think about the deeply entrenched Southern senators and representatives who controlled Congress. For his own good, he should have made Lyndon his number-two man. Instead, he chose to rely on Bobby, whose only congressional experience was working for Senator Joe McCarthy and Senator McClellan. That scarcely qualified him for the difficult job of getting congressmen of different (often conflicting) viewpoints to vote the same way on certain bills. It takes a born compromiser, a healer, to do that kind of work.

As a matter of fact, Bobby's tough prosecutor roles were the worst kind of training for a man who's going to stage-manage a legislative program. I am well aware that Larry O'Brien was the official liaison man between the White House and Congress, but everyone knew it was Bobby Kennedy who was calling most of the signals. They also knew Bobby had no great love for Lyndon and that he was surrounded by a so-called intellectual elite who regarded my brother with contempt.

Thus, in spite of all the high-flown rhetoric about "getting this country to move again," there was nothing much happening. Scores of well-intentioned bills on housing, education, medicare, civil rights, and foreign aid were stalled in some committee or subcommittee with no prospect of being voted upon by either house.

Meanwhile, the New Frontiersmen somehow managed to create an aura of great accomplishment, smugly congratulating each other at hundreds of fancy cocktail parties for those beautiful-beautiful "in" people, who seemed to have an endless supply of Lyndon jokes. Judging from some of the gossip columns of that era, the most popular witticism was "Say, whatever happened to LBJ?"

Although they were obviously referring to my brother's nowhere status in the Washington hierarchy, their question had a certain relevance in respect to his physical whereabouts.

One week he might be in Dakar to observe the first anni-versary of the new Republic of Senegal; the following week he might be on an equally important ceremonial visit to Thailand, the Philippines or Taiwan. He became the most-traveled Vice-President in history, visiting at least thirty-three foreign countries and making more than a hundred and fifty speeches abroad. Quite often he would ask Lady Bird to go along, knowing that she had a way with strangers. Lynda and Luci would stay at home in Washington or at the ranch on the Pedernales River, well cared for by Zephyr but never-theless resenting their parents' frequent absences.

I imagine most politicians' children feel like deserted or-phans and would probably vote against their daddy if given a chance. That was certainly true of Lyndon's kids. Luci has publicly said that she remembers screaming and stomping her feet because her mother would be taken away by Lyndon for some political rally.

"My resentment was aimed at him," she told a reporter, "because he seemed to be always taking my mother away, and I knew I loved her. Even when my father was around, I'm afraid I didn't do much to help our relationship. So even-tually he stopped trying, too. This bothered mama a great deal. She really tried to smooth things over, and to keep us a closely knit family. She loved us both and tried to bring us together. She felt a sense of loyalty to father; but she also felt a tre-mendous sense of conscience toward my sister and me. Quite often she was torn between the two obligations.

"Finally, I decided: Why buck it? So I stopped thinking of him as a father and started thinking of him as a friend. Eventually, I learned to love him as a person—not as a father, because he seldom had time to be a father."

Having lived in their home off and on for many years, watching those little girls trying to get their busy daddy's attention to tell him about a problem at school or about something funny that happened at a playmate's birthday party, sometimes pulling at him in a futile attempt to take his attention away from the Congressional Record—then finally retreating with a pout and a hurt look in their eyes—I can well understand Luci's attitude.

Unfortunately, most politicians have that same problem: They're away from home too often, and their children become part-time orphans. Harry Truman was the wonderful exception. He always doted on little Margaret, and he was publicly willing to defend her against any "sonofabitch" who tried to criticize her singing. Some people felt Truman demeaned himself when he used that word against the *Washington Post* music critic, but I frankly think he made millions of friends with his loyalty.

I felt the same way about his firing of General MacArthur. There was no pussy-footing with Truman. He said exactly what he felt, and to hell with all the niceties. Incidentally, I remember watching General MacArthur dressed in civilian clothes as he waited in the corridor outside the hearing room where he testified before a closed session of the Senate Armed Services Committee. He was a surprisingly short man and his cocky manner seemed slightly comical when he was out of uniform. I saw him fading right there and then.

Getting back to President Kennedy's failure to use Lyndon as his legislative manager, I think one must finally conclude that he had only a limited understanding of how the government really works, and therefore couldn't appreciate my brother's true value. Perhaps he *did* have a certain historical sense, a broad exposure to history books, but he never showed a real grasp of actual governmental operations. He had never been one of the active senators, nor had he ever guided a single important bill through the legislative mill—amending this section to catch that vote or buttonholing Senator X about a different amendment or doing a bit of horse-trading with Senator Z. All that necessary back-stage maneuvering apparently bored John Kennedy, as it later bored his brother Bobby.

One of Lyndon's friendly biographers, Booth Mooney, has

another explanation about why he wasn't used as the chief go-between from the White House to Capitol Hill:

> Johnson had a deep-rooted respect for the traditional separation of governmental powers. It was, in his own words, bred into the marrow of his bones, and now that he was a member of the executive department he would have no more thought of injecting himself into the functions of the legislative department than he would have considered voting the Republican ticket in the next election.

With all due respect to my dear friend Booth and to my brother if he actually approved that statement, I must frankly say it's a bit of hogwash. The minute Lyndon became President he had his hand on every major piece of legislation and personally pushed it through both the House and Senate. That was his great strength—his ability to make Congress enact his programs. No President can be successful unless he strongly injects himself into the legislative process, no matter how much lip service he gives to a theoretical separation of the executive and legislative branches of government. Franklin Roosevelt was the prime example of a strong effective President who knew how to handle Congress, and he was my brother's model.

So I'm afraid Booth Mooney's explanation won't hold water. And if Lyndon actually made such a statement, I think he was merely avoiding the more likely explanation: *that the Kennedys didn't want him to help them get their proposals through Congress.* His pride wouldn't let him admit that. There was also a deep reluctance on his part to say anything publicly that might be taken as a criticism of the President. For all the galling humiliation he suffered under Kennedy, he had a stubborn kind of loyalty to his chief. What's more—as my ex-wife soon found out—he wouldn't tolerate other people criticizing Kennedy in his presence.

Having just returned from Europe, where she was working for our State Department, Mary was invited to have dinner with Lady Bird and Lyndon at the Elms, their home in Spring Valley. (I was in Texas at the time, but she later told me what happened.) It was a very pleasant evening, with the usual chitchat about family affairs. Then, naturally assuming that Lyndon deeply resented the Kennedys, Mary told him that a lot of people in Europe apparently hated or distrusted the President. She even went so far as to repeat a harmless joke about the Kennedy clan. That's when my brother exploded.

"Listen here," he said, with sudden anger in his eyes, "you're making cracks about the man you're working for. If you don't like the President then why don't you quit your job? You have no business holding that position if you can't be loyal to him."

"But I'm only an office worker——" she started to say.

"That makes no difference," he snapped. "Either quit talking about him that way or quit your job!"

When she told me about this unexpected scolding from Lyndon, I was just as surprised as she had been. Since it was fairly common knowledge that he was getting pretty shabby treatment around the White House, such fierce loyalty seemed rather odd and a bit strained. Then it suddenly came clear to me. It wasn't at all strange. He had always felt that way: An employee owes complete loyalty to his employer. That was almost a phobia with him, dating way back to his earliest years as an NYA administrator.

He always demanded complete loyalty from his subordinates. Any shade of criticism or lack of enthusiasm from any staff member could be suspect. He might tolerate sloppiness and occasional stupidity from someone who was dedicated, but his most able people would be leary of crossing him on even the most impersonal matters, no matter how justified their criticism might be. A staffer's duty was to carry out instructions, not to challenge them. He felt the same way about the employees of other people and was deeply suspicious of anyone who criticized his boss.

115

"You better watch out for that guy," he once told me, referring to some senator's administrative aide who had made a harmless crack about his chief. "Anyone who talks that way about the man he's working for can't be trusted. He would double-cross you a lot easier."

As a consequence of his rather excessive demand for complete loyalty from subordinates, he probably got his best advice from people who weren't on his official payroll—outsiders like Abe Fortas, Clark Clifford, A. W. Moursund, Phil Graham, and a few trusted colleagues in the House and Senate. And I guess he took a lot of candid criticism from me because I was his only brother.

Still, despite his loyal-employee notions, I think his reaction to my ex-wife's remark about the Kennedys was a trifle exaggerated. After all, she was merely trying to please him.

His attitude is particularly ironic when you pause to consider the highly publicized hopes of certain Kennedy associates to "dump Lyndon in 1964." At least ten Washington columnists hinted or said outright that Bobby Kennedy was pressuring his brother to get a new Vice-Presidential candidate for the coming election and that he was hoping the Bobby Baker scandal would provide the "right reason" for doing so. It should be noted, incidentally, that no one—despite the most exhaustive investigations—has ever linked my brother to any of the deals for which Bobby Baker was later indicted. They all occurred after he had quit working for Lyndon.

Baker was a sharp wheeler-dealer, no doubt about that. He was bright, charming, ambitious, and he had a nose for money. His chief mentor in financial matters was Senator Robert Kerr, the millionaire oilman from Oklahoma.

Several years ago, just before the senator died, Bobby phoned my office to tell me about a promising oil venture.

"Bob Kerr tells me it's a good bet," he said. "And I thought you might want a piece of the action, Sam."

It sounded like a perfectly legitimate deal, but I had to

say no because I knew Lyndon would give me hell for getting involved in any business involving oil.

"I'm the majority leader and a Texas senator," he once told me. "So I want to be damn sure none of us gets into any ventures where my votes can be misconstrued."

When the Baker scandal eventually hit the headlines, I was damned glad I passed up that offer, but I'll have to admit it was tempting at the time. Lyndon, of course, was obviously aware of the columnists' open speculation about Bobby Kennedy using the Baker case as a reason to dump him, but he seemed confident the President would ask him to stay. On two or three of his visits to the ranch, we had long discussions about his future plans and I asked him about the Bobby rumors (both Bobbys) and he shrugged them aside.

"That's just newspaper talk, Sam Houston. They're always doing that. Some columnists think that if they speculate hard enough about something they can actually make it happen."

"Sometimes they do," I said.

"But not this time," he said. "Jack Kennedy has personally told me that he wants me to stay on the team. Some of the people around him are bastards, but I think he's treated me all right. He's had me briefed by Rusk and some of the other Cabinet members, and I especially like Dean Rusk. He's a damned good man. Hard-working, bright, and loyal as a beagle. You'll never catch him working at cross-purposes with his President. He's just the kind of man I'd want on my Cabinet if I were President."

Little did he know that he would have his own Cabinet within a few short months.

CHAPTER SEVEN

Take-over after Kennedy Assassination

At the very moment President Kennedy was shot, I was having lunch with my brother-in-law, Oscar Bobbitt, at his home in Austin, Texas. It was also my home, for I had been living with him and my sister Becky since my retirement from government service in 1960.

The telephone rang as we were about to have our soup, and Bobbi grabbed it off the cabinet near his chair. Almost instantly he let out a gasp and the phone nearly dropped from his trembling hand. His eyes bulged with fright.

"For God's sake, what happened?" I asked.

"Lyndon's been shot," he said. "So has Kennedy."

The news department of the local television station* had called to give us the first fragmentary reports, which indicated that my brother, rather than Governor Connally, was the second victim. In those first hectic and confused moments,

* It's owned by Lyndon and Lady Bird, and Bobbitt is vice-president and general sales manager.

Senate Majority Leader Johnson with members of his staff.

Lyndon and mother in the hospital as they read through a batch of get-well telegrams and letters after his recovery from a heart attack in 1955.

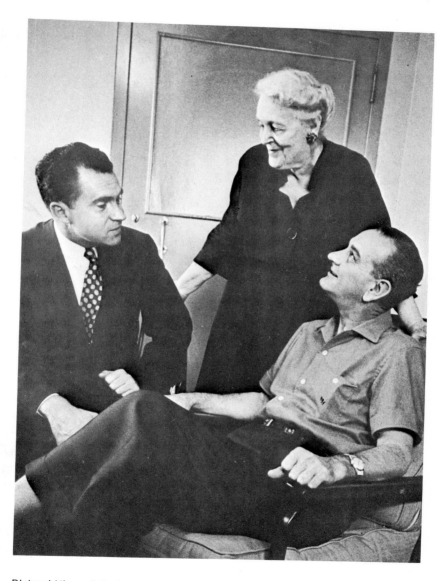

Richard Nixon visits Lyndon during his convalescence.

Lyndon Johnson, Chairman of the Texas delegation and Favorite Son candidate, and the author head for the 1956 Democratic convention in Chicago.

Senator Johnson, with former President Truman and Sam Rayburn, Speaker of the House, visit an old Texas friend, John Nance Garner, at Uvalde, Texas, in November, 1958.

President Kennedy, former President Truman, and Vice-President Johnson at a White House luncheon.

In Jamaica, the Vice-President meets Great Britain's Princess Margaret at ceremonies marking the island's independence.

As Vice-President, Lyndon visited India in June, 1961. He is pictured here with a village child.

Lyndon with Bashir Ahmed, the Pakistani camel driver he invited to visit the LBJ ranch.

Rufus Youngblood had pounced on Lyndon in the second car and slammed him to the floor to protect him. The jolt had injured Lyndon, and he was still in pain when he got to the Parkland Memorial Hospital. Seeing him bent forward and holding his chest, some reporters naturally assumed he had also been shot.

We were still on the phone catching a relay of news bulletins from the TV station when more detailed reports clearly indicated that Lyndon had not been wounded. We then turned on the radio and TV, slightly relieved but still stunned by the horrible news.

Thinking it might be an international conspiracy, I imagined Lyndon would be the next target and the thought chilled me to the bone. Becky and I both expressed that fear as we watched the televised post-assassination events through glazed eyes. Then, as I watched my brother taking the oath of office—Jackie Kennedy, with vacant, staring eyes, standing at his side—I was overwhelmed with a sadness so heavy I could hardly bear it. In spite of all my resentment against the Kennedys, I broke down and wept for the President and his family. Rising from the couch in front of the TV set, I limped into my room and fell on my bed, oppressed by a tremendous sense of sadness. And it wasn't only Kennedy I was sorry for—I was also sorry for my brother, who had just taken over the most thankless job in the world.

Now I realized, as did most people, that it could also be one of the most dangerous jobs. By the very nature of his office, the President is bound to antagonize someone every day he holds office. There must be thousands of demented cranks who think of the man in the White House as a personal enemy they must destroy. The FBI can tell you plenty about that. And the most dismal aspect of this President-hating sickness is that there is no sure way for the President to protect himself against it.

Not long before he died, President Kennedy himself told a reporter that any chief of state is an easy target for a sniper,

119

especially when he is in a parade or making a public speech. Anyone with a high-powered rifle, a telescopic lens, and a good aim can find a thousand places to perch himself for a clear shot at the President—no matter how careful the Secret Service may be in its pre-parade inspections.

"It's simply impossible to guard against everyone," said Kennedy.

Such thoughts passed through *my* mind as I visualized my brother leading a giant parade down Fifth Avenue in New York or standing fully exposed on the platform of a Labor Day rally in Detroit's Cadillac Square, where thousands of windows and hundreds of rooftops overlook the square. But after awhile these morbid fears gave way to the more depressing consideration of the Presidency itself.

No job is more demanding or more onerous, more subject to public abuse. The average citizen couldn't care less what the president of General Motors thinks or does; but as a taxpayer he feels he has every right to think and to say any damn thing he pleases about the President. He and his family are the focal center of all public attention, and everything he does is subject to public approval or disapproval. He can't even pull his dog's ears without raising a storm of criticism from a bunch of old ladies in tennis shoes.

These were minor considerations, however. What concerned me most, as I lay on my rumpled bed in a darkened room, were the awesome responsibilities that had been suddenly thrust upon my brother. Every day, perhaps each working hour, he would have to make decisions affecting millions of people here in America and throughout the world. (He had made certain such decisions as majority leader but never with the ultimate responsibility of a President.) The Vietnam War was heating up, racial conflicts were tearing apart our cities, our educational institutions were at an explosive stage, millions of impoverished citizens were still waiting for the promised benefits of the Kennedy program, and each of these problems was bound to arouse deep and conflicting passions.

120

Lyndon would have to face and try to solve all of these issues without a personal mandate from the people. He was not an elected President and therefore had no way of knowing how much public support he would get.

In fact, it was quickly apparent that many of the Kennedy people resented and even hated Lyndon simply because the assassination had occurred in Texas. They somehow associated Dallas with LBJ—never mind that Oswald was not a Texan—and some of them were heard bitterly asking: "Who had the most to gain from Kennedy's death?" (It's a curious thing that Los Angeles was never condemned as a city when Robert Kennedy was killed there, but all kinds of sick judgments were made about Dallas.) And when the TV camera focused on the faces of certain members of Kennedy's staff and I saw the stiff coolness in their manner when my brother came near them, I feared that Lyndon would never be able to break down that unforgiving, personal resentment. Their attitude frankly angered me because I felt it was far more bitter than was justified by their understandable grief.

After several days of watching the televised accounts of the assassination, the funeral, Oswald's death, the frenzied assumption of power by Lyndon and the commentators' agonized appraisals of all that had happened—my mind and heart perpetually nagged by that persistent resentment against my brother by the Kennedy people—I finally placed a long-distance call to my friend, Sam Shaffer, the Washington correspondent for *Newsweek*. I wanted to let him know how I felt about the personal problems my brother would face around the White House. It was a long conversation and a very personal one (probably cost me more than thirty bucks), but I knew Sam would respect my confidence and print only the things I wanted to say for publication.

"Lyndon was never the number-two man in that administration," I told him. "And we both know that they made some pretty nasty jokes about him around the White House —not the President maybe, but some of those smart alecks

121

around him. They never showed any respect for him then, so there's no reason to expect them to change their minds about him now. Especially under these circumstances."

Well, I went on in that vein for awhile, no doubt showing a bitterness I had long suppressed. Then I capped it off by saying that Lyndon should do a general housecleaning and get rid of most of the Kennedy staff and have his own men replace them.

"You mean right away?" asked Shaffer.

"The sooner, the better," I said. "It'll be sticky for awhile, but he might avoid a lot of trouble later on. And you can quote me on all this."

Being the responsible man that he has always been, Shaffer decided to call Lyndon's office to get their reaction to my comments. He didn't want to intrude on my brother in the confused rush of activity that surrounded him, so he talked at length with Walter Jenkins, who was soon to take over a command post in the East Wing of the White House. Shaffer later told me about their conversation.

"Sam Houston may be right in certain respects," said Walter in his dry, cautious voice, "but I really don't think the President will want to go that far right away. He'll get around to it later on, I guess. But right now I reckon he won't want to ruffle any more feathers than he has to. He'll want to work with the Kennedy people as much as possible and to avoid any appearance of friction with them. So I don't think we gain anything by *Newsweek* quoting Sam Houston that way, though I can certainly understand his feelings. Ain't no one more loyal to Lyndon, I'll say that."

In view of what subsequently happened, I'm not sure who was right, but I tended to agree with Walter that it was best not to air my views in print. So I asked Sam Shaffer to regard our whole conversation as "off the record." Nevertheless, I still wish Lyndon had gotten rid of some of those people sooner than he did.

Except for my talk with Shaffer, I deliberately avoided any contact with the rash of newspapermen who swarmed around us from the moment Lyndon was sworn in. Every member of our family was besieged by the press, all wanting to know the "real LBJ." What was he like as a boy? Did he fight with his kid sisters when they were children? Did he ever play hooky? Who was his girl in high school? Did mama ever spank him? Did he wear long woolen drawers in the winter? Did they itch? They even wanted to know about *our* personal habits. Quite suddenly the whole damn Johnson family was living in a glass bowl. Excluding me. I didn't want any of that snooping into my personal life. Becky talked to some of the reporters who came to our house, but I stayed away from them. I would lock myself in my room until they went away. Once or twice Becky knocked on my door to tell me some photographer wanted to take a picture of the two of us together, and I yelled out that I was naked in the bathtub.

Ordinarily, I'm not that much of a shrinking violet. I was simply too moody, still brooding about Kennedy's death and what it could mean for my brother.

As you might expect, all the members of Lyndon's immediate family (and even a few distant cousins) were suddenly quite popular. People we hadn't seen for a long time would drop in unexpectedly. "Just happened to be driving by your house and just sorta thought we oughta drop in and say hello." That sort of thing. One of Becky's occasional acquaintances called up and asked if she could come by for a little visit, then called back five minutes later to ask if she could bring her boss along.

"Hell, Becky, these people don't give a damn about us personally," I said. "They just want to tell people they've been visiting the President's kin."

I could have sat in front of these people with a huge neck brace, a couple of rubber tubes up my nostrils, and my left leg in a cast, and they would have said, "You're looking fine, Sam. How's ole Lyndon doin' at the White House? You heard from him lately?"

As a matter of plain fact, I hadn't been feeling very well for a long time. Those twelve months in a body cast, following a major operation, had permanently affected my physical condition and forced me to retire from government service sooner than I wished. I hadn't minded being away from Washington during my brother's Vice-Presidency because I wouldn't want to see him humiliated; but now that he was in the White House, I sorely regretted my physical incapacity. With my back almost constantly aching from walking with a pronounced limp or lugging a heavy built-up boot, I had to take more sedatives than one ought to take. Sometimes bourbon and gin were a lot more satisfactory.

Whenever things got too gloomy and oppressive, I might have to go on a toot to get away from it all. That's exactly how I felt a few days after Kennedy was killed. I had been a virtual recluse, holing up in my bedroom to get away from all the yak-yak of people dropping by to gawk at us. Then, when I couldn't stand it anymore, I called up my old friend Judge Jeff Willens (which, of course, isn't his real name) and asked him to join me for a quick holiday in San Antonio.

"I want to get away from everybody," I said. "This damn house has been swarming with reporters and all kinds of sweet-weather friends."

"Sure, Sam, I'll be glad to. But where are you going to hide yourself, buddy?"

"That's easy," I said. "You get us a suite at the El Tropicano Hotel in your name, and we won't let anyone know I'm there except my sister Becky. I want her to know in case Lyndon should call."

That afternoon, as we were getting settled into the largest suite available, Willens asked me when I would be going back to Washington. "I know Lyndon's going to need you there, for all the political stuff," he said. "I remember him telling John Cameron Swazey how you were his chief political adviser."

He was referring to a television broadcast several years earlier. One of his (Swazey's) correspondents had come out to the ranch to do a story, "The Second Most Powerful Man in Washington," the presumption being that Ike was the most powerful. (I doubt that Ike could have gotten an extra set of golf clubs without Lyndon approving the appropriation.) Well, toward the end of the shooting, Lyndon told his cameraman, "I'm not letting you take another shot till you get one of me and my brother together."

"What does he do?" asked the leg man.

"What do you mean, what-does-he-do?" snapped Lyndon. "Why, Sam Houston is my chief political adviser—always has been."

Swazey quoted him directly in a seven-minute sequence on Lyndon a few nights later, and that was the statement Judge Willens brought up when he asked about my possible return to Washington.

"I'm not planning to go back," I said. "That pace would be too much for me, Jeff. I can't tell from one day to the next how I'll feel when I get up the next morning. My working days are over, man."

"Sorry I brung it up," he said.

"Never mind that," I answered. "Let's call up some girls I know and we'll have ourselves a few drinks and forget all this crap."

But just as our lady friends came in—one of them was the secretary of a lobbyist I knew—the phone started ringing and then stopped before I could pick it up. Then it rang again and the hotel operator almost shouted in my ear, "The White House is c-c-calling," she stammered. "It's the r-r-real White H-H-House calling, Mr. J-J-Johnson!"

"Just a moment," I said. "I'll take it in the bedroom. Please switch it there."

But when I got to the next room the operator told me the

125

call had been interrupted—that the President would call me back in a few minutes. Well, I waited on that bed for nearly two hours, not wanting to join Jeff and the ladies until I'd gotten the call. With that phone operator getting so excited, I didn't think I should complicate matters by switching a call from one extension to another.

Finally the call came through, with the operator breathlessly saying, "It's him! It's the President of the United States calling."

Then Lyndon's voice came over the wire. "Hi, Sam Houston, how y' doing?"

"Fine, Lyndon, everything's fine here."

"Sorry about that first call. I got involved in a hurry-up conference with Rusk and MacNamara, so I decided to wait till I got back home to call you. I'm still living at the Elms, you know. Just got in."

"I imagine you're pretty busy," I said.

"Never been busier," he said. "But I've been waiting for a chance to talk with you and to let you know how much I appreciate all you've done for me, Sam Houston. I wouldn't be here if it hadn't been for you."

"Lyndon," I said. "I had nothing to do with Oswald."

He gasped, sputtered, and then exploded. My God, what an explosion! I have never heard him so angry.

"Goddammit, Sam!" he shouted. "What the hell kind of a remark is that? Here I come all the way home to have a serious talk with you, and you come out with a damned stupid crack like that! Why in the hell can't you ever be serious, you crazy ass? You make your lousy sick jokes about everything. . . ."

He went on like that, getting angrier and angrier, for about twenty minutes. And I kept expecting him to slam the phone down like a sledgehammer, but he went on talking at full fury. Finally, in a tired, somewhat despairing voice, he said, "I'll call you some other time."

I certainly couldn't blame him for bawling me out. He was dead right. There is no earthly justification for a remark like that, no possible explanation. I mention this incident now only because it reflects how my brother must have felt about all the ugly insinuations that were made about Kennedy being killed in Texas, most of which he surely read or heard about in one form or another. He could blow up at me and thus release some of the tension, but what could he do about the persistent haters who were willing to spread the vilest rumors about him and all other Texans?

When one considers the stress under which he worked, I think it's remarkable how well Lyndon took over upon Kennedy's sudden death. And I don't have to rely upon my own subjective judgments in this respect. Here are the words of Theodore H. White:

> There is no word less than superb to describe the performance of Lyndon Baines Johnson as he became President of the United States. All accounts of his behavior through the week of tragedy—his calm, his command-presence, his doings, his unlimited energies—endow him with superlative grace. Yet such stories limit the tale only to his positive deed. To measure the true quality of his take-over, one must consider not only these positive acts, but what did *not* happen. So much *might* have gone wrong—yet did not.*

With almost thirty years' experience in the House, the Senate, and the executive branch, Lyndon moved into the Presidency with a sure knowledge of the vast, intricate machinery of government. As the strongest majority leader in recent history, he was no stranger to power and therefore wasn't awed or confused by his new responsibilities. He took to power like a fish to water. I think it had always been his natural habitat. But he didn't swallow it whole or wallow in it. He

* Theodore H. White, *The Making of the President* (New York, The New American Library, 1964), p. 45.

used only what he needed and when he needed it, always acutely aware of the *limits* of power as well as its potential. He also knew there were power brokers at every level of government and in every sector of the community outside the government—people he had to work with in order to maximize the powers of his office.

Lyndon picked Senator Mike Mansfield as his assistant majority leader because he knew Mansfield was not a strong man—certainly no threat. And when he became President he kept Mansfield on as majority leader for the very same reason. Anyone who has followed Mansfield's actions or inactions since he assumed that position will surely agree that my brother had him pegged pretty well.

Since the civil-rights problem was the most pressing matter on the domestic scene, Lyndon gave it top priority in a fireside chat on Thanksgiving Day. Immediately thereafter, during a seven-day period, he invited every major Negro leader in the country—Roy Wilkins of the NAACP, Whitney Young of the Urban League, Martin Luther King, and James Farmer of CORE—to the White House to discuss pending legislation. In between these sessions, he also talked with congressional leaders like Charles Halleck and John McCormack about the urgency of unfreezing civil-rights measures that had been put in cold storage by certain committee chairmen.

They couldn't very well hem and haw with Lyndon about the difficulties involved: He was an old hand at cracking legislative ice. As majority leader, he had moved through a mountain of Southern resistance in 1957 to pass the first Civil Rights Bill of this century. His old senatorial allies, people like Dick Russell and Allen Ellender, thought they would never forgive him but eventually they did. Now Lyndon was about to cause them even greater grief with far more expansive legislation; but, first of all, he had to set the stage and create the proper mood.

Like one of those Broadway producers who has four plays

showing at once and two TV shows in the works, Lyndon was simultaneously setting the stage for passage of the long-delayed tax bill and several other important bills, like medicare and federal aid to education. No less than fifty pieces of major legislation had been jammed in various committees, whose chairmen had stubbornly refused to budge for the Kennedy people.

As all this was going on, my brother was reshuffling his personal staff and also conferring with various officials at the State Department. Dean Rusk later told an interviewer that he was absolutely amazed at Lyndon's instant recognition of scores of foreign dignitaries at the Kennedy funeral and of his personal knowledge of the kinds of problems they faced in their respective countries. He had met most of them on his travels as Vice-President, somehow getting to know them beyond the mere diplomatic level, and he was now able to talk with them like one of those country politicians who knows everyone in his district by their first names. (He has always considered most diplomats cold, fancy-pants snobs who never unbend enough to really know the people with whom they're dealing.)

On one particular day during his first week in office, he chatted with Sir Alec Douglas-Home, Ludwig Erhard, Anastas Mikoyan, Haile Selassie, Eamon de Valera, Ismet Inonu, Diosdado Macapagal, and several Latin American dignitaries, all of whom were frankly surprised by his ready and intimate knowledge of our economic and political relations with each of their countries. This may have surprised Dean Rusk and his aides; but, if they had seen him in the House and Senate, always able to recall the nicknames, hobbies, pet legislation, and even the food habits of all his colleagues—never forgetting a face or a favor—they wouldn't have been a bit surprised.

In the midst of this whirlwind of administrative maneuvering, Lyndon phoned me in mid-December and asked if I would handle the preparations for a big Christmas celebration at the ranch for all the Johnson and Baines relatives, young and old.

"This will be my first Christmas as President," he said. "And I want to spend it with my own kin."

He also said he wanted me to come back to Washington with him after the holidays. I told him we'd have to discuss that later on.

But a few days before Christmas, he was faced with a problem that eventually delayed his arrival at the ranch till the very last minute. With the foreign-aid bill coming up, the House Republican leader (Charles A. Halleck) suddenly proposed an amendment forbidding the U.S. Export-Import Bank to finance a $250,000,000 wheat sale to the Soviet Union. He had timed his move to coincide with the hurried departure of congressmen for the Christmas holidays and to seriously deplete pro-administration forces on the Hill.

Speaker McCormack advised Lyndon to let Congress adjourn for the holidays and then tackle the Halleck amendment when the House reconvened in January. But my brother balked at this, feeling that the amendment was a head-on challenge to his leadership of Congress and to his freedom of action in foreign affairs.

In a strong memorandum to the Democratic leadership, he said ". . . The countries of the free world are watching anxiously to determine whether the new President is so strong that the Communist nations will have to come to terms with him or so weak that they can start hacking away at the free world with impunity. Against this background, it is not difficult to imagine the reaction of the rest of the world if the first disagreement between Congress and the new President results in a restriction upon the powers of the President."

Those were strong words, and Lyndon backed them up with a virtual order to the Democratic leaders to keep Congress in session and to call back any Christmas-absentees so that the foreign-aid bill could be enacted without the crippling Halleck amendment. While the leadership labored hard and long to keep the House in session, even holding one all-night meeting, the White House staff and Lyndon himself started phoning certain absent representatives to summon them back for the crucial vote.

A two-engine jet, fighting a snowstorm, arrived at the Washington airport at 2:30 A.M. with six bleary congressmen from New Mexico and Alabama; a helicopter intercepted the Honorable Elijah "Tic" Forrester as he was driving on a Georgia highway; and Carl Albert was brought back from a Canadian fishing trip—all of them responding to telephone pressure from Lyndon.

To assuage their annoyance (downright anger in some cases), Lyndon gave a big White House party on December 23 for all representatives, senators, Supreme Court justices, and Cabinet members, and he made a special point of sweet-talking Charlie Halleck. And the next morning at a most unusual 7:00 A.M. Christmas Eve session, the House approved the LBJ version of the foreign-aid bill. They voted on strict party lines, with only two Republicans (John V. Lindsay was one of them) supporting the President. With that problem solved, Lyndon, Lady Bird, and the girls hopped on Air Force One and flew to Texas.

Seventy-four of our kinfolk—aunts and uncles, brothers and sisters, nephews and nieces, and in-laws from all branches of both Lyndon's and Lady Bird's families—showed up at the ranch in their Sunday best. I don't imagine anyone had a better time than Aunt Jessie, who was seventy-eight years old and sweet 'n sharp as apple cider. She beamed when Lyndon gave her a bear hug and kissed her cheek.

"How'm I doing?" he asked.

"You're doin' all right so far," she said, arching her back so as to look him in the eye. "But don't you let your britches ride too high, Lyndon. Don't let those people brag on you too much and make you go forgetting you're just plain folks like the rest of us."

"Don't you worry 'bout me, honey," said Lyndon, hugging her again. "I know you won't let me, Aunt Jessie."

When we had finished our huge dinner of turkey, ham, cranberry sauce, yams, stuffed celery, hot biscuits, mashed potatoes, and several kinds of dessert, Aunt Jessie took me aside on the big front porch facing the Pedernales River and gave me some heart-to-heart advice for my brother.

"I didn't want to hog all his time with all these other kin wanting to visit with him," she said, fingering an old jade medallion. "But I want you to tell Lyndon something else for me, Sam Houston. Tell him to stick with the Jews and never do nothing against them. Now, they're God's chosen people, you know. Says so right in the Bible, and don't you ever doubt it. The best thing Harry Truman ever did was create the state of Israel. That was the right thing to do because they didn't have a home land to call their own. Why, when he did that, Sam Houston, whether he figured on it or not, he had that next election right in the bag. Tom Dewey didn't have no more chance than a pig in a dog race. So you tell Lyndon never to let the Jews down. They're the best people in the world to have on your side. In politics or anything else."

I had another long talk with Aunt Jessie in the summer of 1960, when I was interviewing some of our relatives for the family section of the Lyndon Johnson Memorial Library. She was eighty-four years old then and still as charming and salty as ever. With the national nominating conventions coming on, I asked her what she thought of Lyndon being drafted by the Democrats.

"Nossirree," she said, with a snap in her voice. "Don't you let him do it, Sam Houston. You tell Lyndon to stay right where he is, right there on the ranch, and take care of his health. He'll get beat sure as God made green apples if he runs again. He's done some awful good things, mind you—especially for poor folks and old people like me. But then he's done some other dad-gum things that've made him some mighty bad enemies. He sure has.

"Now I'm not talking about this Vietnam War, Sam Houston, because he's right about that. He's got the Bible stand on that. Yessirree, he's got scripture to back him on that. And he's also been right in sticking with the Jews. He's appointed that fella Goldberg to the Supreme Court and that was good.* I understand he's thinking of making this man Abe Fortas the new chief of the Court. Now, he's also a Jew, Sam Houston. I don't know if Lyndon knows that, but he is. So you tell him to stick with him, y'hear."

When I told my brother about our conversation—excluding her gloomy views of his running again—he roared with laughter and said he would have to tell Abe about it.

Aside from Aunt Jessie's candid advice about not letting his britches ride too high, most of the Johnson-Baines kinfolk were content to just bask in the warmth and glory of Lyndon's presence. He seemed bigger than life to them, as if the Presidency had actually increased his size (six feet three inches) and made him too big for an ordinary room. It was his incredible animal vigor and brute magnetism that made him so expansive.

"I never realized he was so tall," several of them said to me. "He looks like a giant."

In so thinking, they treated him with a bit of awe, hardly responding to his rough good humor except with timid smiles and small laughter. I guess that's what happens to all big successes when they come back home and try to be just plain Joes with the kinfolk who haven't "made it."

Curiously enough, I felt a shade of awe myself, though nowhere near as much as the others. After all, he *was* the President, the most powerful man in the world, and that alone made him more than just another brother.

The fact of his Presidency was made all the more impres-

* Arthur Goldberg was a Kennedy appointee.

sive by the complicated communications apparatus that preceded his arrival from Washington. A miniature White House command post, with instant contact to the capital, the Pentagon, the CIA, and various important embassies throughout the world, was set up at the ranch by a squad of technicians who did their chores with the cool precision of a gang of international safecrackers.

"What the hell's that for?" I asked one of them, pointing to a strange object with all kinds of wires poking out of it.

His abrupt answer was a six-syllable word that could have been a Latin phrase meaning "None of your business." (I do know it wasn't *res ipsa loquitur*, which is the only term I remember from law school.) Whatever that instrument was, I know it was put to constant use during that so-called Christmas holiday at the ranch. Right in the middle of some family conversation, Lyndon would be called to his ranch office to talk long distance with some Cabinet secretary, staff member, or a senator handling one of his administrative bills. He never seemed to have a chance to relax for more than a half hour. I wondered how he could possibly avoid another heart attack.

"You've got to slow down," I told him one evening just before the new year. "This pace will kill you, Lyndon."

"Don't you go to worrying about me," he said, leaning back in his chair and stretching his legs out. "I'll pace myself, Sam Houston. These first few weeks have been kinda hectic, but things will settle down pretty soon. Ain't near as bad as being Vice-President. Not being able to do anything will wear you down sooner than hard work."

That's as close as he ever came to admitting that he had been chomping at the bit for three frustrating years, and I could see that the heavy grind of Presidential work was actually good for him. His eyes were clear and sharp, his hands strong and steady, his voice firm and commanding. He was in many ways younger and stronger than he had been since his near-fatal heart attack in 1955.

The surest sign of Lyndon's rejuvenation was his snappy,

quick-tempered manner with members of his personal staff. They all moved on the double at his slightest command, nervously trying to anticipate his wishes and trying to beat each other to the punch. I guess that's been true of palace guards since the beginning of history—someone always giving his partner the shiv to curry favor with the headman. Seeming to ignore their constant maneuvering for petty advantage, my brother treated them all with a bluff first-name familiarity, often teasing some secretary about a personal matter to make her feel more at home, somehow letting her know that a previous rebuke was not all that serious. I've always said, "If he doesn't bawl you out now and then, you ain't part of the family."

Bearing in mind his explosive reaction when I made that crack about Oswald (incidentally, not a word was said about that during the entire holidays), I wasn't quite sure what he had in mind when he again asked me to come back to Washington with him.

"I want you to stay at the White House, Sam Houston," he said. "There's a room ready for you in the family quarters."

"Well, now, that's fine, Lyndon. But what do you want me to do around there?"

"Come and see how you like it first, and we'll talk about that later on."

Still wondering what might be in store for me, I packed my bags on New Year's Eve and took my heaviest coat out of mothballs. The winters in Washington could be miserable. I particularly remembered the blizzard that immobilized the capital on the week of the inauguration festivities for John Kennedy and my brother Lyndon.

CHAPTER EIGHT

The Promise of Greatness

Lyndon worked on his "State of the Union" speech as we flew back to Washington, carefully checking each word of an initial draft that had been prepared by Ted Sorenson and two or three members of his staff. Having heard at least twenty-five Presidential addresses by Roosevelt, Truman, Eisenhower, and Kennedy—most of them long dull recitations at least twenty-five thousand words in length—he was determined to make his very first one brief and to the point.

"Keep it down to three thousand words," he told the writers. "And carve out all the fat."

He sat in his private quarters on Air Force One, a sort of bedroom-office with all sorts of instruments that could put him in instant contact with the White House or the Pentagon. As he read each page, hunched over in a big chair, he would hand it to a waiting secretary who had been told to pass it on to me. I frankly didn't know why he wanted *me* to read the corrected pages, for I was certainly not prepared to make any suggestions or criticisms. It was more or less a courtesy on his part, a thoughtful gesture when you think about it.

As I recall, the main thrust of the speech was a strong request for legislation dealing with domestic issues, especially poverty. The language was sharp and direct and would get sharper as Lyndon blue-penciled an occasional fat phrase.

Sitting across the aisle from me, perhaps wondering what I was reading with such intensity, was a very quiet man who carried a black briefcase. He had been at the ranch all week, hovering around Lyndon wherever he went, yet never a part of his inner group. Later on I learned that the briefcase contains a secret code by which the President (and he alone) can order the launching of atomic missiles against an enemy. By law, the bearer must accompany the President every time he leaves the White House, always keeping within easy earshot. He must look strange on a golf course with that damned briefcase.

The day after Nixon's inauguration my brother told a reporter, "the thing I'm most happy about is not having that man with the black bag following on my heels."

That man was a constant nagging symbol of a possible nuclear war—a grim reminder that Lyndon had the power to press a button that could blow Russia and China off the map. And several thousand miles away, in the Kremlin, there was someone else who could push another button that could blast the U.S. and all its allies off the map. Between them they could blow almost every living creature off the face of the earth. Those who survived might just as well be dead.

During the various times I stayed at the White House, several different men carried that secret code, but I never learned the names of any of them. They were deliberately unobtrusive and seemed to be human ciphers, so I guess I didn't think of them as having names. Or perhaps I was subconsciously trying to wish away that black bag. I'm certainly glad Lyndon never had to use it.

I would have tried to start a conversation with that first black-bagger I saw on Air Force One, but his manner was

137

so withdrawn and so self-contained that I soon decided not to. By the time we got off the plane at Andrews Air Force Base three hours later, I was no longer aware of him.

We arrived at the white "penitentiary" located at 1600 Pennsylvania Avenue in a special helicopter that made the trip from Andrews in about fifteen minutes. That beautiful Presidential mansion didn't seem like a penitentiary at first sight, but I soon found out that it was. There were security people all over the place. My bedroom was in the family section on the second floor, which is as difficult to penetrate as the high-security cell block of a prison. Secret Service men guard every access, and any visitor you have must get specific permission from the President—yes, even the guests of Lady Bird and the girls had to get that special permission.

The reasons were obvious, of course. If Lyndon wanted to see someone on a very confidential basis—some foreign ambassador, a prominent industrialist during a big strike, Clark Clifford before he joined the cabinet, and, later on, Justice Abe Fortas—such persons would come through the outer gate least frequented by reporters, enter the White House through a side door, and sneak up the back stairs to the family sitting room. Needless to say, Lyndon wouldn't want any of his secret visitors to be seen on that second floor by anyone who had come to visit Lady Bird, Luci, Lynda, or Sam Houston. Washington is one of the most gossip-plagued cities in the world—no one could be trusted to keep his mouth shut about seeing some specific individual conferring privately with the President. Since Lyndon would often see someone on the spur of the moment, I might have to get rid of some friend who was already visiting or ask him to stay closeted in my room until I got an all-clear from one of my brother's aides.

Somewhat amused by all these security measures, my friend Marie Wilson once said, "I'll have to bring you a big cake next time—with a steel saw inside it." She and her husband, Dr. Glenn Wilson, were among my few visitors.

Glenn and Marie knew exactly what I meant when I gave

the guard at the East Gate my favorite signal, raising my two wrists together as if they were hand-cuffed, and yelled, "Back to my cell on the second tier."

But I really shouldn't complain about life in the White House. The room and board were free, with Zephyr's cooking better than ever. My room was elegant and more than ample, with all kinds of historical doodads strewn about. (Lynda once told me, "It sure feels funny sleeping in Lincoln's bed.") There was also a beautiful solarium and a fine swimming pool with tropical scenes that had been painted on the walls at Jackie Kennedy's request. And we could see the latest movies in a small projection room with the most comfortable seats imaginable. Later on I have a story about the night we saw Sidney Poitier in *Guess Who's Coming to Dinner?*

The thing I enjoyed most, however, was the wonderful conversations we had at breakfast and dinner. If you ever really want to know what's on Lyndon's mind (or to present a new idea to him), it's best to catch him around breakfast time. He's more relaxed then, with a sort of it's-a-new-day attitude, no matter how little sleep he's gotten. Consequently, his breakfast talk was usually wide-ranging and optimistic. Yet once in a while his face might cloud over as he started thinking about some pending legislation.

"That damned fool, Senator Gooch," he would say, slipping an extra spoon of sugar in his coffee. "I got him two defense plants last year, and now he's giving me nothing but trouble."

"Maybe you ain't been bragging on him enough," I might say. "Those old bastards need that kinda thing, especially someone like Emmett Gooch. He probably thinks the whole world's slipping right by him and nobody giving a damn about him."

Lyndon would think about that awhile, sneaking some more sugar in his coffee while Lady Bird was looking the other way. "That's not a bad idea, Sam Houston. And I think I've got just the right thing to do it with. Emmett made a little speech on the Senate floor about three days ago. Read part of it in the Congressional Record."

He was an avid reader of the Record, which he had delivered to his room fresh off the press at seven o'clock every morning. It was one of his most useful political weapons.

Grabbing the phone near his chair, he would ask the White House operator to contact Senator Gooch at his home. Then he would go into his familiar LBJ pitch: "Say, Emmett, I've been meaning to call you about that fine speech you made the other day . . . Yep, I read all of it in the Congressional Record, and I can't understand why the goddamned newspapers didn't run it. Your people must have forgot to put out a release . . . Sure, you've got to send 'em out. Those damned lazy reporters don't read the Record. You've just got to do their work for them, Emmett . . . Anyway, I liked the way you said it. Too bad it wasn't covered. . . ."

Then Gooch, in a fluster of guilt, would start to mention the pending bill he was dragging his feet on.

"Well, that's not what I called you about, Emmett, but now that you're on the phone, I want to tell you how important it is for me to have your support. We've always been together you know. . . ."

Well, it wouldn't take long for Senator Gooch to see the light. It's always nice to be bragged on by the President of the United States, especially if he takes the time to call you at home around breakfast time. Everyone thought it was a lot of hogwash when he said it to someone else, but when Lyndon said it to them it sounded like God's holy truth.

Of the several important legislative measures that had been stalled in Congress during the Kennedy era, the items that engaged Lyndon's most immediate concern were the Tax Bill and the Civil Rights Act. The Tax Bill had been approved by the House before he took office, but it faced considerable difficulty in the Senate. Although he frankly opposed the bill, Senator Byrd had promised my brother he would let the bill out of his powerful Senate Finance Committee, but there was still a threat that major amendments could cripple the measure and cause serious economic problems.

The threat became a harsh fact on the morning of January 23, 1964, when Minority Leader Everett Dirksen offered an amendment to the committee that would cut at least $445 million in taxes by eliminating excises on jewelry, cosmetics, furs, and other luxuries. Realizing this amendment would probably lead to a rash of other changes, Larry O'Brien immediately phoned the White House and got hold of Lyndon as he was having lunch; he never finished his soup. Within the next two hours he phoned almost every member of the committee, appealing to one man's patriotism, another man's personal interest, a third man's party loyalty—hard-talking, sweet-talking, joking, pressuring, telling an anecdote to prove a point, quoting scripture, counterarguing, horse-trading, and, if necessary, gently threatening with the full force of the Presidency to back him. One has to see and hear him in action to appreciate his great skills of persuasion on a person-to-person level. By midafternoon the Dirksen amendment was voted down in the committee, nine to eight, and the original bill reached the Senate floor without any significant changes.

Now came the second stage of the battle. Several senators, who presumably supported the bill, nevertheless began to offer a few "minor" amendments designed to appease certain pressure groups from their respective states. Even Senator Russell Long, *who was the floor leader for the bill,* tried to cut $30 million from the proposed $80-million increase in taxes on oil companies. Hubert Humphrey asked for a $365 tax credit for each child attending college, but he voted against his own amendment after Lyndon contacted him.

Responding to pressure from costume jewelry manufacturers from his native state of Rhode Island, Senator John O. Pastore tried to revive Dirksen's effort to eliminate taxes on luxury items. But whenever a particular amendment seemed to make headway, my brother would get on the phone and chop

141

it off. He knew from long experience that one supposedly minor change could start a flood of amendments.

"You let 'em start scratching each other's backs and it's all over," he often said. "There isn't a single senator who doesn't feel an itch of one kind or other."

He maintained the pressure on various senators for thirty-three days, tenaciously warding off any attempt to amend the bill. It was finally approved on February 26, with no significant changes. Thus, after being stalled in Congress for thirteen months, the first of John Kennedy's four major proposals became a law just ninety-six days after my brother took over. He saved three of the many pens he used to sign the Tax Bill and later presented them to Mrs. Kennedy and her two children, Caroline and John.

While the tax struggle was building to a climax, he was already involved in the far tougher battle on the Civil Rights Bill. On February 17, the clerk of the House of Representatives presented the House-approved measure to the Senate, and Majority Leader Mike J. Mansfield immediately asked that it be read for the first time, then objected to a second reading. His move was obviously designed to keep House Bill 7152 from being referred to the Judiciary Committee, whose chairman, Senator James O. Eastland of Mississippi, would most certainly try to strangle the bill before it could ever be brought to the floor.

Mansfield's strategy had been worked out with Lyndon in several conferences and their principal aim would be to impose cloture on an inevitable filibuster by the Southern bloc. The opposition leader was Dick Russell, an old friend of ours and a past master of Senate procedure. Although I am sure Russell would never say it, I am equally sure that some of his Southern colleagues were calling Lyndon "a goddamned nigger-loving traitor."

Their only hope was to delay the vote at least five months, until July 13, when the Republican National Convention would convene in Frisco. Knowing this, Lyndon soon made it clear to everyone that he would take all necessary steps to counter Russell's strategy of parliamentary delay, even to the point of sacrificing all other legislation to keep the civil-rights debate going. If necessary, he hinted, he might call a special session after the two nominating conventions were over.

"I'm shoving in all my stack on this bill," he kept telling his staff.

He was referring to a poker-player statement John Nance Garner made whenever he was faced with a hard decision: "There comes a time in every game when a man has to put in all his stack."

Lyndon also realized that each of the Southern senators would have to shove in *his* stack—that his constituents would demand it. Therefore, he instructed his Senate leadership to bide their time, to give Russell and his people plenty of talking space.

"You've got to give them a chance to show folks back home that they're doing their job, that they're willing to talk themselves hoarse day after day—a few nights maybe—to keep us from passing this bill."

That was Lyndon's way. He had an acute sense of the pressures faced by any elected representative. He knew you could make a permanent enemy of someone if you deliberately prevented him from talking for his people, but that he might still be your friend (even if he were finally out-voted) if you would let him talk long enough to show his constituency that he wasn't loafing on the job. It isn't enough for a Southerner to vote against civil rights; he's got to participate actively in a filibuster, or face possible defeat in the next election.

So Lyndon let them talk awhile, occasionally noting in the Congressional Record that Senator X had given his Senate colleagues a new formula for cough medicine and that Senator Y was deeply concerned about the mating habits of Northern sparrows. Sometimes there would be less frivolous talk about the "mongrelization of the races" and the crime rate in Harlem; but much of it was the usual filibuster menu, prepared by eighteen expert chefs working in three platoons of six each, one platoon for each successive day.

Meanwhile, my brother was helping to build up public pressure for civil rights by making a number of well-publicized statements to various groups. He told the leaders of the Southern Baptist Convention that "I have seen firsthand how basic spiritual beliefs and deeds can shatter barriers of politics and bigotry," reminding them that it was their duty to involve themselves in this process. And he told an audience of business executives about the problems faced by Zephyr Wright because of her color.

"She has been with us twenty years, she is a college graduate, but when she comes from Texas to Washington she never knows where she can get a cup of coffee. She never knows when she can go to a bathroom. She has to take three or four hours out of her time to go across to the other side of the tracks to locate a place where she can sit down and buy a meal. You wouldn't want that to happen to your wife or your mother or your sister, but somehow or other you take it for granted when it happens to someone way off there." There were tears in Zephyr's eyes when she later read what he had said in one of the Washington newspapers.

As the time approached for cutting off the filibuster, it was quite apparent that Senator Dirksen would have to be persuaded to get his Republican followers to vote for cloture. Consequently, Lyndon had several friendly chats with the minority leader, appealing to his patriotism, his ego, and to his self-interest as a senator from a state with an increasingly powerful Negro population.

"Ev is too intelligent and too good a Republican," Lyndon said one morning at breakfast. "He won't want his party to take responsibility for defeating civil rights—not with the public mood we've got now."

The opposition was also doing a bit of wooing. Still hopefully assuming Dirksen would vote against the bill, Dick Russell said to his colleagues on the floor, "I cannot refrain, even if it does harm to the senator from Illinois, from expressing to him my great admiration for his political courage. It gives one hope for the future of the Republic to see a man who has convictions and the courage to sustain them, even though it may endanger his seat in the Senate."

That was a very pretty sentiment and the good senator responded with an equal but somewhat ponderous prettiness: "I trust that the time will never come in my public career when the waters of partisanship will flow so swift and so deep as to obscure my estimate of the national interest."

Having stated that lofty principle in his usual majestic manner that we all will miss now that he's gone, "Old Ev" got down to the more earthy practical consideration of certain amendments that would make the Civil Rights Bill more acceptable to him and his fellow Republicans.

With Lyndon finally giving the signal for "action now," applying whatever last-minute pressures were necessary, the Senate leadership cut off debate after fifty-seven working days; and soon thereafter the measure was approved without any serious amendments.

On July 2, 1964—less than eight months after he became President—Lyndon Johnson walked into the East Room of the White House and signed the most important pro-Negro legislation of this century.

Since I am a Texan, a white man, and Lyndon Johnson's only brother, my comments on his accomplishments in the field of civil rights will undoubtedly arouse considerable skepticism among certain readers. Therefore, I would invite their attention to the following appraisal by the distinguished black novelist, Ralph Ellison:

> When I was growing up, a Negro Oklahoman always listened for a threat in the accent of a white Texan, but one learned to listen to the individual intonation, to *what* was said as well as to *how* it was said, to content and implication

145

as well as to style. Black provincials cannot afford the luxury of being either snobbish or provincial. Nor can they ignore the evidence of concrete acts. . .

It is possible that much of the intellectuals' distrust of President Johnson springs from a false knowledge drawn from the shabby myths purveyed by Western movies. Perhaps they feel that a Texan intoning the values of humanism in an unreconstructed Texas accent is to be regarded as suspiciously as a Greek bearing gifts; thus they can listen to what he says with provincial ears and can ignore the President's concrete achievements here at home while staring blindly at the fires of a distant war. . .

Lyndon B. Johnson is credited even by his enemies as being a political genius, but the phenomenon of a great politician becoming President confronts us with a dual figure, for even while entangled in the difficulties of his office he is identified by role with the achievements of the proven great who preceded him there. . .

No one has initiated more legislation for education, for health, for racial justice, for the arts, for urban reform than Lyndon Johnson. Presently it is the fashion of many intellectuals to ignore these accomplishments, these promises of a broader freedom to come, but if those of other backgrounds and interests can afford to be blind to their existence, my own interests and background compel me to bear witness. . .

When all of the returns are in, perhaps President Johnson will have to settle for being recognized as the greatest American President for the poor and for the Negroes, but that, as I see it, is a very great honor indeed."*

Coming from the pen of a highly regarded black novelist, I feel those words carry special weight. I should also mention that, in addition to his civil-rights legislation, Lyndon appointed a large number of Negroes to important positions in the administration. He also appointed the first Negro Supreme

* Ralph Ellison, "The Myth of the Flamed White Southerner," in *To Heal and to Build*, James MacGregor, ed. (New York, McGraw-Hill, Inc.), pp. 211–216.

Court justice—Thurgood Marshall, the lawyer who success-fully argued the case of *Brown vs. the State of Kansas*, which resulted in the Court's famous desegregation decision in 1954.

But, important as it was, the Civil Rights bill was not the only domestic legislation that occupied his time. He was also pushing for broad-scale programs for medicare, the war on poverty, federal aid to education, model cities, expansion of social security, highway construction, the prevention of air pollution, and several other programs that had been frozen in various congressional committees during JFK's administration.

Tackling all these problems at once with enormous driving energy and bulldog determination, Lyndon demanded more from his staff than ever before, threatening to fire someone at least once a day but never letting them quit on their own. His quick outbursts of temper were somehow balanced by impulsive, often embarrassed generosity. However, the ulcer rate among his closest aides probably doubled as they scurried in and out of his office with the forward-leaning stance of someone who is about ready to break into a fast trot. (With my crippled right leg, I wouldn't have been able to join them in what some people called "the LBJ trot.")

I was about to describe the atmosphere around the White House as a "human beehive," but I think "hornets nest" would be a more accurate phrase. They were all busy helping Lyndon—no doubt about that—yet most of them were equally busy helping themselves. At any given moment, A would be giving the barbed shaft to B, who would be shafting C, who would shaft D, who would join B in shafting A, who would then join C in shafting D. Then A, B and D would get to-gether and shaft C, with B and D simultaneously shafting A, like so many hornets buzzing around the same flower. In all probability, the personal staffs of all previous Presidents were pretty much the same, one assistant vying with another for status and power and the personal affluence that often results from having them.

When I flew back to Washington with Lyndon early in

January, I could sense that some of his aides were wondering how I would fit into the picture. Three or four of them had seen me in close association with my brother during his many years in the House and Senate, sometimes as a political trouble-shooter and at other times as a sort of general overseer in his office.

Walter Jenkins and George Reedy would probably remember that shortly after Lyndon became majority leader in 1955, he had told them, "Nothing goes out of this office, press release or anything else, without Sam Houston or me giving an okay."

They also knew I had been forced to retire because of ill health; that I had been totally inactive during his tenure as Vice-President. Yet there I was again, living in the family quarters of the White House, having breakfast and dinner with Lyndon and Lady Bird almost every day and apparently privy to confidences of a highly personal nature. And knowing Lyndon as I do (I have often said I know him a lot better than he knows me because he's been too damned busy with other matters to think about me, while I've had practically nothing to do except study him), I am sure he kept his staff completely in the dark about his reasons for having me there.

Consequently, during the few times I visited the West Wing or the Oval Office, some of the principal staff people treated me with an uncomfortably wary deference, as if they thought I might be spying on them. Others seemed too friendly, too ready to kowtow. Very few seemed disposed to treat me on a plain man-to-Sam basis. Walter Jenkins and George Reedy were in this latter group.

I first met Walter many years ago, about 1940, when my brother had him appointed as a special policeman on Capitol Hill. Born on a poor farm near Jolly, Texas, he had attended Wichita Falls Junior College and then moved on to the University of Texas, which he attended for a couple of years before his money ran out and he came to Washington.

Later he went to work as a clerk-accountant in Lyndon's

congressional office in Austin, a job suddenly cut short when he was drafted into the army. After serving in the Quartermaster Corps in Africa and Italy during World War II, he passed through Washington on his way to Texas; and when he called the office, Lady Bird invited him out to the house for supper.

Until that particular evening Lyndon had paid very little attention to Walter and, as far as I knew, he wasn't planning to give him a job. Then, in a most casual way, he asked Walter what he planned to do now that he was out of service.

"Well, I'm hoping to get married right soon," said Walter. "I've been corresponding with this girl back home, and she's agreed to it."

"But what will you live on?" asked Lady Bird. "You haven't a job yet."

"I've got my savings, ma'am," he answered. "I managed to save more than five thousand dollars while I was in the service."

Assuming he had won all that loot in some nice crap games, though he certainly didn't look like a gambling man, I said, "You musta been pretty lucky with the dice."

"No, sir, Mr. Sam," he quickly protested. "I never gamble or anything like that. Those are my savings. I saved every penny of my army pay."

"You saved it all?" asked Lyndon, suddenly alert. "All your pay as an enlisted man?"

"Yes, sir, that's what I did," said Walter. "I told the paymaster to put it all in savings bonds."

As of that moment, Walter Jenkins' career was settled: He became a permanent member of the LBJ senatorial staff. Nothing could have impressed Lyndon more than Walter's incredible feat of frugality and discipline. I was flabbergasted for entirely different reasons. Remembering how I was usually flat broke within forty-eight hours after getting my pay as an intelligence officer in Morocco and other parts of North Africa, I simply couldn't visualize anyone saving even 10 percent of his pay—much less 100 percent. I was dead certain of one thing: Walter Jenkins couldn't have been much of a hell-raiser around the barracks. But my brother wasn't looking for a hell-raiser to put on his staff; he already had one too many.

"You go home and get married," he said to Walter. "Then I want you to come to work for me."

Soon thereafter Walter married Marjorie Whitehill, a lively and pretty Catholic girl for whom he abandoned his Protestant religion. Then he settled down in Lyndon's branch office in Austin, gradually working himself up to general manager of the office and eventually moving to the Washington office as a chief administrator. Always cautious, thorough in every detail, and completely loyal to his chief, he was like a top sergeant at a command post.

Later, when he moved into the West Wing, right next to the Oval Office, there could be no doubt that he was the President's chief executive officer. Almost no memoranda or any other important documents could get to the President's desk without first being screened by Jenkins.

He was not a "policy man," nor did he pretend to be. His responsibility was to get things done, to carry out the hundreds of administrative details that were involved in the policy decisions flowing from Lyndon's office. From his long experience, he could often anticipate some of the things the boss would want done the next week. He also determined, to a great extent, who could or could not see the President—which, when you think about it, gave him a considerable influence in matters of profound importance. Knowing that he had that kind of power, quite a few senators, congressmen, Cabinet members, and other high officials made a special point of cultivating his friendship.

Quite apart from his official duties, Walter had been for many years a close personal friend and confidant of Lyndon. On the night Lyndon and Lady Bird finally moved into the White House, they had a quiet family dinner at the Jenkins' home, and it was Marjorie who gave a very private party for Lady Bird on her first birthday as First Lady. Their daughters were also good friends. In fact, it was Beth Jenkins who got Luci to attend Catholic Marquette University in Milwaukee, where she became a convert and met Pat Nugent.

It was because of their close friendship as families that the Johnsons (that means all of us) were so painfully saddened when Walter was arrested for disorderly conduct in the basement of the YMCA, which the newspapers blatantly characterized as a hangout for sexual perverts.

When I read the charges that hit all the headlines about a month before the 1964 Presidential election, I simply couldn't believe any of it. The last time I had seen Walter, he was behind a desk stacked high with urgent papers that he was reading in snatches between hurried phone calls from this man, then that man, then from Lyndon or a Cabinet minister or some congressman from Texas—a steady, nerve-racking torrent of phone calls that he answered in a low, tense voice edged with impatience. As usual, his suit was rumpled and his shirt collar slightly wilted, reminding me of the time Lyndon had given him one of his special monogrammed LBJ shirts and how proudly Walter had worn it, though the sleeves were too long and the collar a bit loose. His face was flushed now, his hair noticeably grayer than the year before, and his paunch just a bit flabbier.

Knowing that he was a man with only a limited capacity for relaxation, I wanted to tell him to get away from his office, to get out while the getting was good. If ever I saw a man hell-bent for a nervous breakdown, it was Walter Jenkins. He is one of the best and most loyal friends Lyndon has ever had, a man who drove himself too hard, who was perhaps too dedicated to his work.

George Reedy was also an extremely loyal worker and a devoted friend, and probably the brainiest man on my brother's personal staff. He had been one of the famous Chicago Quiz Kids, and a member of the intellectual elite at

151

the University of Chicago during the early days of President Robert M. Hutchins.

Following in the footsteps of his father, who was a crime reporter for the Chicago *Tribune*, George had a summer job on the Philadelphia *Inquirer* and later became a full-time reporter for the Washington office of United Press International. Interrupting his newspaper career, he served as an Air Force intelligence officer in World War II, then returned to UPI, assigned to Capitol Hill.

It was during this phase that he met the new Senator from the state of Texas, Lyndon B. Johnson. They liked each other from the very start, and George happily left his newspaper work in 1951 to affiliate with our senatorial staff. Not long after he joined us, Reedy told me that Lyndon had more power of concentration than anyone he had ever known. "He gives a problem all he's got, Sam Houston. That's why he gets things done." He told his friends way back then that he was going to work for a man who would be President someday.

Once in awhile, during their many years of close association, Lyndon would get impatient with George's casual, lumbering manner. He's six feet two inches tall and generally has a weight problem, sometimes scaling as much as 280 pounds when he's not dieting, and his slow, ponderous gait is often matched by a slow, deliberate way of talking.

"I sometimes hesitate to ask old George what time it is," Lyndon said to me one morning. "He's liable to tell you all about the solar system before letting you know it's ten thirty."

But that slow speech is often a convenient cover for a mind that works like a steel trap. I've seen the White House correspondents, especially after he took over the job of press secretary from Pierre Salinger, get annoyed and downright angry at George when he started answering their questions in a curious, frustrating roundabout way. He knew damned well what they wanted, but he was deliberately avoiding a direct answer because he knew Lyndon would want him to avoid it. He was simply protecting his boss, the way he often protected other people.

I remember one occasion when Reedy tried to protect his secretary at great personal risk. He had shown Lyndon a press release on the poverty program and he'd been instructed to delete a particular paragraph that could be misinterpreted by a hostile press. He readily agreed it could be damaging and promised to strike the passage forthwith. But somehow, in the madhouse flurry of activity around the White House, George's secretary mineographed the release without changing it, thereby causing a minor flap. When Lyndon heard about it the next day, he blew a gasket in his lower groin. Summoning George to his office, he listened impatiently to a wordy explanation, then fired him on the spot.

When I saw him a few minutes later, George told me what had happened, how he had avoided telling Lyndon the truth so as to protect his secretary. "I knew damned well he would fire *her*, but I didn't expect him to do it to *me* after all these years, though I fully expected him to chew me out."

"Don't worry about it," I told him. "Take the afternoon off and come back tomorrow. I'll talk to Lyndon. I'm sure he didn't mean it."

A few hours later I had a long heart-to-heart with Lyndon, explaining how George was merely protecting some poor girl and reminding him of how loyal he had always been. He was still grumpy and, as usual, unwilling to admit he might have reacted too hastily.

"George was still wrong, goddammit," he snapped. "But if you want him, you go on and hire him back."

Reedy was in his office the next morning and nothing further was said about the press release. About two or three weeks later he came up to my room in a very low mood. The competitive pressures in the West Wing were getting him down.

"I've never seen so much backbiting," he said in a soft,

weary voice. "All those people giving each other the shaft and still pretending to be friends. I never realized ambition could be so ugly."

"Anybody shafting you?" I asked.

He looked down at his huge, fleshy hands, apparently reluctant to mention anyone and yet wanting to. "There might be someone," he finally said. "As a matter of fact, I have a hunch Bill Moyers is putting me down to Lyndon and Walter Jenkins. Probably wants my job."

"Hell, George, you ought to be able to take care of that skinny boy," I said. "Big guy like you could mash him to a pulp."

I was joking, of course. That's not the way you settle differences in a political jungle. The in-fighting within a President's "palace guard" is more subtle and devious than the man-to-man confrontations I had mentioned, and George was too nice a guy to play that game. But Bill Moyers was perfectly suited for that type of intramural squabbling. He was young, bright, hard-working, and totally dedicated to his own personal advancement. When I first met him in Lyndon's private office where he worked during a summer vacation, I had him classified as a little go-for who wanted to please everybody: "Shall I go for coffee . . . go for cigarettes . . . go for sandwiches?" Always volunteering to do something for you *and also wanting to learn all there was to learn about our office.* So he was more than a mere bootlicker; he was a kid who had his eye on the main chance.

Having spent a year at the University of Edinburgh on a Rotary Fellowship after attending North Texas State College and the University of Texas, he got a job at KTBC-TV, the Johnson television station in Austin. Somewhere along the line, he attended the Southwestern Theological Seminary and did a little preaching here and there. Then, when the 1960 Presidential campaign got under way, he worked full time on Lyndon's staff and subsequently joined the Peace

Corps at a high administrative level. The day Kennedy died, my brother took him on as a special assistant.

His duties on the loosely structured staff of the White House were numerous and varied, a mixture of administrative and policy functions that gave him ready access to the President. There was political power in that kind of position, and Bill was aggressive enough to make it work for him. Needless to say, his influence increased when he replaced George Reedy as press secretary. (Contrary to some reports, George was not fired. He had to quit to get medical attention for an old ailment, and my brother volunteered to absorb the hospital bills for both him and his son, who apparently had the same ailment.)

Moyers viewed the job in a much different light from Reedy. Where George had been somewhat self-effacing, Bill was inclined to bask in the spotlight and to become a spokesman for administrative policy rather than a convenient channel for Presidential views. Knowing how much Lyndon disliked being upstaged by subordinates, I was rather surprised at his almost paternal tolerance when Moyers moved onto stage center. I mentioned this at dinner one night, and Lyndon passed it off with a slight shrug. He was less casual when I told him that Bill Moyers was overexposing him to television.

"That's not your medium," I said. "You don't come across on TV, Lyndon. You look pretty damned awful, to be brutally frank about it. You'd better stay away from those cameras."

Well, no man wants to hear that kind of talk, especially someone like my brother.

"What the hell's wrong with me?" he asked in a curt voice. "What don't you like about me?"

"You're too damned stiff in front of the cameras," I said. "And your voice sounds kind of phony when you're reading off the teleprompter. Television just doesn't work for you, Lyndon, particularly when you're making a formal speech."

Many people who have seen him on TV have expressed surprise on seeing him in the flesh talking with a small group of people. The senior editor of a large publishing firm put it this way: "I was frankly unimpressed with LBJ on the tube, but when I saw him in action at an informal gathering at the White House, I was amazed by his personal magnetism and his sheer animal vitality. Everyone else felt the same way. He was an entirely different Johnson from the pallid, uncertain guy you see on the screen."

Bill Moyers and Jack Valenti should have realized that, yet they kept on encouraging Lyndon to go on television—at least they didn't *discourage* him. But my personal gripe against Moyers isn't related to his performance, good or bad, as press secretary. The thing that annoyed hell out of me was the way he was bootlicking around the Kennedy crowd at the same time Bobby was giving my brother a royal shafting.

Though at the beginning Lyndon seemed rather indulgent about Moyers' frequent contacts with Bobby, he eventually started dropping remarks at our dinner-table conversations that clearly indicated his displeasure. Most of the time Lady Bird would pretend to ignore his digs at Moyers. She had always been partial to Bill because he had a certain boyish appeal to women. They seemed to like his high-flown preacher talk and his life-long willingness to run errands for his superiors.

When Moyers finally left Washington to join a Long Island newspaper, some of the press reported that he had become disenchanted with LBJ. I imagine this was prompted by a prior disenchantment on Lyndon's part.

Before leaving the subject of Bill Moyers, I must admit that he showed occasional flashes of humor. When the formation of the Lyndon Johnson Library was announced, Juanita Roberts (Lyndon's personal secretary) started collecting every conceivable item that related to the boss. The most innocuous memo was filed away for posterity.

Then one afternoon Moyers came by her office and dropped a pile of chicken bones on her desk. "Here's something else for the library," he said in a mock-solemn voice. "These are the leftovers from the President's lunch today." Even his worst enemies would have to admit that's a pretty good crack.

Moyers was apparently friendly with Dick Goodwin, another special assistant who was part of the Kennedy inner circle. I caught only an occasional glimpse of Goodwin and probably never had a personal conversation with him, and yet he made a fairly definite impression. Dark-eyed and swarthy, his dark suits slightly rumpled and loose, he looked like a young Svengali with a million secrets behind that half smile. And from what I've heard and read about (and by) him, I imagine he's a great hand at playing both sides against the middle.

During the 1968 primaries, I was quite amused by his ability to jump back and forth from Kennedy to McCarthy to Kennedy and back to McCarthy again. Had Humphrey won the election, I wouldn't have been surprised to see Goodwin back in the West Wing, writing whatever kind of speech was called for. He wasn't tied down by the kind of loyalty you found in people like Jenkins, Reedy, Busby, and Valenti.

Jack Valenti, who is married to Lyndon's former secretary, was one of the first men to join the White House staff after the assassination. He came to Washington aboard Air Force One on that famous flight that carried John Kennedy back to the capital, and he stuck right close to Lyndon from the very beginning. He was a bright, friendly little guy who was always being kidded by my brother, especially about his degree from Harvard.*

Some people thought of him as a court jester, the willing butt of LBJ jokes, but Jack's role was far more important than that. He dealt directly with the President on all kinds of important matters and was often the final editor of Lyndon's speeches, sometimes inserting a couple of quotes from famous authors.

* *Editor's Note:* Valenti attended the Harvard Business School, which most Harvardians snobbishly regard as "not quite Harvard."

As my brother once said to some reporter, "Jack is really an intellectual, and people would admit it if he didn't come from the wrong side of the Mason-Dixon line."

Valenti was awfully pleased with that comment, and he was certainly loyal enough to merit any kind of praise from his chief. I can't think of anything more loyal than the sentiment he expressed in a speech to the Advertising Federation of America in June, 1965, when he said, "I sleep each night a little better, a little more confidently because Lyndon Johnson is my President."

That kind of hero worship would have made me a little uncomfortable, but I don't think the President minded it very much. Now, I couldn't honestly say that about Lyndon, because I was always afraid he'd jerk me out of bed in the middle of the night and tell me to turn off my damned light.

CHAPTER NINE

The Bobby Problem

The Bobby problem, which had been simmering since February, came to a boil in July, 1964. I am referring, of course, to Bobby Kennedy rather than Bobby Baker.

Everyone knew that Kennedy wanted to be the Vice-Presidential candidate in the coming elections, and some of his followers apparently felt he had a God-given right to his party's nomination. From Boston to Los Angeles and all points in between, the well-organized Kennedy machine was busily engaged in creating a "spontaneous" ground swell for Bobby, hoping the voters' postassassination sentiment would turn the trick for them. No one was more keenly aware of this effort than my brother Lyndon, and he was dead set against it. Not for a single moment did he ever consider having Bobby Kennedy as his running mate. And the reasons were quite obvious:

a) Lyndon hated Bobby.

b) Bobby hated Lyndon.

c) He didn't need Bobby to win.

d) Lyndon didn't trust Bobby.

e) Bobby didn't trust Lyndon.

f) And each of them knew damned well he was hated and mistrusted by the other.

Under these circumstances, it was naïve of the RFK crowd to think they could force their man on the President, and their so-called "ground swell" was being organized against all historical precedent. Theodore H. White says in *The Making of the President 1964* that Kennedy either disapproved or was unaware of his supporters' spirited campaign—a statement that sounds incredibly innocent coming from an otherwise sophisticated political observer.

I have never in my life seen a campaign that couldn't be stopped by a candidate who didn't want it. No politician ever gets drafted against his will. Consequently, any mild disclaimers by Bobby were simply an outward acknowledgment of the time-honored rule that no one actively runs for Vice-President.

I know that the delegates to the national convention legally nominate the Vice-Presidential candidate, but that is all sham. The Presidential candidate—and *only* he—selects the man he wants. Any other method would be ridiculous. To force him to take someone he doesn't want could be extremely impractical and even dangerous. Ordinarily, as Truman once said, a Vice-President is "about as useful as a cow's fifth teat."

Nevertheless, he does have a great deal of potential power, and he could raise all kinds of hell if he should suddenly decide to oppose the President, especially if the President were ill or absent for other reasons. There are all kinds of opportunities for a scheming, dissident Vice-President to sabotage the President and to wreck all semblance of unity within his administration. I, of course, realize that a President might be double-crossed by a man of his own choosing, but that is less likely to happen.

Even though the Presidential nominee has the final say about his running mate, he still might feel it necessary to choose someone he doesn't completely want. I seriously doubt that my brother was John F. Kennedy's *personal* preference (he certainly wasn't Bobby's choice), yet Jack had to give some practical consideration to the Southern and Protestant vote. He also knew Lyndon was better prepared for the Presidency than anyone else, including himself—though I am sure that wasn't his primary reason. Once having made his choice against the advice of certain bleeding-heart liberals and labor leaders, he ordered the convention to nominate Lyndon.

Four years earlier, when Adlai Stevenson was nominated for the second time, he tried a different method; Stevenson actually gave the delegates a free choice on the Vice-Presidential nomination. The ensuing Kefauver-Kennedy floor fight may have been a nice dramatic touch at an otherwise dull convention, but it was mostly a sign of weakness and poor judgment.

Not long after the convention I heard Lyndon telling Sam Rayburn that Stevenson had been a damn fool for running such a risk. Mr. Sam agreed. Having beaten Adlai in the primaries, Estes Kefauver naturally resented his defeat by Stevenson; and now that he had won the Vice-Presidential nomination *on his own steam*, he could very logically have considered himself more independent than most Vice-Presidents. He had his own personal power base, and he might have used it had the Stevenson-Kefauver ticket been elected.

We could all rest assured Lyndon wouldn't run that kind of risk—he wasn't about to let Bobby Kennedy establish an independent power base inside his administration. That decision was made right away, from the moment we first heard the rumors of a "Bobby Draft" in January.

My brother's only concern was how and when to squelch the campaign. Quite obviously, it would be premature to take action in the spring or early summer; that would give Bobby's followers a chance for a countermove. It would be better to wait until shortly before the convention in late August, when it would be too late for the Kennedy people to stage a comeback. One thing was certain—there would not be a Stevenson type of "open choice" by the delegates in electing the number-two man. Lyndon would make that decision for himself, and it wouldn't be his attorney general.

Having carefully pushed the Bobby problem onto a back burner, Lyndon could devote himself to the much more important consideration of an overall strategy for the November election. His chief political advisers outside the White House staff would be James Rowe, Abe Fortas, and Clark Clifford —all old friends from the early New Deal days.

During the first few weeks of 1964, as we sometimes sat in his room sipping an occasional after-dinner drink, he would think aloud about the way he ought to approach the campaign.

"I guess the best thing for me to do," he often said, "is to stay around here and let people know I'm real busy tending the store, that I'm taking good care of their business."

He knew, of course, that an incumbent President has a natural advantage over his opponent because he can *act* instead of just talk. Aside from his bold decisive actions on civil rights, the Tax Bill, medicare, the war on poverty, and other major legislation, he prevented a threatened railroad strike by personally pressuring both sides to settle a dispute that had been going on for four and one-half years. That was a great feat of painless arm-twisting. He had used a modified version of the same LBJ technique in settling a minor uproar down in Panama, although some of the Kennedyites thought he was a bit too tough.

And he played the role of President-in-action right up to the hilt in less controversial matters—making a fourteen-hour tour of the Appalachian region to discover ways to tackle poverty there, flying over the Ohio River flood to emphasize his immediate concern for stricken families, and visiting other areas to dedicate public works of various kinds.

Wherever he went, Lyndon was able to point out how prosperous Americans were under two Democratic regimes, JFK's and his own. On November 21, 1963, the day before he became President, the Dow Jones stock-market average stood at 733; then climbed rapidly to 827 in April; to 837 in May; and to 851 in July. Even for the millions of ordinary citizens who never read the market quotations, the signs of prosperity were visible everywhere—new buildings, new cars and appliances, more expensive vacations, more private homes for working people, more kids going to college, more of everything for almost everyone. Certain persistent pockets of poverty merely emphasized the look of general prosperity.

The economic prospects in midsummer looked even brighter because most of the business community had confidence in Lyndon. So did labor. And this was no accident. In his day-to-day striving for a consensus of all socio-economic groups, he would invite a flock of high business executives to a White House dinner one night, and on the following day he would have steak and potatoes with George Meany and some of his boys from the AFL-CIO. His personal charm and great energy seemed to work wonders in these small face-to-face meetings.

Late in May, 1964, Henry Ford II announced that he would support LBJ for President, no matter whom his Republican party nominated; and most of the members of the powerful Business Council, polled at their annual conference at Hot Springs, Virginia, also declared themselves in favor of Lyndon. From the other side of the fence came another boost from Walter Reuther, president of the United Auto Workers, who had begged John Kennedy *not* to take my brother as his Vice-Presidential running mate in 1960.

It was everybody-loves-Lyndon season, poor and rich alike. Some news columnists would argue that the voters didn't really love Lyndon—not the way they did JFK. But I don't think a politician expects people to fall all over him; all he wants is their vote on Election Day, with or without hugs and kisses.

Lyndon certainly wasn't complaining. He was in great spirits and bursting with self-charging energy, working harder than ever and demanding more and more from his staff. Once in awhile I would hear a complaint from one of the older staffers who had just gotten a tongue-lashing or, worse yet, the old LBJ silent treatment.

"Sure wish you were down here more often," a long-time employee confided. "You were sort of a lightning rod."

He was referring to some of the scoldings I supposedly got from Lyndon when he actually intended to chew out someone else. Quite suddenly, he would turn on me and pretend to bawl me out about something that had never happened, just some wild, made-up accusation. Knowing it was all pretense, I would take his crap with a proper show of resentment. Then he would turn to the person he really intended to burn and would let him have it full blast. Since that particular person had already seen *me* getting hell from my brother, he would find it a little easier to absorb the harsh criticism he received. It seemed less personal that way. In other words, he'd be thinking Lyndon had treated him no worse than a member of his own family. Such explosions were bound to happen, no matter how well things were going outside the office.

Things could hardly have been better than they were as that summer began. The public-opinion polls were especially pleasing. With the civil-rights filibuster going on in the Senate, we had been a little worried about George Wallace's strong showing in the Democratic primary in Maryland. He had gotten 43 percent of the vote, indicating a fairly significant backlash movement. But a subsequent poll in that state by Oliver Quayle showed that the backlash was more a *potential* threat than a *real* threat, and that Lyndon still ranked very high. Several other polls in Maine, Indiana, and Wisconsin produced similar results. By early summer some follow-up polls showed Lyndon getting 77 percent of the vote in Maine, with 50 percent of the former Nixon supporters saying they would desert their Republican ranks and vote for LBJ. He also pulled a heavy vote in traditional Republican states in the Midwest.

With certain exceptions, we had always been rather partial to public-opinion polls, but Lyndon was now particularly impressed with the Quayle organization. They weren't just ordinary pollsters; they went right to the heart of an issue, with detailed analyses of voter profiles, depth perception, potential shifts in sentiment, and all kinds of testing.

For example, they might show that LBJ was losing votes on one issue (civil rights) but still picking up more votes on another issue (farm price supports). That was the kind of balance and counterbalance that had always fascinated my brother—the business of weighing one thing against another.

He never tired of reading and rereading the polls, generally stuffing them into his pockets for another look later on, or just to show them to somebody else. Like most politicians, he was always asking "How'm I doing?" and those surveys gave him the answer right down to the last percentage point.

The figures that brought him the greatest satisfaction were those that demonstrated he could win quite easily *without having Bobby Kennedy as the Vice-Presidential candidate.* The Kennedy crowd had been trying to convince everyone the Democrats couldn't possibly win without Bobby's name on the ticket. Nonsense! According to any Quayle poll, none of his potential running mates (Kennedy, Humphrey, Stevenson, McCarthy, Dodd, Pastore, Wagner) could add or subtract more than 2 percent from the probable vote for LBJ. He could pick any partner he wanted.

"Look't here," he said one night at the supper table, waving a news clipping over his coffee, "I don't need that little runt to win. I can take anybody I damn well please."

He wouldn't have made that kind of statement in public, for he was generally pretty closemouthed about his resentment against any of the Kennedys or their clique. If nothing else, his pride wouldn't allow him to reveal how much they had humiliated him. One particular incident he wasn't likely to forget for a long time occurred when Air Force One arrived in Washington just after the assassination.

Realizing how important it was to establish a sense of continuity, my brother naturally wanted to accompany the casket from the plane to the ground in the cargo lift, along with the Kennedy family. But Robert Kennedy shoved him aside, flatly refusing to let him do this, thus giving millions of television viewers the clear, unmistakable impression that he resented the new President as an unwanted intruder.

I was heartstruck when that happened, and I could feel the shame and embarrassment Lyndon must have experienced at that moment. I mentioned this to him several months later and noticed his mouth suddenly draw tight.

"That's all past," he said. "I don't want to talk about it."

I really couldn't tell how much or how long he resented that public snub (or the many other snubs that must have preceded it), because he has always managed to keep such things to himself. Even as a boy, he would bottle up certain angers inside himself, tightening his lips and refusing to complain to mama or daddy or anyone else. But with respect to less personal matters—perhaps those having nothing to do with self-pride—he's always been capable of exploding like a can of hot steam and then quickly simmering down.

Whatever his natural tendencies, he was always able to "keep his cool" in moments of political stress. He was particularly cool in his handling of the Bobby problem when it came to a fast boil late in July. A memorial film to John F. Kennedy (with a personal introduction by Bobby) had been scheduled for the first evening session of the National Democratic Convention, an arrangement that could lead to trouble. We all knew this highly emotional film could easily trigger a draft for RFK as Vice-President, and that Lyndon might be forced into crushing the move before millions of television spectators. Accordingly, Lyndon invited the Arrangements Committee to the White House, examined their proposed schedule, then casually informed them that he preferred to have the Kennedy film shown later in the week when he could attend himself. They got the point right away. The film was rescheduled for the evening *after* the nomination.

That still wasn't enough. Quite suddenly, rumors started

floating around Washington hinting that Jackie Kennedy would dramatically appear at Atlantic City to "help Bobby." Whether true or not, Lyndon realized it was time to take more direct action. Bobby Kennedy would have to be told he wasn't going to be Vice-President and, if possible, he should be persuaded to take himself out of the race. This was easier said than done.

On July 29 my brother called the Justice Department and asked Kennedy to meet him at the White House at 1:00 P.M. Apparently wishing to give the meeting a somewhat formal air, Lyndon sat behind his big desk with Kennedy in a chair to his right. In a less formal, friendly chat, they would have sat at the rocking chair and sofa at the far end of the Oval Office.

As Lyndon later recalled, Bobby was obviously unhappy when he was told he had been eliminated from the list of prospective candidates. He gulped like a fat fish pulling in a mouthful of air. Lyndon's imitation of him was pretty amusing. Then, for some reason or other, Kennedy brought up the Bobby Baker case, as if to show that his name on the Democratic ticket would somehow soften the effect of a possible scandal. Well, that didn't faze Lyndon one bit. He simply reminded Kennedy that there were too many Republicans involved with Baker, so that the GOP candidate wasn't likely to harp on it. The flack would hit both parties.

Since Kennedy hadn't volunteered to announce his own withdrawal, Lyndon asked McGeorge Bundy (he was a family friend of the Kennedys and an old Bostonian) to talk with him about a simple statement to the press announcing he had other plans. But Bundy wasn't very successful. In fact, he alienated some of the faithful, who immediately tagged him as a no-good traitor.

With no other recourse left to him, Lyndon called a press conference the next day and told the reporters: "I have reached the conclusion that it would be inadvisable for me to recommend to the convention (as my running mate) any member of the Cabinet or any of those who meet regularly with the Cabinet."

That last phrase was meant for Adlai Stevenson, but everyone knew the statement was principally directed at Bobby Kennedy. Later on, my brother told a few reporters that he wasn't directing it at RFK, but I doubt that anyone took him seriously.

I would have advised him to say it in more positive terms —something like this: "I have decided to recommend a Vice-Presidential candidate who has a broad practical experience in the *legislative* branch of government, because I will expect him to be my personal liaison man with the Congress," or words to that effect.

In the long run, however, the language made no difference. The point that really mattered was squelching the "Bobby draft" and keeping it squelched.

Shortly before the convention I came down with something resembling the Asiatic flu and reluctantly checked into the army hospital at Kimbrough, Maryland. In my generally poor condition, I had decided not to go to Atlantic City, knowing it would be hectic, tiring, and dull. Then, just after the convention got under way, I received a call from Lyndon asking me to accompany him and Lady Bird, probably on Thursday. That was the night he would make his acceptance speech.

"I don't know, Lyndon," I said. "I've got this damned cold, so maybe I better stick around here and rest awhile." (My condition seemed far worse than that, but I knew how much he tended to worry about my health and I didn't want to get him in a fret.)

"Well, you might be okay by then, so we'll just leave it open," he said. "But now that you're on the phone, I might as well get your ideas on whom I should pick for Vice-President."

Now, I knew damned well he had probably made up his mind several weeks back, but I decided to go along with his cat-and-mouse game. As a matter of fact, this would be a good chance to smoke him out, the way our daddy would do it. Having already assumed it was Hubert Humphrey, I tried my old reverse-elimination gambit.

"I kinda like Senator Pastore myself," I said. "He made a damned good speech this evening."

He actually snorted when I said that. "Goddammit, Sam Houston, what in the hell's gone wrong with you? How could an Italian from a dinky state like Rhode Island possibly help me?"

"There's Adlai," I said. "He's got the egghead vote good and solid."

"Don't need him," said Lyndon. "With Barry Goldwater running, I look like a Harvard professor to the eggheads."

"Maybe you oughta get a Catholic like Gene McCarthy. He's awful strong in the Midwest."

"He's not exactly what I'm looking for. There's something sort of stuck-up about Gene," he said. "You get the impression that he's got a special pipeline to God and that they talk only Latin to each other."

"How about Mayor Wagner or Daley?"

"With Goldwater running, I don't have to worry about the big-city vote," he said.

"Well, hell, Lyndon," I said with a fake whine in my voice. "That leaves only Hubert, and you sure ain't picking him, are you?"

That really got to him. He didn't expect such a negative attitude. "Now what the damn hell have you got against Hubert?" he asked.

"Plenty, Lyndon," I said. "For God's sake, he's been fighting you for years. No one's bugged you more on civil rights; and look at the way he's always harping about the oil people. He's a damned maverick, Lyndon."

Now, that was a pretty extreme picture of poor old Hubert, but it really drew my brother out of that secret shell of his.

"Dammit, Sam Houston, you've got him all wrong," he

said. "Hubert's a good man. I've made a goddamned Christian out of him. He's gone along with me on a lot of things. And you can bet your bottom dollar he ain't no Kennedy man. He also happens to be a helluva good campaigner."

"He talks too much," I said.

"Don't worry about that," he said. "I'll get Muriel to keep him short."

"So you've already made up your mind," I said, smiling to myself.

"Not yet," he said, forgetting I wasn't some stupid reporter he wanted to string along. "I'm keeping it open awhile. I want to talk with some more people."

The moment he hung up, I called my friend and doctor, Colonel Pete Scoles, and told him to put all the money he could bet that Hubert Humphrey would be Vice-President. But Pete couldn't get anyone to bet him. They all knew he was my best pal and that I had probably given him some inside dope.

Meanwhile, Lyndon kept talking to people right up to the last moment, holding Humphrey in suspense until the day before he was nominated. Even after he informed Hubert by way of Jim Rowe, he pretended to "keep his options open." It was pretty good theater, though, a welcome distraction from a boring convention. And by "consulting" with everyone about his choice for Vice-President (scores of governors, mayors, senators, and janitors got personal phone calls), Lyndon flattered them into thinking their opinions really mattered, which is always good politics. "You might have a point there, George. I'll certainly keep it in mind, and I'm much obliged to you for telling me." Then George could go tell his friends —and the local newspaper—that the President himself had called him to get his views on Senator Peewinkle as a potential running mate. That's great stuff for people out in the boondocks, and it works pretty well with a few city slickers from places like New York and Chicago. No one's immune to the glamour of the White House.

Some people on Lyndon's staff thought he used the phone too often, that it was some kind of strange addiction. They simply didn't understand his technique. They took all his "trifling" phone calls at face value, not realizing that the mere act of calling was often more important than anything he had to say. It was his way of "pressing the flesh" through the telephone wires, always keeping in touch, often bragging on people, and storing up a lot of goodwill for some future date.

He may have done this by design at first, way back in his early years in the House, but it soon became almost totally unconscious, as natural to him as breathing. And his favorite breathing apparatus was a desk phone with forty-two buttons (Nixon has only six, so I must assume he's kind of short-winded). He also had plenty of other communicating gadgets, including a huge three-screen television console in his bedroom, with a built-in playback device that enabled him to see three network news programs simultaneously and to get a second viewing of any portion he desired. I'm told that Nixon has only one screen and that he never watches a newscast or public-affairs program—just Ed Sullivan and an occasional ball game. As Zephyr would say, "Curiosity will never kill that cat."

Except for the artificial suspense about the Vice-Presidency, all cleverly managed by Lyndon, the National Democratic Convention was even duller than I had expected. I knew from previous conversations with him that Lyndon was hoping to make a strong and lasting impression with his acceptance speech, but I thought it was rather disappointing. Too many different writers had worked on it—Horace Busby, Willard Wirtz, Bill Moyers, McGeorge Bundy, and Dick Goodwin —and they had produced a patchwork of dull clichés that Lyndon read with a passion he didn't feel. Watching him on television from my hospital bed, I saw once more how poorly that medium works for him. He looked stiff and unnatural, and you could tell he was reading someone else's words. He would have been a lot more effective speaking off the cuff, as he would later on in the campaign.

Humphrey's speech was much better. Although frequently long-winded, he has a great deal of warmth and natural energy, and his sense of humor can be very sharp. I guess you would have to credit him with the most humorous remark of the fall campaign. Goldwater and Miller had been sarcastically referring to him by his full name, Hubert Horatio Humphrey, with a heavy stress on "Horatio." Then one day Hubert got back at them.

"Senator Goldwater thinks he has found a real issue in my middle name," he told his audience, "but in the spirit of charity, I must warn him. The hidden middle-name vote—all those youngsters blessed by loving parents with a middle name they choose to convert to an initial—may rise against him. He should beware of 'midlash.' "

Once he got out on the hustings, meeting the people face to face, my brother was also more humorous and forceful, especially when he spoke spontaneously instead of reading a canned speech. It was the old Lyndon stumping around the country from one city to another, reaching out to the crowds and shaking hands while his Secret Service men went crazy with worry. He made more than two hundred speeches in forty-five days of tireless campaigning, rushing back and forth from Washington to Detroit to Boston to Providence to Washington to Chicago to Denver—on and on in a fury of activity that exhausted the reporters who trailed after him.

The crowds were larger than any he had ever seen, larger than any other Presidential candidate had ever seen. He drew more people in New England than John F. Kennedy, and the mayor of Louisville told him what Oliver Quayle and the other pollsters had been saying all along: LBJ would give Barry Goldwater a terrible shellacking in all parts of the country.

Poor old Barry. He was the best campaign manager Lyndon

ever had. About a month before the Republicans' mass suicide at the San Francisco Cow Palace, my brother had told Marianne Means that he considered Goldwater the toughest man to beat, and she actually believed him—quoted him word for word in her newspaper column. When I started to tease her about it later on, Marianne blushed a little but insisted that Lyndon was probably sincere when he said it.

Knowing how he really felt about Barry, I still can't figure out how he managed to keep a straight face when he told her that, even though I've seen him bluff his way into winning a big pot in a poker game with only a pair of deuces in his hand. I wonder if he ever apologized to that sweet, trusting woman for pulling her leg that way. There were, of course, many other reporters who were bamboozled by Lyndon's appraisal of Barry.

Even more curious than Miss Means' momentary lapse was the Republicans' apparent conviction that Barry *was* the toughest man to beat. Obviously, they couldn't have anticipated the kind of campaign he would run: that he would argue against Social Security before a group of retired pensioners in St. Petersburg, Florida; that he would condemn the TVA as communism in Tennessee, which had prospered from cheap electric power; that he would talk against the antipoverty program in West Virginia and against reapportionment in a grossly under-represented city like Atlanta. That was indeed a strange performance.

I got to thinking that his speeches and travel plans were being prepared by the Democratic National Committee. I'm surprised he didn't propose compulsory birth control in Boston or that he failed to promise diplomatic relations with the Vatican at the Baptist Convention in Houston. Whatever a candidate shouldn't do, Goldwater was bound to do it.

With that kind of opposition, Lyndon could have stayed home without a moment's worry. The only thing that posed even a mild threat—and it was only temporary—was the Walter Jenkins affair, which suddenly hit the headlines in early October. I was back home in Texas when the scandal broke, but I heard most of the sad details from Lyndon and other people after the election.

Jenkins had gone to a cocktail party given by *Newsweek* Magazine on October 7, celebrating the opening of its new offices in Washington. It was one of those splashy affairs attended by several Cabinet members, two or three justices, and the usual number of senators, congressmen, and high government officials. Generally speaking, Jenkins avoided the day-to-day social whirl that makes the capital one of the drinkingest places in the country. But this seemed to be a pretty special occasion and, with Lyndon out of town, he apparently decided to relax a bit from his grueling schedule at the White House.

Exhausted as he always was toward the end of the day, the few drinks he took affected him more than usual. Leaving the party alone at about seven o'clock, he wandered over to the basement of the YMCA, about two blocks away from the *Newsweek* office. The newspapers later revealed that the "Y" was a fairly notorious hangout for homosexuals, and the District had a kind of peeping-Tom operation staked out in the basement and steam baths.

Although the specific accusation was never made public, Jenkins was arrested about a half hour after his arrival and later booked (along with an army veteran) on a rather vague charge of "disorderly conduct." A couple of days later an alert fink in the FBI leaked the story to some Republican friends, who later conveyed it to certain officials on their national committee. By the following Monday afternoon the news had gotten to Barry Goldwater, who chose to play it down at that particular moment.

That same day two newspapers that were supporting him (the Chicago *Tribune* and the Cincinnati *Enquirer*) got the story but decided not to publish it. On Tuesday evening the Washington *Star* finally learned about the rumor, which, if I know Capitol Hill, must already have been known to everyone in town. The very next morning, Charles Seib, the *Star*'s assistant managing editor, reluctantly decided to phone the White House to get some kind of clarification on the story.

The call was relayed directly to Jenkins' office by some assistant in George Reedy's press office. With the Washington rumor mill grinding away at full speed, Walter couldn't have been too surprised when it came, but I imagine he kept hoping the dirty mess would suddenly and miraculously fade away. Consequently, Seib's phone call was like a knee kick to the solar plexis. Caught in the worst crisis of his life, he had no one to turn to. Lyndon was out of town, campaigning in New York, and no other close friends were around.

In obvious panic, he rushed out of the White House and hurried to Abe Fortas' office. After listening to an incoherent outpouring of anguish and fear, Fortas called Clark Clifford, who joined them immediately. Realizing Jenkins was on the verge of a nervous breakdown (which, as I've said before, could have been caused by sheer overwork), they got him hospitalized shortly after noon.

Meanwhile, Fortas and Clifford made the rounds of Washington newspapers and major news services, and asked them —literally pleaded with them—not to print the story, simply on the grounds of common humanity.

"You can't condemn a man for one single moment of weakness," they said.

Perhaps believing they had been unduly put on the spot, two or three of the editors apparently felt compelled to tell Fortas and Clifford that the October 7 incident had not been an isolated incident. Jenkins had been arrested under similar conditions in 1959, and on that occasion he had been specifically accused of being a "pervert."

I have very little knowledge of such matters, and I have never considered it any of my business to pass judgment on what people do in their private lives. But there would have to be some incredible excruciating inner pressures or brutal outward demands to cause a man to sacrifice a whole lifetime for whatever momentary release he hoped to find. I can only say that the relentless pressures of his job and his intense dedication might eventually unsettle even the most stable human being.

In any event, the Fortas-Clifford pleas to the press were unavailing. Exactly a week after Jenkins' arrest, on the evening of October 14, United Press International sent the entire tawdry story over the wires to hundreds of newspapers, radio stations, and TV channels throughout the country. Most of the ensuing articles and editorial comments stressed the fact that he was the President's most important personal assistant, who regularly attended meetings of the National Security Council and was privy to the most confidential matters in the White House. There were tentative hints of the old McCarthy scare about sexual deviants being high security risks, but a wonderfully expressed statement from Lady Bird (who has remarkable grace under great stress) created a mood of thoughtful sympathy rather than rash hysteria.

In a brief statement from the White House, she said: "My heart is aching today for someone who has reached the end point of exhaustion in dedicated service to his country. Walter Jenkins has been carrying incredible hours and burdens since President Kennedy's assassination. He is now receiving the medical attention which he needs. I know our family and all of his friends—and I hope all others—pray for his recovery. I know that the love of his wife and six fine children and his profound religious faith will sustain him through this period of anguish."

Traveling with Lyndon to several rallies in New York State, George Reedy was besieged by reporters asking questions about the Jenkins case. Though advised of the persistent rumors and increasingly insistent inquiries by the press, Lyndon declined to make any comments one way or the other, no doubt feeling that Lady Bird's statement would suffice for the moment. On his arrival at the Waldorf Astoria Hotel that evening, he got a call from Clark Clifford and Abe

Fortas filling him in on all the bleak details, and they all subsequently agreed that Clifford should quietly request Jenkins' resignation.

When Reedy met with the press to confirm the whole story, there were tears in his eyes and his voice trembled with unabashed grief. He later told me it was one of the saddest duties he had ever performed. Though deeply affected by what had happened (one must bear in mind that Jenkins had been a close personal friend and long-time confidant) and also suffering from a nasty cold, Lyndon somehow managed to mask his inner concern when he went downstairs to the Waldorf's main ballroom to make a brief address at Cardinal Spellman's annual dinner in memory of Alfred E. Smith. He would have preferred to bypass the banquet but realized his absence would simply magnify the Jenkins affair.

Leaving the dinner before it was over, he went back to his suite for a series of long phone conversations with Fortas, Clifford, and other trusted advisers, meanwhile using a vaporizer to fight off the cold. After discussing a number of alternative courses and gradually eliminating the more drastic ones, he finally decided to ask for a prompt FBI investigation to determine if there had been any attempted blackmail or breach of security.

Then, of course, Lyndon had to face up to the possible political consequences of the sudden scandal. He had to decide almost immediately whether to call off his campaign until the matter quieted down or to go on as if it were an incident of no political importance. Perhaps an instant public-opinion poll would offer some clue as to what direction he should take. There was no one he trusted more in such matters than Oliver Quayle, who was conveniently nearby.

After getting a call around midnight at his home in nearby Westchester County, Quayle hopped into his car and arrived at the hotel a half hour later. Working through most of the night, he drafted the appropriate questions and organized a nationwide telephone poll that got underway the next morning.

By midafternoon he had gathered sufficient findings to indicate there had been no visible negative reaction to the Jenkins' case. LBJ could resume his campaign, including his scheduled Thursday night telecast speech on the Test Ban Treaty, without having to concern himself—at least publicly—with the problem of Walter Jenkins.

Even if there *had* been some furor about the arrest, it would have been immediately overshadowed by three events that were of much greater concern internationally. Within a space of forty-eight hours Nikita Khrushchev was booted out as dictator of Russia, the Red Chinese exploded their first nuclear bomb, and the thirteen-year reign of the Tory party in England came to an abrupt end with the election of Harold Wilson. Not even the juiciest Washington scandal could have competed for the headlines with any of these events.

Plowing ahead with perhaps greater intensity than before, Lyndon shuttled back and forth from Washington to all parts of the country on a work-and-campaign schedule that would have worn down most younger men. I was frankly worried about him, especially when I thought of his previous heart attack. But I wouldn't have tried to dissuade him because he was doing what he believed had to be done. Besides, the very act of campaigning was a necessary life tonic for him. Like most politicians, he has always felt a need for public approval, a need to reach out and actually touch some part of the huge crowds that were greeting him everywhere he went.

I have been with him on the campaign trail (between rallies) when he seemed totally exhausted—slouched in the rear seat of a car, his eyes glazed and his face gray and slack with a weariness that verged on sadness. Then, quite suddenly, as we got near the crowd that was waiting to hear him, he would straighten up and lean forward as the color flowed back to his face and an eager glint came back to his eyes. You would think someone had just given him a massive dose of adrenalin. And, from what George Reedy later told me, that's exactly what happened in the closing days of the 1964 campaign.

"I've never seen anything like it," said George. "The cheers and applause were like new blood in his veins."

It was, by all accounts, a triumphant October. His voice was somewhat raw from too many speeches and both hands swollen from "pressing the flesh" of thousands of supporters, he came home to Austin, Texas, on election eve. The evening was warm but rather cloudy, and the crowd at the State Capitol was the largest we had ever witnessed in that part of the country. When the college band had finished playing and the cheers had finally subsided, Lyndon made a short and simple talk that was completely "LBJ"—with not a single trace of a speech writer's stilted language.

"It was here," he said as his eyes looked beyond the crowd, "as a barefoot boy around my daddy's desk in that great hall of the House of Representatives, where he served for six terms and where my grandfather served ahead of him, that I first learned that government is not an enemy of the people. It is the people. The only attacks that I have resented in this campaign are the charges which are based on the idea that the Presidency is something apart from the people, opposed to them, against them. I learned here, when I was the NYA administrator, that poverty and ignorance are the only basic weaknesses of a free society, and that both of them are only bad habits and can be stopped."

That was the real Lyndon talking in his own personal fashion. He had made some far less effective speeches, especially on television, when he was obviously reading an awkward mixture of bad Busby and mediocre Goodwin, occasionally flavored with an unmistakable touch of corny Valenti. This particular speech at Austin was his own. But no matter how unevenly my brother performed on the speaker's platform, Goldwater's performance was so inept that he could afford an occasional lapse.

After this final speech on the steps of the Capitol, Lyndon

went to the Jim Hogg suite at the historic Driskill Hotel, where he had a few drinks with some local friends who listened with rapt attention as he speculated about the probable electoral count. As you might expect, he was pretty cagey about that.

"The way I see it right now," he said, "I figure Barry might carry Alabama, Mississippi, Louisiana, South Carolina, North Carolina, Virginia, North and South Dakota, Wyoming, Iowa, Maine, and Vermont."

Now, that's what I call a first-class job of poor-mouthing. Lyndon knew damned well (and he had Quayle's polls stuffed in his pockets to prove it) that Goldwater couldn't possibly do that well. He was merely setting him up for a huge shellacking, as the results the next night clearly demonstrated.

When the votes were finally tabulated, Lyndon had won by a margin of 15,951,320 votes, receiving 43,126,218 against Goldwater's 27,174,898. It was the greatest victory margin ever received by a Presidential candidate. It was the best percentage (61 percent) and the largest number of votes any President ever received. And of the 13 states that Lyndon said "Barry might get," Goldwater won only 6: Arizona, Mississippi, Alabama, Louisiana, South Carolina, and Georgia.

Proving that his coattails were exceptionally long, Lyndon helped elect 37 new Democratic representatives and 2 new senators. Bobby Kennedy was one of the 2 new senators who benefited from the Johnson landslide. There would now be a heavy Democratic advantage in both houses: 68 to 32 in the Senate and 295 to 140 Republicans in the House. Lyndon's effect on local elections was just as impressive: The Democrats gained over 500 seats in state legislatures around the country, giving the party control over 12 states previously in the hands of Republicans.

He was his own man now. He had been elected on his own personal strength. You could see it in his eyes as he scanned through some of the thousands of telegrams that poured into the LBJ Ranch on the banks of the Pedernales

River, where the family had gathered after getting the results on television. His victory clearly overshadowed Kennedy's hairbreadth victory four years earlier. He had, in fact, drawn a better vote than JFK in his native region of New England.

"How'm I doing?" he kept asking everyone with a big happy grin, knowing they would have to say, "You're doing mighty fine, Lyndon!"

Looking back on that joyous, triumphant night, it's almost impossible to believe that things would change so drastically in the next four years.

CHAPTER TEN

Troubles Ahead

Lyndon's inauguration was a big, gaudy, expensive bore—just like any other inauguration. I have been to several, and they all follow the same dull pattern. Thousands of politicians and their local fat-cat contributors who could afford the jacked-up hotel and restaurant prices converged on Washington to pay homage to their leader and possibly raise a little hell on the side. From all the advance publicity, I imagine they had visions of an exciting luxurious Roman holiday and casually rubbing elbows with the great and near-great and perhaps having a private little chat with LBJ.

On their home grounds most of them were men and women of considerable substance, acknowledged bigwigs boasting cozy first-name relations with the governor or senator—certainly their congressman. Then suddenly they were nobodys, mere ciphers lost in a mob of pushy, sweating bigwigs from other states, grumbling about their lousy rooms, lousy food, lousy valet service, lousy transportation, lousy tickets for the gala, lousy phone service, and lousy weather.

I particularly felt sorry for the women. They had spent

Vice-President Johnson and Hobart Taylor on September 27, 1962, as LBJ welcomes him to the Presidential Committee on Equal Employment Opportunities.

The Vice-President is host to the Shah of Iran during the monarch's visit to this country in August, 1962.

Teen-ager Lynda, Lady Bird, Lyndon, and mother at the ranch. Behind them stand the author and a family friend.

Lady Bird relaxing at the LBJ ranch after a horseback ride.

Lyndon during a conference in his Presidential office in 1964.

Lyndon, Luci, Lynda Bird, and Lady Bird at the ranch.

Lyndon with President John F. Kennedy and Jawaharlal Nehru of India during the latter's visit to the U.S. in 1961.

Lyndon on the Presidential campaign trail in 1964.

Lyndon and Sam Houston Johnson at the LBJ ranch.

hundreds (perhaps thousands) of dollars for lovely ball gowns that were immediately wrinkled and sometimes torn as they struggled through dense, unhappy crowds at every function.

"I don't know why I bought this damned dress," I heard one woman complaining. "Nobody can possibly see it in this mob. Even if I were naked no one would notice me."

Although Lyndon had publicly announced he would not wear a top hat or formal attire for the swearing-in ceremony, most of the men wore tails or tuxes for the various parties and the final gala ball. I had two top hats, neither of which fit me. One was too damned small, and the other seesawed on my ears until I stuffed the sweatband with a pound of cotton. The stiff celluloid collar sliced my Adam's apple to the core, and my pants were so tight around the crotch I was afraid to sit down. No wonder I was so grumpy.

Having suffered through previous inaugural "festivities" (when both my legs were sturdy), I had halfway planned not to attend my brother's inauguration. It's hard enough to get through those human traffic jams when you're perfectly healthy, but it can be hell when you're crippled like me.

Nevertheless Lyndon stubbornly demanded that I come. "How the hell will it look if my only brother doesn't show up?"

Aware that he had not invited some of our relatives, I decided to ask for a *quid pro quo*. "Okay, Lyndon," I said, "I'll come, but I think you ought to invite all our kinfolk. I wouldn't want to go without them."

It took a little pressuring here and there, but they all got invitations and a set of free tickets to all the events. As the President's brother, I got two extra sets of tickets and then purchased five more for some friends I had invited from Texas, three of whom were Republicans. I insisted on giving the Finance Committee my personal check because I didn't want them to think I was throwing my weight around. However, I was happy to learn later on that my check was never cashed

—all of which probably proves a moral I can't seem to recall. Perhaps it's something like: "It's always good luck to invite Republicans to a Democratic shindig."

I had, incidentally, come to Washington about two weeks before the big brawl. Lyndon had assigned me a very nice bedroom on the third floor of the White House and pointedly told me, "You're now sleeping in the room once occupied by Harry Hopkins, and I want you to act accordingly."

In view of Hopkins' exalted status as Roosevelt's chief adviser, one might conclude that he had suddenly created a special job for me. Far from it. He was simply telling me that I had to behave, that I was expected to follow a straight and narrow path worthy of a tenant in the nation's most prestigious house. And to make damned sure I wouldn't stray too far off that terribly slender path, he assigned a Secret Service man (Mike Howard) to hound my steps morning, noon, and night—especially at night.

My SS code number was 007—it really was! But that was about the only resemblance between me and Ian Fleming's lucky swinger. If James Bond had been chaperoned the way I was, he would have been a teetotaling bore without a woman in sight. My input of martinis, single or double, was drastically cut down. Not that Mike Howard actually stopped me from drinking or wenching; he never said a word of prevention. Yet I knew from long experience that Lyndon would be subjecting him to one of his grueling prosecutor's cross-examinations every day. "Where d'you and Sam Houston go yesterday? . . . Whom did he talk to? . . . What did he drink? . . . Who's he fooling around with . . . When did y'all come home?"

So help me Billy Graham, I swear Lyndon has the most persistent "big brother" complex of anyone I've ever known. He's been that way since early childhood. Always checking on his three sisters and only brother to make damn sure none of them get out of line.

Well, Mike was only 90 percent effective in guarding 007.

Once in awhile I'd slip out a back door and go off on my own. Weary of my confinement in the White House fish bowl, I would occasionally stay away altogether. Sometimes I would sleep at a hotel, but most of the time I would spend the night with my good friends, Glenn and Marie Wilson. They understood my need to get away from the world's least private home. On my return, however, Lyndon would be waiting to quiz me.

"Ain't seen you around for a couple days," he would say as we sat down for supper. "Where've you been keeping yourself, Sam Houston?"

"I spent the night at Dr. Wilson's place," I would say, knowing that Glenn and Marie were on his "approved" list, since he himself had appointed Glenn to the Senate Space Committee. "We got to gabbin' till all hours, and I figured it was too late to come struggling home at three or four in the morning, so I sacked out on their couch."

There were times when I was tempted to tell him I'd been kidnapped by a whore and confined in a cathouse for forty-eight hours, but I resisted the temptation. He doesn't take kindly to that kind of humor.

On one occasion, when I had been away for two whole days, I was spared a third-degree quizzing by the presence of A. W. Moursund, his oldest friend and personal adviser, who was having a private preinaugural dinner with us. Lyndon gave me the old fish-eye stare when I came in, but said nothing.

Though the conversation was fairly animated, I was rather quiet and withdrawn that evening—not out of any sense of boredom or discomfort, but simply because Moursund's presence reminded me of something I had done many, many years ago.

His brother, Johnny Moursund, had been a classmate of mine all through grammar and high school in Johnson City. We had been the top students and fierce competitors every year—perhaps too competitive. When we were about to have

185

our final exams in the sixth grade, we decided to study together. That afternoon I came home early, rushed through my chores, and immediately started to review my math problems, concentrating like mad for two hours.

When Johnny came over I said, "Let's study social science." Then it was spelling, then history, then English. And whenever he suggested math, I would say, "We'll do that later." Finally, it was bedtime for both of us. I had kept him from studying math, just as I had planned all afternoon. Well, the next day we both got hundreds in all our subjects, except for the eighty he got in math. My dirty little trick had worked. It had helped me beat him. But it wasn't much fun for me when I saw the tears brimming in Johnny's eyes. He broke down and cried all the way home, and I felt like hell.

That's what I was thinking about as I sat quietly across the table from Johnny's brother, A. W. Moursund, about forty years later. That tiny needle of guilt was still stabbing at me after all that time. I once told Lyndon about how I'd tricked Johnny Moursund, and he looked at me as if I were pulling a scab off an old sore.

"Why in the hell do you want to brood about a little old thing like that?" he said. "The past has passed, and there's no sense harping on it."

I imagine my ruminations about Johnny were prompted by the inauguration itself. Such events are like watersheds in our own personal histories. There is always a summing-up of the might-have-happeneds and the might-*not*-have-happeneds. And you see people you haven't seen in a long time. During that mad, hectic week, for example, I ran into Governor John Connally and he asked me to come along with him to some fancy party.

"I can't right now," I said. "I'm going to a party somewhere else. Why don't y'all come with me? It's over at Ralph Yarborough's suite."

I was only needling him, of course. I knew damned well he hated Senator Yarborough, and the feeling was mutual on

Ralph's part. "You go ahead," John said, not knowing if I were really serious. "I'm going to be pretty busy."

My guess is that Lyndon would also have been "too busy" to attend any party given by Ralph Yarborough. I can't remember what started the feuding between Yarborough and the Johnson-Connally faction of the Texas Democratic party, and I frankly don't care.

Ralph has always been a good friend of mine, in spite of anything Lyndon might hold against him. Connally probably thinks he's too radical, too solid with labor and the minority groups, too much of a maverick; but none of that can possibly affect my attitude toward him. In my book, he has been a fine senator and a loyal friend. Not long after LBJ removed himself from the Presidential race, Ralph took me to a luncheon meeting of the Texas congressional delegation —the same group I used to give Allen Shivers the shiv back in 1953.

In a short speech following the usual introductions, Senator Yarborough turned to me and said, "I'm happy and proud to have as my guest, Sam Houston Johnson, the man who quietly but effectively helped his brother become President of the United States. Most people—certainly those outside of Texas —have no idea how much he contributed to his brother's career. But I do. And I frankly don't think Lyndon would have gone as far as he did without Brother Sam behind him."

That was highly exaggerated praise, but I wouldn't want to embarrass my good friend by denying it. Accepting the comment with my usual gracious humility, I said, "That's the God's honest truth."

I didn't really say *that*, of course, but I did seize the opportunity to remind them of the occasion on which we maneuvered Governor Allen Shivers into a very tight corner, so that he talked himself out of a probable race against Lyndon in 1954. (I may as well confess that we were damned worried about that possibility.)

"The last time I was here in this room was on February

13, 1953," I said. "Two men were here who are no longer with us—Sam Rayburn and Allen Shivers. As you all know, Mr. Sam died just a few years ago. And Shivers is also dead —*politically*. We buried him right in this room, and he's stayed dead ever since. And most of you attended that political funeral."

They all had a big laugh on that one, especially Lyndon's old congressional colleagues, like Wright Patman, Jake Pickle, and a couple of others who had helped us plan the burial.

Curiously enough, I started musing about the Shivers episode right in the middle of Lyndon's inaugural address. It was not one of his better speeches, so I probably wasn't the only listener whose mind strayed to other matters. He was reciting another patchwork of stilted phrases prepared by too many different people, none of whom really knew how Lyndon thought or felt. With all the TV cameras trained on him, mercilessly recording every gesture and grimace, he seemed stiff and unnatural, straining too hard to be earnest and forceful in language that wasn't suited to him. Having only his television image by which to judge him, millions of Americans never got to know the real LBJ and no doubt wondered how he had ever become the most effective political leader in congressional history.

Somewhere along the latter part of his speech, he must have mentioned Mexico or Latin America because my vagrant thoughts suddenly focused on Judge Bob Bibb, a very wealthy businessman from Eagle Pass, Texas, who once got himself into a mess with the Mexican government back in 1951.

Bibb had an official government concession to feed hundreds of *braceros* who had been brought from Mexico to work on vegetable farms along the border. Like most other concessionaires, he had been feeding them canned beef surreptitiously imported from Mexican sources at prices lower than local ones. The average family in Chihuahua and Sonora purchased and ate that meat all the time; but, because of an alleged foot-and-mouth disease in their cattle, Mexican meat packers were not permitted to sell their canned beef in this country unless it was labeled "dog food" or "unfit for human consumption."

That's where the rub came. One of Bibb's disgruntled employees went to the local Mexican consul and showed him one of the cans clearly labeled "dog food." Then all hell broke. Formal protests were made, and the story made headlines all over the country.

Realizing he was in deep trouble, Bibb flew into Washington to try to save his government concession. When he called me at Lyndon's senatorial office, I quickly suggested he contact his local congressman (Lloyd Benson) or the senior senator from Texas, Tom Connally. An hour later he called back to complain, "Neither of those mealy-mouthed bastards want to see me; and, by God, I've given them both some fairly good contributions."

"Well, I sure can't promise anything," I said. "But I'll talk to my brother and see what he can do."

The following day Lyndon put in a call to the Labor Department to ask what action was contemplated, and he was told, "The case is out of our hands, Senator. It's an international incident and now entirely up to the State Department." That was enough for him. There was no point in getting involved at that level.

"You take over, Sam Houston," he said. "I'm taking a plane for Dallas in a couple of hours. Just let Bibb know that I tried but couldn't do anything for him."

The judge took it pretty hard when I told him, but he felt slightly better after a few drinks. "Well, anyway, your brother tried, at least. Those other bastards wouldn't even talk to me."

"You've got a lost cause," I told him. "Your name is mud with the federal government. You better put that feeding camp under someone else's name—some relative, maybe—and start all over again."

That's exactly what he did, and he somehow managed to

189

prosper more than ever. Since he was always a fairly regular contributor to the Democratic party, I thought he might show up at Lyndon's inauguration. However, I don't remember seeing him during that long and tedious week of overcrowded private parties and dull public events.

Only slightly less boring than most of the functions I attended was the big fund-raising "gala" that featured a lot of entertainers from Broadway and Hollywood, most of whom were obviously making "duty" appearances that they clearly resented. To make matters worse, the acoustics were bad, the staging less than mediocre, and the audience too self-centered to care what happened on stage. Johnny Carson was the master of ceremonies, and he came on like a tired balloon. I should confess, however, that my retroactive opinion of him is undoubtedly tainted by my angry reaction to one of his subsequent *Tonight* shows.

One of his guests was Mark Lane, the lawyer who continuously insinuated that Kennedy's assassination was a devious plot by wealthy Texans who had a lot to gain by having Lyndon in the White House. It was a backhanded, treacherous attack on my brother ("Who had the most to gain?"), and I frankly thought Johnny Carson, with his phony arched eyebrows and surprised innocent expression, was deliberately encouraging Lane to spill his dirty guts.

Im not in favor of precensorship in newspapers or television, but there ought to be some degree of public responsibility from directors of TV panel shows. When I saw that particular Carson program, I immediately asked for a full transcript, intending to show it to Lyndon. But, after considering the number of snide insinuations he had to face every day, I decided to spare him this additional irritation. It wouldn't have done any good, anyway.

Perhaps I am too harsh on Johnny Carson. After all, he did volunteer to m.c. the inaugural "gala," no doubt anticipating it would be a dull, thankless job. He was happily spared the exhausting boredom of the several inaugural balls that took place on the night before the swearing-in. Each one of them was like an enclosed Coney Island, with millions of fancily dressed Democrats trying to have a good time inside five brilliantly lit sardine cans.

The number-one ball was held at the Mayflower Hotel, where 2,417,126 women were trying to dance with 2,714,000 men. I was supposed to sit in the Presidential box near the orchestra, but I couldn't even get my cane inside the place. All the friends, relatives, and booklickers of the White House staff were jammed into that small space, so I quickly abandoned any notion of getting my assigned seat. I really didn't mind, however. I preferred to sit with my own friends at a table on the far side of the room. But when Bill Moyers and Jack Valenti spotted me, they sort of panicked.

"You've got to sit in the Presidential box," said Moyers, nervously glancing at my guests.

"That's right, Sam Houston," said Valenti. "It doesn't look right for Lyndon's brother to be way over here. People are liable to start talking."

"It's too damned crowded over there," I said. "With a lotta people I've never seen. I'd rather stay right here with my friends."

Well, they finally got the Secret Service people to clear out some of the hangers-on in the Presidential box, but I chose to stay where I was. It was better that way. Made it easy for me and my few guests to make an early getaway. We spent most of the night at Dr. Wilson's place. Larry King* was there and three or four of my Texas Republican friends, all of us enjoying the customary warm and gracious hospitality that Glenn and Marie always provide. It was the only party I fully enjoyed.

Considering my own boredom with the inaugural festivities, I imagine poor old Lyndon was doubly bored—particularly since he was forced to attend all of the functions and to keep

---

* A fellow Texan, whose recent book, ". . . And Other Dirty Stories, I highly recommend.

smiling throughout the whole damned extravaganza. You've got to have strong cheek muscles to keep grinning like that night and day. It finally wore him down, and Lady Bird's poor brother Tony had to suffer for it.

Just after Inauguration Day, when everyone else was hurrying out of town, Tony Taylor received permission to give a dinner at the White House for a few of his friends. It was supposed to be a small affair at first; but, as the word got around, Tony had to expand his guest list to accommodate the overflow. When Lyndon (in one of his more petulant moods) learned about the impending "banquet," he grabbed the phone and summarily canceled everything. He wasn't being stingy about the food, mind you—he just didn't want to make another speech!

With the inauguration ceremonies happily out of the way, Lyndon resumed his man-killing schedule in the Oval Office. Using all of his great legislative and executive skills, he channeled a virtual flood of major bills through various congressional committees and then through the House and the Senate. Most newspaper columnists and television commentators grudgingly admitted that he was doing an amazing job, yet they couldn't resist sniping at him whenever they could.

Theodore White has written: "A President is like a horse in a horse market—experts in political livestock examine him daily, poke him, pinch him, stare at him, prod him. The gait, the stride, the breathing, the sound are all examined minutely hour by hour, day by day, until one wonders whether any human being can stand up to the strain. Even a normal man entering the White House becomes abnormally sensitive under such attention, and Lyndon Johnson was certainly no exception to the rule."*

That is a fairly accurate observation, but I still think my brother was subjected to greater and different pressures than most other Presidents before him—some of which he brought

* *Making of the President* (New York, Atheneum Publishers, 1964).

upon himself, and others that were unjustly and cruelly thrust upon him.

First of all, he was a Texan—and that alone was enough to curse him in the eyes of a vast number of snob reporters throughout the country. His accent, his manner, his country-boy candor—all worked against him. Whenever possible, the press deliberately tried to picture him as an uncouth, prairie-town bumpkin, with no dignity or social graces. And once in awhile Lyndon seemed to be perversely and defiantly courting their disdain, as if to say, "Here's what I'm like—just an ordinary Joe from Johnson City—and if you don't like it, that's your problem."

So he playfully picked up a dog by his ears, and offended millions of oversensitive doglovers.

He pulled up his shirt and showed some reporters the big scar from his gallbladder operation, no doubt distressing a lot of squeamish old ladies.

He impulsively invited a Pakistan camel driver to visit him on the ranch, thus horrifying the striped-pants dandies from the State Department.

He went swimming in the nude in the White House pool, causing great concern among church groups.

He raced along a country road at ninety miles an hour, sipping beer from a can and scaring hell out of some women reporters in the back seat of his Lincoln Continental sedan.

Lyndon must have realized that each of these incidents would get a negative public reaction. Anyone with his keen sensitivity to popular attitudes would know. Therefore, I'm convinced that each episode was a conscious or subconscious act of defiance, a compulsive strain against the tight discipline that is constantly demanded of a President. He also wanted to show he was not ashamed to be himself.

However, the repeated and widespread publicity given to each of these events simply proves that the news media were all too ready to emphasize even the most trifling false steps by LBJ. Yet in all fairness to the press, I must say that Lyndon himself did a great deal to irritate them. He was often testy and petulant when there was no reason to be.

Take, for example, his annoyed reaction to the news photos that showed him kissing Senator Harry Byrd's hand at the funeral of Mrs. Byrd. That was a very touching gesture on Lyndon's part (he had interrupted his stay at the 1964 national convention to attend the burial), and it was certainly nothing to be embarrassed about. There has always been a tradition of men kissing men on certain emotional occasions in our part of the country, and we do it without the slightest concern that it might appear unmasculine.

But aside from his quick-tempered reactions to certain piddling matters that he should have ignored or simply joked about, my brother's main problem with the press was the so-called "credibility gap." There were several things he did— some of which were purely capricious—that caused White House correspondents to regard him with a certain degree of suspicion. He often hinted the opposite from what he meant; omitted important elements of some report; made outright denials of things that were obviously true; avoided direct answers to simple straightforward questions; needlessly kept the press guessing about certain things he planned to do; waited until the last minute to tell them where he was going; and often treated reporters as if they were "the enemy."

He was not, however, unique in this respect. Every President in our history has done the same things. Sometimes our national security has required them to make evasive statements or tell outright lies. And certain sensitive domestic issues have also demanded oblique statements. Franklin D. Roosevelt was often described as a devious manipulator by his enemies, and even his loyal friends admitted he occasionally "fudged" in dealing with Congress. Knowing what a cool, sophisticated pragmatist he was, I can imagine him smilingly admitting, "Of course, I lie when it's necessary"—and fully expecting you to understand.

At the outset John F. Kennedy felt he had to lie about

the Bay of Pigs fiasco (in fact, he had Adlai Stevenson deny our involvement therein before the United Nations); but when all the smoke had cleared away, it was poor old Adlai Stevenson who emerged as the devious culprit. Although Stevenson lost many of his idealistic supporters, Kennedy somehow survived that miserable episode as a kind of hero. That's when I realized that the Kennedy mystique—much of which is a product of a mesmerized press—can work the strangest miracles. Never has defeat tasted so sweet.

Lacking the sophisticated flexibility of a Roosevelt or Kennedy, honest Ike Eisenhower innocently (and I think mistakenly) admitted that he authorized the spy flights of Gary Powers over the Soviet Union. The experienced and cynical Russians undoubtedly expected and *hoped* Ike would deny any knowledge of the flights, thus making it possible to avoid an embarrassing confrontation. They would have been content to blame the CIA and to publicly picture Ike as a nice man who doesn't do such things. When he forthrightly admitted it, they had no recourse but to cancel his projected visit to Moscow.

Had this happened during Lyndon's administration, I am sure he would have followed the customary practice of denying any knowledge of an espionage mission, and the press would probably have left the matter rest without raising a big fuss. They are well aware these things are happening all over, and that the Russians and other dictators have a distinct advantage over us because they control their press and can suppress any news they wish. With two or three exceptions, most of the newspapers, magazines, and television networks in this country have shown a fairly responsible and discrete attitude in matters of such magnitude.

What the press clearly resented were Lyndon's occasional lapses on matters of no consequence whatsoever. Back in 1966, for example, he had obviously planned to make certain campaign appearances for gubernatorial and senatorial candidates in California, New York, and perhaps Illinois. The press knew the Secret Service had been dispatched to check security measures and local officials had been informed of his probable arrival time. But when Lyndon got back from an exhausting conference with the South Vietnamese leaders in Hawaii, he decided not to go through with the campaign schedule.

Then, rather than simply saying he was too tired or was getting a cold or Asiatic flu (any such excuse would have been acceptable), he told the White House press corps that he had never made any definite plans to campaign in the afore-mentioned states. I don't know what prompted him to say that, but it was certainly a mistake. It was, in a sense, an insult to their intelligence and a rather needless fib—especially since he didn't smile when he said it.

That particular incident left him wide open to charges of "credibility gaposis," on a matter that wasn't worth lying about. He also annoyed the press when he was cat-and-mousing on his choice of a Vice-Presidential running mate in 1964. Having already decided on Hubert Humphrey, he asked both Hubert and Senator Thomas Dodd to fly back from the convention, evidently wishing to give the impression that Dodd was also seriously being considered. Some of the reporters hurriedly filed stories on Dodd's background and even speculated on why LBJ might choose him. They probably felt like fools when they found out it was just a ploy, and naturally resented my brother for leading them up a blind alley.

As I said earlier, the press gave him a pretty rough time through most of his years in the Presidency, but he sometimes irritated them needlessly.

The Kennedys, on the other hand, have all enjoyed un-usually friendly treatment by many of the same journalists who bugged LBJ. The news media have always participated in the Kennedy mystique, sometimes to their own chagrin. For years they assiduously pictured Jackie Kennedy as the very essence of womanhood—the perfect, loyal, and regal Presidential wife, then the tragic, still-perfect widow. But when she suddenly married a rich old Greek who wears funny dark glasses and pants baggier than Lyndon's, the bloom was off the rose and some of the press did a complete turnaround. She's probably the same person she has always been, a very attractive, stylish woman; but our news media can't bear it when one of their heroines or heroes quite humanly fails to conform to their mythical image.

CHAPTER ELEVEN

The Vietnam War

As far as Vietnam is concerned, it is important to remember that Lyndon not only inherited a going war from Kennedy but he also inherited the men who were Kennedy's principal advisers—Dean Rusk, McGeorge Bundy, and Robert McNamara—all of whom supported the domino theory and, therefore, advocated a strong and continuing effort against the Vietcong.

Time and again, I have read and heard the repeated accusation that my brother had no rapport with intellectuals, that he disdained anyone with a fine education, especially if he had attended a fancy Ivy League college. Yet who could be more intellectual than Rusk, Bundy, McNamara, Rostow, Acheson, Fortas, and Ball?

Take McGeorge Bundy, for example. Can anyone be more intellectual and Ivy League-ish than a former dean of Harvard University, a direct descendant of the famous Lowell family, and the director of the Ford Foundation? Some people say he was the best brain in the Kennedy administration and was the only man who would dare argue with JFK. He had been so close to the President that some of the New Frontier people considered him a sellout when he stayed on with the new administration.

Obviously disturbed by such criticism, Bundy publicly stated, "Loyalty to President Kennedy and loyalty to President Johnson are not merely naturally compatible, but logically necessary, a part of a larger loyalty to their common cause."

I recently read an article that says he got pretty damned impatient with some of his friends and associates who apparently considered Lyndon too uncouth for their fancy tastes.

"You people are snobs," Bundy told them. "You don't understand Texans and you don't understand this man. He can become one of the greatest forces for good. This man has a gut power which gets things done."

From what I heard during numerous breakfast and dinner conversations with Lyndon and Lady Bird, (with an occasional visitor popping in now and then), I gathered that McGeorge Bundy had considerable influence in shaping our policy in Vietnam and in the Dominican Republic. He was also one of the administration's principal spokesmen for that policy. I particularly remember how forcefully he defended our stepped-up campaign against Hanoi in a televised debate on CBS against that leftist professor from Chicago, Hans Morgenthau.

Bundy had been to Saigon and knew what he was talking about, whereas Morgenthau could merely theorize from his ivory tower. Eventually, Lyndon and his "favorite hawk" had a slight falling-out, though not with respect to our stand on Vietnam. Some people say Bundy was pushing too hard to become secretary of state, but I imagine it was something more personal than that. Perhaps, as Aunt Jessie would say, he was letting his britches ride too high.

Whatever their final feelings may have been, I think you would have to say that Bundy was a fairly loyal LBJ man. I, for one, can't say the same for Robert McNamara.

From the very beginning Lyndon relied to a great extent

upon the expertise and advice of McNamara, who seemed deeply committed to a firm and aggressive policy in Vietnam. With his practical know-how as head of the Ford Motor Company, McNamara seemed to be a tough, pragmatic man who was able to view the war with the cool eye of a top-notch systems analyst. Flanked by his top aides, he made several trips to the battle front; and on the basis of his personal observations and careful technical calculations, he advanced some convincing arguments for a continued escalation of our military effort.

Adlai Stevenson once criticized McNamara for opposing the so-called "U Thant initiative with Hanoi" in 1964. He told Eric Sevareid that "McNamara flatly opposed the attempt. He said the South Vietnamese government would have to be informed and this would have a demoralizing effect on them; that government was shaky enough as it was. . . ."

I think that was a logical assumption on McNamara's part: Thant's plan would certainly have demoralized Saigon. But then McNamara tried to deny he had said it. That's precisely why I developed my doubts about him and subsequently wrote a long memorandum to my brother expressing those doubts.

Quite obviously, there were two McNamaras—one a hawk and the other a dove. It was fairly common knowledge in Washington that when he was around certain liberals—his Kennedy friends—McNamara would express all sorts of doubts about our course in Vietnam; but when he talked to Lyndon he was the gung-ho advocate of increased military pressure, always ready to prove his point with impressive charts and figures. He wanted it both ways, he wanted to be an agonized liberal and a tough pragmatist at the same time.

If he really felt this country was on the wrong course, he was obviously deceiving his President and doing a great disservice to all of us. But if he was actually sincere in his advice to Lyndon, he had no business expressing contrary views to dovish liberals in order to curry favor with the Kennedy crowd.

Although Lyndon took no immediate action on my memo castigating McNamara for his wishy-washy, double-dealing attitude and his covert loyalty to Bobby Kennedy, I am sure he harbored increasing doubts about him. None of us were unhappy when Lyndon finally greased McNamara's path to the presidency of the World Bank.

Of the three principal Kennedy advisers who stayed on after the assassination, Dean Rusk was much more consistent than either Bundy or McNamara—certainly more loyal to the Johnson administration. At no time did he waver in his support of an escalated war against the Vietcong, arguing again and again that the freedom of Southeast Asia hung in the balance. He stuck to his guns in the face of mounting opposition from his intellectual friends in the universities and foundations.

Perhaps history will show that Bundy, McNamara, and Rusk were mistaken in their advice to Lyndon and that Generals Westmoreland and Abrams underestimated the enemy's will and capacity to fight. But certainly no man can say that Lyndon Johnson acted arbitrarily, that he was shooting from the hip like a Texas sheriff. He not only consulted at great length with his inherited Kennedy brain trusters, he also sought the outside counsel of people like Dean Acheson, Clark Clifford, and Abe Fortas. Later on he had the benefit of the advice of a brilliant professor from MIT, Walt Rostow.

Anyone who ever talked privately with my brother soon realized that he was continuously weighing the pros and cons of every facet of the Vietnam conflict. Nothing depressed him more than the cruel statistics from the battlefields, the number of Americans killed every day, the number wounded, civilian casualties on both sides, the devastation of property —all of which made the day-to-day decisions more difficult to make.

Believing that his policies would prevent even greater casualties at some future date, he was naturally hurt and angered by the accusations of beatnik students, misled peace movements, college professors, and certain metropolitan editors who readily published cartoons depicting him as a bloody war-monger. It was some comfort to know that most Americans supported him, that the public-opinion polls showed heavy majorities in favor of stopping the Communists now; but the mass demonstrations and certain televised Senate hearings were bound to affect him.

His entire family—even I—was exposed to the same flack. Several times, as I was sitting in a restaurant or bar minding my own business, someone would come up to me and make horrible accusations about my brother. Two or three of them had obviously stoked their courage with liquor.

"Watch me tell that sonofabitch off," they would say to a wife or girl friend. "I don't give a damn who he is—President's brother or no President's brother."

Then I'd get the big grand-stand play, a bleary, mush-mouthed lecture on Vietnam with floppy gestures and a few threats. I would simply listen with a blank stare, knowing it would be useless and silly for me to say anything. One of them, a chubby middle-aged man with horn-rimmed glasses and thin frizzy hair, was pulled back to his booth by an embarrassed wife. She came over to apologize afterward and then shyly asked me for my autograph.

Professor James MacGregor Burns once invited me to Williams College in Massachusetts, where I was publicly insulted by a grand-standing member of the faculty, whose hatred of my brother seemed pathological. His attack was so vicious and personal that several members of the audience—many of whom probably shared his opposition to the war in Vietnam—hissed at him and finally forced him to sit down. It was a very tense and embarrassing moment for me, and just a bit frightening. Mike Howard, my faithful Secret Service chaperone, had not accompanied me on that trip, and, for once, I began to wish that he had. When supposedly mature people get so impassioned and virulent, you can never tell what may happen.

Two or three days later I mentioned the incident to Lyndon, not to point out any personal dangers but merely to let him know about the intensity of feelings aroused by the war.

"Stay away from those meetings," he told me. "You can't tell what kind of nuts are floating around these days."

"It wasn't as bad as you think," I said. "He was just blowing off steam. He's probably the meekest milk-toast in town."

"They can be the most dangerous ones," he said. "You can't be too careful about those quiet little guys. They often carry the deepest grudges—against everybody. So don't go taking any chances. After all, you're my brother, and that alone might be enough to make some crazy bastard go off his rocker."

I couldn't tell to what extent, if any, Lyndon worried about being assassinated (that's not the kind of thing he would discuss, not even with Lady Bird—particularly not with her), but I must frankly say I worried about it occasionally. In an atmosphere of hatred and violence, anything can trigger a sick mind, and there was certainly plenty of hatred simmering near the surface during my brother's last three years in the Presidency. Some of the television newscasts we saw provided close-up views of demonstrators, men and women alike, with pure venom shining in their eyes.

I realized the anger in most of them would not go beyond participation in mass insults and vague threats, yet their rabid feelings could easily influence at least one lunatic, one man out of a hundred ninety million. That's all it would take—another Harvey Oswald nursing who-knows-what kind of grudges against the world at large, some small insignificant nobody hungering for the instant prominence of a Presidential assassin.

One also had to consider the violent mood in Washington itself. Aside from the periodic invasions of peace groups who came to picket the White House, the ever-increasing racial conflicts added to an atmosphere of explosive tension. More than once, when the subject came up at breakfast or dinner,

Lyndon would wearily nod his head and look away with a baffled expression in his eyes.

Now that I've touched upon the problem of violence in Washington, I would like to comment on Richard Nixon's glib accusation in a campaign speech that Lyndon was responsible for increased crime in America, on the grounds that the President is obliged to provide a "public climate with regard to law." He blamed the incidence of crime and violence on my brother's alleged failure to create such a climate, and then confidently promised to establish a new climate in which there would be respect for law and order.

Nixon's "new climate" produced a 10 percent increase in serious crime throughout the country and an even greater rise in Washington, D.C., where there was a 63.4 percent increase in robberies, a 37.5 percent rise in murders, and 66.7 percent more rapes than the year before. I am certainly not blaming Nixon for this startling increase in crime, but I cite these statistics to show how irresponsible, opportunistic, and tricky-Dicky he was when he blamed Lyndon.

Some of the anti-Vietnam critics showed the same kind of irresponsibility when they insisted on calling it "Lyndon Johnson's war." It was conveniently forgotten, certainly de-emphasized, that my brother was continuing a policy set by John F. Kennedy and relying on the advice of the same experts Kennedy himself had chosen—Rusk, Bundy, and McNamara. He believed, as did Kennedy, in the so-called "domino theory," which held that if South Vietnam collapsed so would Thailand and the rest of Southeast Asia, possibly the Philippines, so that we had a vital strategic interest in South Vietnam.

On September 9, 1963, not long before he was killed, Kennedy had a television interview with Chet Huntley and David Brinkley, in which he definitely said he believed in the domino theory because "China is so large, looms so high . . . that if South Vietnam went, it would not only give them an improved geographic position for a guerrilla assault on Malaya, but would also give the impression that the wave of the future in Southeast Asia was China and the Communists." He also said the goal of American policy in Vietnam was the creation of ". . . *a stable government there, carrying on a struggle to maintain its national independence. We believe strongly in that. In my opinion, for us to withdraw from that effort would mean a collapse not only of South Vietnam but Southeast Asia.*"

I have italicized the latter portion of Kennedy's statement because it clearly demonstrates that Lyndon was not alone in his convictions about the war. I should also add that on the famous Gulf of Tonkin Resolution, perhaps the most crucial turning point, Lyndon won the unanimous support of the House of Representatives and the almost-unanimous support of the Senate.

When the U.S. destroyers *Maddox* and *C. Turner Joy* were attacked by North Vietnamese torpedo boats in the Gulf of Tonkin on August 2 and 4, 1964, Lyndon immediately ordered a retaliatory bombing raid on enemy torpedo boats and their bases and also informed the American people: "Aggression by terror against the peaceful villages of South Vietnam has now been joined by open aggression on the high seas against the United States of America."

Before the actual bombing, however, he phoned Barry Goldwater and got his public support for the projected air strike: "We cannot allow the American flag to be shot at anywhere on earth if we are to retain our respect and prestige." Then, of greater importance, he asked Congress to pass a joint resolution supporting his plan. Senator Fulbright was the floor leader pushing for the resolution which consisted of three basic points:

1. Congressional approval of the air strike;
2. Authorization for the President to take whatever further

steps he might deem necessary to combat aggression in Southeast Asia, with said "aggression" to be defined by the President himself; and

3. A provision stating the resolution would remain in force until the President declared it was no longer necessary or until it was replaced by Congress.

It was a fairly broad resolution, but not too different from others that had been passed since World War II. In this age of advanced technology, when super powers like Russia and China can strike without much notice to anyone, the President may need to make critical decisions and then act within hours—perhaps minutes. (That's why that scary "man with the bag" has to follow him around like a damned shadow.)

There were some misgivings about the scope and duration of the Tonkin Resolution, but the Senate readily approved it by a vote of 88 to 2, and the House gave its unanimous support, 414 to 0. On the day the document was signed, August 7, there was an attack on North Vietnam by 64 planes, which destroyed at least 25 PT boats and severely damaged 4 bases. The operation was considered highly successful by Secretary of Defense McNamara.

As everyone knows, Fulbright subsequently accused Lyndon of going far beyond the intended scope of the resolution, and his Senate Foreign Relations Committee was used as a convenient platform for continuous public assaults against our Vietnam policy.

To say that my brother was annoyed with the Arkansas senator (he was called "Halfbright" around the White House) would be a gross understatement. He occasionally reminded people that Harry Truman had called Fulbright "an overeducated sonofabitch" when he suggested (on Roosevelt's death) that Truman should step aside so that Secretary of State Stettinius might become President. Like many other officials around the capital, Lyndon resented Fulbright's intellectual Rhodes-scholar snobbery and his sarcastic questioning of Rusk, McNamara, and other Johnson supporters.

The often-repeated contention that the Tonkin Resolution had been stretched beyond its original meaning was firmly denied by Under Secretary Nicholas Katzenbach, a former professor of law at Yale, who told the Foreign Affairs Committee that the administration's policy of escalation was legally within the purview of the resolution. The learned Senator Fulbright naturally dissented from that view, once again reminding us of Truman's classic remark.

My brother was never too impressed with Fulbright, probably because he knew him too well and realized he was naïve and inept in the day-to-day maneuvering inside the Senate ("Hell, he can't even park a bicycle.") But I'm afraid he was sometimes overly impressed with certain other people who had more formal education than he had.

Bright, scholarly men like McNamara, Bundy, and Fortas had a lot of influence on his thinking because he regarded them as part of an intellectual elite. There was a hint of awe in his attitude toward them. He knew he was basically as smart as they were—smarter in some respects—but their way of talking and their whole educational background—Harvard, Yale, and all that—somehow got to him more than it should.

He had known plenty of book-loving ignoramuses with Phi Beta Kappa keys from fancy colleges, had seen them pull damn-fool boners on the simplest matters, yet he could suddenly be self-conscious about his own limited schooling at a small Texas college. I know he sometimes wished he had obtained a law degree, the same as I had, even though he could talk circles around some of the most prominent lawyers in this country. He once told me, "Some of those boys are so smart, they're dumb."

There were some lawyers, however, who commanded his total respect. One of them was Clark Clifford, who replaced McNamara as secretary of defense. Shortly after he was appointed to that position, Lynda broached the subject at one of our family dinners at the White House.

"Daddy," she said, "does Mr. Clifford know anything about military matters—or is that just a political appointment?" She glanced at Captain Robb when she said it, clearly indicating that it was *he* who had expressed doubts about Clifford's qualifications.

"Well, now," said Lyndon, giving his future son-in-law the cold-fish eye, "let me tell you a few things about him. Though there are some professional military people who think that only a military man knows about defense, I happen to feel that Clark Clifford knows a lot more about the Defense Department than most generals."

I could see Robb starting to squirm a little, but Lyndon pressed on. "He's the man who drafted the law reorganizing our military branches into one single defense department, and he had to know an awful lot about the army, navy, *and the marines* when he did it. So if anybody starts telling you he's not qualified, you can tell him I've got the best man I could possibly get for that job. And I'm damned lucky to get him."

Lynda looked at Robb as if to say, "So, there! My daddy was right after all."

Well, poor Captain Robb got red as a beet, tiny beads of sweat surfacing near his hairline, but he couldn't find his tongue to say anything. Everyone around the table grew embarrassingly quiet till I finally switched the conversation to some inane topic like candy addiction among nuns and square dancers, citing some wild statistics from *Reader's Digest*. My clumsy ploy got the good captain off the hook, though I don't think it necessarily endeared him to papa.

By the time Clifford came into the picture in March, 1968, we were bogged down in what seemed like an endless war. The Bundy-McNamara-Rusk-Rostow policies of semiescalation had not worked. Lyndon had been caught in limbo between the totally conflicting views of the doves and hawks.

He didn't want to tuck tail and run, as he was continuously urged to do by Fulbright, McGovern, Morse, Church, and others, but he still resisted the advice of some of his generals who wanted to bomb Haiphong and escalate the bombing of Hanoi.

I frankly think his biggest mistake was allowing himself to be caught in this nowhere position. He should have gone with the hawks for an outright victory or he should have pulled out. The kind of strategy we were following merely emphasized the grim truth of General McArthur's famous statement, "The U.S. should never get involved in a land war in Asia."

My personal inclination was to step up the bombing and to blast the harbor at Haiphong; but since I'm not a military man, I didn't want to bother Lyndon with my advice. He had too much of that, anyway.

I did, however, act as a sort of sounding board from time to time. Whenever or however I could, I would conduct my own little public-opinion polls among taxi drivers, waiters, clerks, insurance adjusters, government workers, tailors, bartenders, shoe-shine boys, and a few personal friends. The results weren't very encouraging.

One bartender expressed a view that I heard from many other people. "I'm bored with this war," he said. "I don't even read about it anymore. The reports you read today are exactly the same as I was reading three or four years ago. We keep fighting over and over again for the same goddamned little villages. We force them out one day, and the next night the V.C. are back again. What the hell kind of war is that?"

Some people—I suspect they total several million throughout the country—didn't even know who our enemy was. I heard them actually say that we were fighting South Vietnam!

Then, of course, many other individuals were disgusted by our inability to beat a "dinky little country nobody ever heard about." That was a constant refrain. "Here we are—

the biggest, most powerful nation on earth," complained a barber shaving the man next to me, "and we can't beat these little bastards who don't even have an air force."

And there were those who were convinced we had no business being there and called it an immoral, imperialistic venture. Nothing the Johnson administration did would ever satisfy them.

The country was undeniably becoming demoralized on the Vietnam issue, and the race riots and student unrest were making matters a lot worse. Knowing how depressed he felt about the growing discontent among the millions who fully supported him back in 1965, I didn't want to tell him the remarks I heard in my informal surveys. Actually, I didn't have to—he knew what they were. As a master politician with long experience in feeling the public pulse, he obviously knew that neither friend nor foe was satisfied with the bogged-down situation in Vietnam. But public opinion didn't bother him half as much as the casualty reports from the battlefield.

Almost every morning at three o'clock he would crawl out of bed, often without ever having gone to sleep, wearily slip on his robe and slippers, then go down to the Situation Room in the basement of the White House to get the latest reports coming in from Saigon. Even the loss of one American soldier (it was never that few) could bring on a mood of sadness and frustrated anger that would keep him awake the rest of the night.

Sitting down to breakfast with him and Lady Bird, I could always tell what kind of news had come from Vietnam. There would be dark hollows under his eyes, his face appeared somewhat gray and drawn, his shoulders slumped forward, his voice was slightly raspy. Pretending not to know he had had another restless, worried night, I would try to make light conversation about any silly thing that came to mind. It seldom did any good. His mood remained somber and uncommunicative.

Convinced, however, that the future of Vietnam was of vital strategic importance to this country and that we had to stay in there, Lyndon naturally couldn't permit himself to show any sign of weakness or doubt. Acutely aware of his responsibilities as Commander in Chief, he had to be outwardly confident, firm, and unruffled by the mixture of good and bad news from the front. He was also compelled to deal with a vast number of continuing domestic crises, any of which could drive an ordinary man up the wall. He pushed himself harder than ever, and the harsh, irritating pressures were felt by everyone on his staff—Jenkins, Moyers, Valenti, Reedy, Busby, and various secretaries who worked with or near him. Some of his staffers privately complained to friends in the press corps but never quite dared to confront Lyndon himself.

Fortunately, a few light moments offered some respite from the tense atmosphere around the White House. One of them was Lynda's wedding to Charles Robb. I had been hospitalized for an old and chronic ailment and consequently didn't plan to attend the ceremony, but friends of mine persuaded me to go.

"You might offend both Lynda and Lady Bird," one of them said.

So I left my hospital bed and really enjoyed myself in spite of a certain weakness in my limbs. The Washington *Post* subsequently reported that "only two people showed up in wheelchairs—Alice Longworth Roosevelt and Sam Houston Johnson." (That was pretty good company, I thought.) It was, as you might expect, a pretty fancy affair attended by diplomats, Supreme Court justices, politicians from everywhere, and numerous reporters.

As I watched my lovely niece coming down the aisle with her proud, smiling daddy, I couldn't help thinking of the many times I had been her baby-sitter and how, back in their less affluent days, my sister-in-law would say, "Oh, let's not bother with a baby-sitter. Sam Houston will be home."

Well, sometimes Sam Houston would get kind of bored sitting with his two lovely nieces, both of whom could cry up a storm when they had a mind to do so. When she was less than two years old, Lynda wouldn't go to sleep unless I let her crawl into my bed. And if I ever started snoring, she'd wake me up and tell me to stop it.

Now, as much as I loved that child, it was damned uncomfortable having her hands across my face or her feet dug into my back, so I had to devise a strategy to save myself. Knowing that Lady Bird and Lyndon preferred not to disturb her sleep when they got in—no doubt assuming it made no difference to me if she stayed in my room—I finally decided to take advantage of that squeaky ninth step my brother used as a signal to catch me coming in after a few drinks. The moment I heard the familiar squeak as Lyndon's heavy foot pressed on the loose board, I would reach over and pinch Lynda's thigh. She'd wake up immediately, screaming like a baby banshee.

Needless to say, Lady Bird would come running into my room with a worried look on her face. "Oh, Lynda baby darling, did you have a bad dream?"

"She's been crying most of the night," I'd say. "That little child really misses her mommy and daddy."

Then Lady Bird naturally would take her into their big bed, and Lyndon would have to put up with a pile of fingers on *his* nose. (*Moral of this story: Squeaky steps can work both ways.*)

I had to use that same tactic on another occasion when Lady Bird asked me to drive her down to the Mayflower Hotel because she had arranged to meet Lyndon for a political dinner. Lynda was obliged to come along since there was no one at home to take care of her, Zephyr having her day off. After depositing Lady Bird at the hotel, I started home by way of Dupont Circle, which I have always considered the worst traffic trap in Washington. It's impossible to navigate without going through a red light, one way or another. And, sure enough, it happened on this particular afternoon. Within a few seconds after I got through the circle, I heard a police siren.

Glancing toward Lynda, who had fallen asleep right close to me on the front seat, I suddenly thought of an "easy out." I reached over and carefully pinched her thigh, and she came out of her sleep like a wildcat, screaming her lungs out.

"I'm awful sorry," I said to the traffic cop when he poked his head inside the window. "Something's wrong with my daughter, and I've got to get her home right away."

"Sure, Mac, I know how it is," he said. "You go ahead. I've got kids of my own."

It took two popsicles and a root beer to quiet her down afterward, but it was worth every penny. (*Second moral: A pinch in time saves you from crime.*)

Such were my thoughts about Lynda as she came down the aisle in her lovely wedding gown, never having known how she had been used by that wicked old uncle sitting up front in a wheelchair, winking at her as she came by.

Another bright moment in that solemn period was the peacock episode that occurred at the LBJ Ranch during the 1967 Christmas vacation. This was preceded by Lyndon's whirlwind trip to Australia, South Vietnam, and the Vatican on his way home. The principal reason for the quickly planned trip was to attend the funeral of Harold Holt, the Prime Minister of Australia.

Lyndon stopped at my room the morning he learned that Holt had disappeared in the surf while swimming off Cheviot Beach in Portsea, Victoria. Lyndon and I had planned to go swimming together, but I knew something had gone wrong when he came in wearing his street clothes.

"Sam Houston," he said in a low, sad voice. "I've just lost one of the best friends this country ever had. He's stuck with us when a lot of other leaders have backed off. And I'm going to his funeral right away."

After attending the funeral rites and then visiting Thailand

and our troops in South Vietnam, he flew back to the U.S. via Italy, where he met with Pope Paul VI. Thousands of anti-Johnson demonstrators had gathered at the main airport in Rome, but he managed to out-maneuver them. Landing at a different airport, he took a helicopter to the Vatican, had a nice chat with the Pope, then rushed back to the airport and out of the country before the antiwar crowd knew what had happened.

"The Pope is a very great man," he told me on the morning after his return from that grueling seventy-two-hour journey.

"What makes you say that, Lyndon?" I asked.

"Well, first of all, he has a very profound understanding of our need to stop Communism in Southeast Asia and also a sympathetic appreciation of the kind of problems I'm facing here at home." He paused to let that sink in, then added this little aside: "Incidentally, the Pope said I was one of the great leaders of our time. What d'you think of that, Sam Houston?"

Of course, I told him I was quite proud of him and congratulated him on the general success of his entire trip. Then the moment he left my room, I grabbed the phone and called Glenn Wilson.

"I just want to tell you about the world's most exclusive mutual-admiration society," I said. "It stretches from the Vatican to the White House, but has only two members— the Pope and Lyndon Johnson." Then I told him about how they had bragged on one another, each one modestly accepting the other's high esteem.

Quickly recovering from the rigors of his long trip and no doubt cheered by the Pope's good wishes, Lyndon was in fine spirits on Christmas Eve. He gave me a beautiful waterproof watch with the Presidential seal stamped on the back.

"This watch won't lose you more than ten minutes a year," he said. "But maybe you'll want to lose them, anyway."

We all got an abundance of nice gifts from him, some of

which he had purchased during the trip, but he himself apparently failed to get something he'd been expecting. The next day, during our family Christmas dinner, he looked at Lady Bird with a look of puzzled disappointment.

"I can't understand it," he said. "Julia Benson apparently forgot me this year. She always sends me a box of candy—that wonderful homemade candy she's been sending me every Christmas since I first moved to Washington."

"Maybe she's been too busy this year . . . or perhaps she's ill," said Lady Bird, not quite meeting his searching stare.

"That's not true, mama," blurted Luci, realizing her daddy was genuinely disturbed by the possibility that he'd been forgotten by an old friend. "She didn't forget. She sent you a five-pound box, but I think mama hid it to keep you from putting on weight."

Caught totally off guard by Luci's outburst, Lady Bird tried to pass it off as a harmless joke, but Lyndon didn't completely accept it in that vein.

"You had no business doing that, Bird," he said with a hint of controlled annoyance. "I want you to bring me that candy right now. That's not only deceit—it's a damned fraud. I'll take care of my own weight problem." Then, noticing a slight frown on her face, he leaned over and kissed her cheek. "But thanks for worrying about me. I'll just eat one or two pieces," he said, stuffing three or four pieces in his mouth. "Sam Houston can have the rest; he could use a little weight."

"Don't need it," I said, palming my after-dinner drink. "This will satisfy my sweet tooth."

We were all in a high good mood as we boarded Air Force One to fly down to the ranch for a brief holiday. For the first time in months I saw Lyndon completely relaxed and apparently ready to enjoy himself.

"We'll have to do a little swimming," he told me. "Help you build up those flabby muscles."

215

I had been using the White House pool fairly regularly, specifically for that purpose, but I certainly didn't intend to go swimming in his outdoor pool at the ranch. Although the water was heated, it was cold outside during December, the temperature dropping to the low thirties most of the time.

"I don't think I'll want to swim, Lyndon," I said. "It's liable to be pretty cold out there."

"Not this year," he said, with a funny sly look in his eyes. "We won't have a bit of trouble."

About an hour later I found out what he had in mind. Looking out the window as we were passing over the LBJ Ranch at a decreasing altitude, Lady Bird gasped. "Good heavens! What's that?" she exclaimed. "Look at that horrible green thing at the ranch."

"Nothing horrible about that," said Lyndon, a broad grin stretching across his face. "That's Sam Houston's special Christmas present. It's a big plastic hood that fits over the pool, so he can go swimming on the coldest day and still not freeze when he comes out of the water."

I choked up when he said that. It was one of the nicest things he's ever done for me. But it wasn't an altogether perfect gift—at least not in a *technical* sense. We soon discovered that the vapor rising from the pool created a warm foggy atmosphere inside the big hood, making it impossible for us to see from one side to the other.

"Get me Abe Fortas on the phone," Lyndon yelled through a muffling cloud of steam. "He'll tell us what to do about this. He's got one over his pool."

Fortas' remedy was more complicated than my brother had expected. "He says we have to put a lot of big green plants around the pool. They absorb all the moisture."

Remembering Lyndon's chronic distaste for "jungle foliage," especially when it was indoors, I knew that was rather unpleasant advice from Abe. But he realized there was no other solution. "I sure hate to mess up this place with a bunch of damn plants, but I guess we'll have to," he said.

But that wasn't the only problem we had with my special Christmas gift. On the following afternoon, as I was returning from a brief shopping trip to Austin, I saw a mad flurry of activity around the big green hood. A squad of Air Corps enlisted men were chasing a bunch of peacocks in, around, and on top of the hood. Lady Bird's peacocks had gotten out of hand and were staging an all-out attack on the new plastic monster, pecking holes all over it and fluttering away whenever one of the soldiers came near them.

Working like demons under the frenzied direction of Colonel James Cross (chief pilot and commander of Air Force One), those poor men were trying to patch the previous punctures as new ones were being made by those lovely, angry birds. It was the funniest scene I've ever witnessed, but Lyndon apparently felt otherwise.

"Get those goddamned peacocks outa there!" he kept yelling, his shouts somehow rising above the excited babble of human voices and the shrill, piercing cries of the peacocks.

The siege was finally repelled by the colonel's valiant forces, who also repaired most of the damage that same afternoon. Sometime later, perhaps that same day, one of Lyndon's aides came to the guest cottage to invite me to a ceremony at the ranch house.

"The President is going to decorate Colonel Cross with a special medal," he informed me. "And he wants you to be there, Mr. Sam."

"What's the medal for?" I asked.

"For distinguished service on this recent trip around the world," he answered. "The President says he did a real fine job, and he's inviting everybody to the ceremony, including the press."

"Hell, that's not why he's getting decorated," I said. "That trip had nothing to do with it. Colonel Cross is getting that medal for chasing away those damned peacocks. From now on he's to be officially known as Colonel Peacock. Mark my words."

217

I am happy to say that the colonel's singular effort did not go unrecognized. Thereafter, quite a few people used the new title I had suggested. But never to his face. Now that he's a general (pursuant to my brother's urgent suggestion), I think that name has even greater dignity.

CHAPTER TWELVE

The McCarthy-Kennedy Challenge

In a strictly political sense, 1968 was undoubtedly the most unusual year in American history. An incumbent President was challenged for reelection by two prominent members of his own party; the President unexpectedly announced he would not seek reelection; one of the major candidates was assassinated; a third-party candidate seemed to have a chance of depriving either of the two principal parties of a clear victory in the Electoral College; and a man who had once been considered a "has-been" was finally elected President.

As for me, the year 1968 meant a sudden reinvolvement in the political life of my brother. Although the elections were several months away and Lyndon had not yet announced his plans, I was given some space at the Democratic National Committee and asked to serve as an informal liaison man between the committee and Lyndon.

The fact that my duties were not sharply defined obviously caused a certain unease at DNC headquarters. Some members of the regular staff probably felt I was a sort of spy or hatchet man, whose principal function was to pry into the internal affairs of the office. Others may have assumed my brother was just finding something for me to do, so that I wouldn't get bored with my premature retirement. This latter assumption may have caused John Criswell *not* to invite me to a meeting of state chairmen when I first moved into the committee, and his failure to do so created a slight problem with Lyndon.

On the first morning the chairmen got together, Lyndon asked me why I wasn't attending. "I haven't been asked," I said.

"Like hell you weren't," he snapped. "That's why I asked you to go over there. I want you in on everything that goes on."

In no time at all, he let Criswell know how annoyed he was, and within an hour I was ushered into the meeting. Later that afternoon the President dropped in on the group and made a special point of introducing me to the assembled chairmen.

"I don't know if he's been formally presented to you, but I just want to take a moment to get you acquainted with my brother, Sam Houston. He's been one of my close advisers for a long time, and I imagine he'll be contacting some of you later on."

Having never seen me till that day, State Chairman of Massachusetts Lester Hyman subsequently asked syndicated columnist Robert Novack about me: "What about this brother of LBJ's? He certainly seems to pull a lot of weight around the committee."

His interest aroused by Hyman's remark, Novack later got in touch with my friend Glenn Wilson, who set up a private off-the-record interview with me. (I'll have more to say about that subsequently.)

I specifically asked that the interview, which was held at Glenn's home, be kept strictly off-the-record because I had always believed in keeping myself in the background as much as possible. I could be more valuable and effective that way. As a matter of fact, I sent the following memorandum to all staffers on the national committee:

> If anyone should ask Criswell or others what position I hold with the committee, I suggest they reply: "Sam Houston was retired for physical disability several years ago and is now living with his brother at the White House. He has primarily been working in collecting material that will be put in the Lyndon Johnson Library in Austin. Since he has been associated with the President in most of his campaign for the past thirty years, we thought he might be able to help us some way while he is here. He has been spending some time observing what we do."

After observing the operations around DNC headquarters, I came to certain conclusions on how I should function in Lyndon's unannounced campaign for reelection, and I wrote the following memo to our chief of staff:

To: W. Marvin Watson
From: Samuel H. Johnson

Marvin, in talking with the President this morning, he suggested that I make calls during this weekend and, I guess, throughout the campaign. I want to serve where you think I can be most helpful to the President.

I think it best for me to make my telephone calls from my room here in the White House and not from the committee. I think that, as long as I am not identified with the Citizens' Committee, the Democratic Committee, or the White House staff, I could be more or less a listening post and be more helpful along that line. If people should have something negative to say about the committee, they can tell me about it without the feeling that I will run to Mr. Bailey or Mr. Criswell. The same thing applies to the Citizens' Committee and your office. I can tell them that I will be glad to tell

221

my brother about it, and so forth, and then all of it will be turned over to you for whatever you might think it is worth. I will talk with anyone you, Rowe, or Criswell want me to talk with, and report back to you on any of the conversations I might have. Then you can decide what the President should see.

I would like to have someone whom I can trust and whom I can use at night or early in the morning like I have been using Willie Day. I have dictated to her early and late in in order to get memos in. The only person that I can think of at the moment is Maurine Ray. She used to work for Charlie Herring and is now with Governor John Connally. I have not seen her in several years and, of course, do not know whether or not she will be available. If not, then I want you to suggest someone you think could listen to my confidential conversations without leaking anything to the press later on. If you think that Maurine would be all right, I would appreciate your asking John about it in the next few days. In the meantime, I intend to use Willie Day and will appreciate your giving me your advice this afternoon.

To a certain degree my memo to Watson was just a matter of protocol, an informal acknowledgment of his role in the chain of command. There were, in fact, quite a few things I didn't bring to his attention.

Actually, my attitude was that I ought to operate as much as possible in the background, because I felt that by staying away from the Democratic Committee, people could come and tell me things they wouldn't tell me there at the office. That's why I met with some of them at my suite at the Watergate Hotel, or in my room on the third floor of the White House. I really wanted to know what was going on —if there was any friction within the campaign committee; if there was any friction at the DNC.

Obviously people wouldn't tell me about it if I were there at the office, or in the East Wing of the White House. But they could come to me very privately and air whatever gripes they had without going through the various echelons of Marvin Watson and Jim Rowe and the campaign staff, or through John Criswell at the National Committee.

A great number of people would keep their mouths shut if they had to work through channels, but if they felt they had someone they could talk to privately and who had the ear of the President, they might be inclined to speak their mind. And that's actually the way Lyndon meant it to be. As a consequence, Lester Hyman realized from the introduction that Lyndon gave me at the meeting of the state chairmen that he could probably level with me about things he probably couldn't say to Criswell or anybody else. The same thing was true with Warren Spanneous, the chairman of the Minnesota committee. John Burns from New York was able to sit with me over a long period of time and level with me about particular problems—knowing I would respect his confidence, but that it was necessary for me to know what was really going on in his state so that I could keep the President aware of some of the voters' gut reactions.

I think Lyndon realized that in me he had someone who had no reason to hide anything. Very frequently, a President (or any executive) will have around him people who are afraid to tell him facts he doesn't want to hear. They're afraid he'll be annoyed with them if they are relaying bad news or if they pose problems difficult for him to resolve. With Lyndon's notoriously short temper a matter of common knowledge, some of his aides felt it was best not to broach any unpleasant subjects for fear of being put on the fire themselves.

In my position I didn't give a damn whether Lyndon blew up or not. My concern was to give it to him straight, to tell him what was actually on my mind and to relay, if possible, any feelings—good or bad—other people had on their minds. He knew I was a disinterested party, that I was his brother, had his best interests in mind; that I had no special ax to grind, and that he couldn't really fire me. You can't fire your own kin. I knew that. So I had this peculiar role, and it was soon apparent to people in the political structure that I was a sounding board placed close to the President. I might be able to get their views directly to the President, which they wouldn't be able to do through normal channels. And they surely must have realized from my long association with Lyndon in every critical situation he'd ever confronted, that I probably had a sixth sense about how he thought, because our minds operated pretty much the same way.

Complaints against him or Criswell, internal or external, were relayed by me directly to Lyndon. There were a number of gripes against Lyndon himself that I kept under my hat because they were complaints he couldn't do anything about. They would merely irritate him—perhaps make him mad as hell—without serving any useful purpose. This was particularly true after the Tet Offensive in late January and early February, when all the Monday-morning quarterbacks in America burst forth with the most severe criticism we had ever received.

The gloom around the White House at this point in time was so thick you could slice it with a knife. As Clark Clifford wrote: "The confidence of the American people had been badly shaken. The ability of the South Vietnamese Government to restore order and morale in the populace, and discipline and espirit in the armed forces, was being questioned."

General Earle G. Wheeler, chairman of the Joint Chiefs of Staff, was sent to Saigon to confer at great length with General Westmoreland, and he came back with a request for 200,000 more troops. This was in addition to the 525,000 already authorized.

To determine how Wheeler's new requirement should be met, Lyndon appointed a special task force headed by Clifford, the man who had been designated to succeed McNamara as Secretary of Defense. Other members of the group were Secretary Rusk, Secretary Henry Fowler, Under Secretary of State Nicholas Katzenbach, Deputy Secretary of Defense Paul Nitze, General Wheeler, General Maxwell Taylor, CIA

Director Richard Helms, and the President's Special Assistant, Walt Rostow.

Though they were not instructed to assess the *need* for substantial increases in men and matériel, but simply to devise a means for training and deploying the additional 200,000 troops, their frank and vigorous discussions inevitably touched upon that fundamental question. Thinking back on the deliberations of the task force he chaired, Clifford wrote the following in an article that appeared in the July, 1969 issue of *Foreign Affairs:*

> . . . All that is pertinent to this essay are the impressions I formed, and the conclusions I ultimately reached in those days of exhausting scrutiny. In the colloquial style of those meetings, here are some of the principal issues raised and some of the answers as I understand them.
>
> "Will 200,000 more men do the job?" I found no assurance that they would.
>
> "If not, how many more might be needed—and when?" There was no way of knowing.
>
> "What would be involved in committing 200,000 more men to Viet Nam?" A reserve call-up of approximately 280,000, an increased draft call, and an extension of tours of duty of most men then in service.
>
> "Can the enemy respond with a build-up of his own?" He could and he probably would.
>
> "What are the estimated costs of the latest requests?" First calculations were on the order of $2 billion for the remaining four months of that fiscal year, and an increase of $10 to $12 billion for the year beginning July 1, 1968.
>
> "What will be the impact on the economy?" So great that we would face the possibility of credit restrictions, a tax increase, and even wage and price controls. The balance of payments would be worsened by at least half a billion dollars a year.
>
> "Can bombing stop the war?" Never by itself. It was inflicting heavy personnel and matériel losses, but bombing by itself would not stop the war.

"Will stepping up the bombing decrease American casualties?" Very little, if at all. Our casualties were due to the intensity of the ground fighting in the South. We had already dropped a heavier tonnage of bombs than in all the theaters of World War II. During 1967, an estimated 90,000 North Vietnamese had infiltrated into South Viet Nam. In the opening weeks of 1968, infiltrators were coming in at three to four times the rate of a year earlier, despite the ferocity and intensity of our campaign of aerial interdiction.

"How long must we keep on sending our men and carrying the main burden of combat?" The South Vietnamese were doing better, but they were not ready yet to replace our troops and we did not know when they would be.

When I asked for a presentation of the military plan for attaining victory in Viet Nam, I was told that there was no plan for victory in the historic American sense. Why not? Because our forces were operating under three major political restrictions:

The President had forbidden the invasion of North Viet Nam because this could trigger the mutual assistance pact between North Viet Nam and China; the President had forbidden the mining of the harbor at Haiphong, the principal port through which the North received military supplies, because a Soviet vessel might be sunk; the President had forbidden our forces to pursue the enemy into Laos and Cambodia, for to do so would spread the war, politically and geographically, with no discernible advantage. These and other restrictions which precluded an all-out, no-holds-barred military effort were wisely designed to prevent our being drawn into a larger war. We had no inclination to recommend to the President their cancellation.

"Given these circumstances, how can we win?" We would, I was told, continue to evidence our superiority over the enemy; we would continue to attack in the belief that he would reach the stage where he would find it inadvisable to go on with the war. . . .

After days of this type of analysis, my concern had greatly deepened. I could not find out when the war was going to end; I could not find out the manner in which it was going to end; I could not find out whether the new requests for men and equipment were going to be enough, or whether it would take more, and, if more, when and how much; I could not find out how soon the South Vietnamese forces would be ready to take over.

And so I asked, "Does anyone see any diminution in the will of the enemy after four years of our having been there, after enormous casualties, and after massive destruction from our bombing?"

(The answer was, "No.")

Having probed all the grim aspects of the situation, Clifford said, "*And so, after these exhausting days, I was convinced that the military course we were pursuing was not only endless, but hopeless. . . .*"*

Lyndon had heard more optimistic views from Rusk, McNamara, Rostow, and some of his generals, but now he was beginning to feel the sharp cutting edge of Clifford's steel-trap mind. With the McCarthy people hacking away at him from all directions, the hawks demanding more aerial bombing, and the casualty figures mounting day by day, the bad news he got from his old and trusted friend (who had no ax to grind) was all the more depressing. His eyes were almost always bloodshot now, his face drawn and haggard. Nothing seemed to be going his way.

But even in the gloomy aftermath of the Tet offensive, there were a few light moments around the White House— small, trifling episodes that delivered a much-needed chuckle. One such occasion occurred on the night Marietta Brooks joined us for dinner in the family dining room.

She was one of Lady Bird's closest friends, a bright, attractive woman who had helped us in a number of campaigns and often served as chairman of the women's division. Her husband was a wealthy and successful architect who had received, perhaps, more than his share of government contracts

* My italics.

227

down through the years. Their home was one of the show-places of Austin, an elegant, very expensive house surrounded by lovely grounds anyone would envy. Perhaps it was a touch of civic envy that finally plagued them. It all came to the surface as we were having our coffee.

"Lady Bird, we're having the most awful time," said Marietta, giving Lyndon a side glance. "The government is going to put a highway right through our property."

"What government?" asked Lady Bird.

"The city government—right there in Austin. They're going to cut our place down the middle."

"Why, you can't let them ruin your home that way," said Lady Bird. "You've got to stop them."

"That's exactly what I intend to do, and Alice Kleberg says she's going to help me," stated Marietta, again glancing at Lyndon, who was pretending not to hear anything.

"Well, I'm going to help you, too," said Lady Bird. "You let me know what I can do."

That's where Lyndon came in. I knew it was coming, especially when Alice Kleberg's name was mentioned. Lyndon and I, you will recall, had both worked for Congressman Kleberg, the owner of the fabulous King Ranch that sprawled over four counties; and we had had our problems dealing with complaints from people who resented his successful resistance to public highways going through his property. The political implications were obvious.

"Now, just a moment, Bird," said Lyndon when she made her offer of help. "You're not helping anyone. You stay out of that. You've already got enough problems with Eartha Kitt."

He was referring, of course, to Miss Kitt's much-publicized outburst against Lady Bird during a meeting of the Women Doers, a group of fifty women who had met in Washington on January 18. Though they had gathered to discuss crime and violence among juveniles, Miss Kitt had somehow managed to drag in the Vietnam War. But I frankly don't know why my brother spoke of it as a "problem." I think everybody agreed that Lady Bird, with her fine instincts, handled the situation in the best possible manner. All the public sympathy flowed to her. Eartha Kitt was the villain of that little drama. Nevertheless, it was implicitly agreed that my sister-in-law would steer clear of Marietta's problem with the city fathers of Austin.

If memory serves me right, we all attended a movie that same night in the White House projection room. The picture was *Guess Who's Coming to Dinner?*, starring Sidney Poitier, Katherine Hepburn, Spencer Tracy, and a very pretty girl whose name I can't remember. Halfway through the movie, where Poitier snuggles up to his fiancée, Lyndon nudged Lady Bird and said, "Look at old Sam Houston squirming over there. Just like Spencer Tracy."

I wasn't squirming at all—couldn't care less about how people choose to lead their private lives—but I went along with his joshing, pretending to be more agitated than the girl's father up there on the screen. It got a few chuckles, but after awhile Lady Bird asked us to hush. She wanted to concentrate on the movie.

As we were leaving the projection room, the women walking several paces ahead, Lyndon told me the picture had reminded him of a conversation he'd had with Dean Rusk shortly before the news broke about his daughter's impending marriage to a young Negro from Washington.

"He came by to see me and offered to resign," said Lyndon. "He thought it might hurt my chances for reelection if he stayed on. So I told him to stop talking nonsense. His daughter's marriage had nothing to do with me or my administration. That was her own business. You know, Sam, I was pretty damned annoyed by his offer. He ought to know me better than that."

"Rusk is also naïve," I said. "I mean in a political sense. If you had let him resign, Lyndon, you really would have caught hell. Everybody would have naturally assumed that you'd pressured him into quitting. You would have made a lot of enemies and no friends."

Aside from such momentary diversions as the Poitier movie, Lyndon was working much too hard and finally had to get away from Washington for a short breather. At Lady Bird's suggestion, he planned a brief vacation in the Caribbean but kept his plans highly secret till the very last minute.

I was told about the trip during a formal White House dinner for state governors. (Having lost a lot of weight because of my accident, my tux no longer fit me, so I had tried to avoid the affair; but Lyndon thought otherwise.

"Just wear a dark suit and bow tie," he said. "I want you there, Sam. There'll be some governors you'll need to see later on during the campaign.")

Just after he introduced me, one of his aides took me aside and said, "The President asked me to remind you to get ready for the trip tomorrow."

"Remind me?" I said, "Hell, he hasn't told me a damn thing about a trip."

"Well, the whole family's leaving tomorrow morning."

"Where are we going?" I asked.

"We don't know yet, but the President says to pack some summer clothes."

Well, I knew there would be no point in asking my brother. When he's on one of his secrecy kicks, no one can pry anything out of him. In fact, his own secretary didn't know where we were going. Anyway, I felt sorry for the poor reporters who were going along: They weren't told about the summer clothes they would need. I really couldn't blame them for being annoyed and grumbling about "all this silly childish secrecy." They didn't get any happier as we hopped from one place to another, still not knowing our destination.

First of all, we stopped at Houston for a short visit to NASA headquarters, without having been told we would go there until we had taken off from Washington. Then, after Air Force One was airborne out of Houston, Lyndon told the correspondents he was headed for Beaumont, Texas, to speak at a political dinner for his friend, Congressman Jack Brooks.

I passed up the dinner in order to visit Paul Barnhart, a close friend of Lyndon's and mine, in Houston. Paul was among several close acquaintances who had met us when we got off the plane at Houston. In order to make sure that I joined the rest of the party the next morning to continue the journey southward, Lyndon took a very special photograph of himself and autographed it as follows: "To Paul and Virginia Barnhart from their friend, Lyndon Baines Johnson," handed it to Paul and said, "Paul, I'll give you this picture provided you bring Sam to the Beaumont Airport by 7:00 A.M. or I'll take it back."

Though Paul and I stayed up most of the night talking and I only got about one hour's sleep (Paul didn't get any), Paul had me up early enough to drink some coffee he had prepared and got me to Beaumont in time to join Lyndon.

After leaving Beaumont we were told our next stop would be Marietta, Georgia, though we were *still* unaware of our final destination. Needless to say, this had some of the older reporters fuming.

"What kind of crap is this?" one of them snapped.

At the Marietta air base we watched Lyndon inspecting the world's largest aircraft, and we were joined by Private Pat Nugent. Finally, just after we had taken off again, we were told that Air Force One was headed for Puerto Rico, where the President and his family would spend a brief vacation at Ramey Air Force Base.

"Jesus H. Christ!" said one correspondent. "I don't have a goddamned thing to wear in the tropics!"

Noticing the angry resentment on the faces of several other men, I wondered why Lyndon insisted on playing "I've Got a Secret" knowing it would inevitably antagonize the press. Later on, he would give me some rationale for his tactics, but it wasn't very persuasive.

Our landing at Ramey Air Force Base was smooth as silk, and Air Force Chief, General McConnell, commented on it in the presence of the U.S. Air Force's high brass, who were meeting there with Air Force chiefs from other countries.

"That was a mighty fine landing, Mr. President," said the general. "You must have an excellent pilot."

"He's not only the finest pilot around," said Lyndon, "but he also happens to be a great administrator." Glancing at me with that sly look he gets when he's up to something and wants a bit of moral support or approval, he added, "As a matter of fact, Colonel Cross is waiting around for the board to approve a recommendation for his promotion to general, and I want to tell you this, General: If I have to bump eight or nine or twenty men who happen to be ahead of him on the list of recommended people, by God, I'm going to see that he's a general before I leave office."

As General Cross will testify, Lyndon made good on his promise.

On the day following our arrival, I heard that a helicopter would be flying into San Juan and immediately asked for a lift, but my plan was nipped in the bud.

"I can't let you go into town that way," said Lyndon. "There are a lot of damn peaceniks down there, and if they see the President's brother stepping off an Air Force helicopter all hell could break loose. If you've got to go in, Sam Houston, you'd better go in a nonmilitary car with a civilian driver. And make it all on the q.t."

Later, as I sat in the sumptuous dining room of the most elegant hotel in San Juan, having a restful after-dinner drink and thanking the good Lord that I had never become well known to the general public, I sort of pitied my brother and his family. They were prisoners on that base, poor important shut-ins with no place to go. He could never get around like his anonymous brother, dropping into a nightclub or restaurant or just mingling with an ordinary crowd in a public place. His principal concern would be the thousands of antiwar demonstrators who had read about his presence in Puerto Rico, but even a friendly crowd could be a nuisance.

He did manage, however, to get in a few rounds of golf with his first son-in-law, Pat Nugent. I don't know precisely what they talked about as they strolled across the course at the airbase, yet it's interesting to note that a few days later Pat volunteered for an immediate assignment in Vietnam.

I'm not saying that LBJ pressured the boy—nor that he pressured Captain Robb, his other son-in-law, who also went to Saigon—but I certainly remember telling Lyndon that it was politically embarrassing to have them both several thousand miles away from the fighting while the sons-in-law of other people were getting shot at every day.

It's ironic that their marriages worked against them. Had they been married to someone else, they would have gone overseas according to the regular timetable. Now, if Lynda had married that actor named Hamilton (neither Lyndon nor I could ever remember his first name), the situation would have gotten rather complicated. He had a special deferment to support his destitute mother, who would have had a terribly hard time keeping that huge Hollywood mansion without his help. I really don't know how my brother would have handled a touchy matter like that.

It was my perpetual concern about the public-relations aspects of such matters that prompted me to suggest the re-enlistment of George Reedy. "We ought to get George back in here," I said to Lyndon shortly after I got myself settled at the DNC.

"Might be a good idea," he said. "What's old George been doing these days?"

"He's got a big-paying job in public relations," I said. "But when I talked to him yesterday, I got the feeling he wants to come back, especially now that we're getting our campaign ready."

"Okay," he said. "I'll fix it with Marv Watson to get him back right away."

Two days later George came by to ask me how he should announce his new position as "director of research." He was thinking of holding a press conference.

"Don't you announce anything," I told him. "You're liable to upset a few people if you hold a damned press conference. George Christian, for example—he might get the idea you're bucking for his job. Just take it easy, George. I'll see that you get the right publicity."

A few days later I invited Holmes Alexander, a conservative columnist but a loyal friend, to drop in at the White House for a chat. We spent a couple of hours in the solarium, discussing the approaching campaign, and then I mentioned George Reedy's return to the fold. Feeling as I do about George, I laid it on pretty thick, and Holmes responded in kind.

The following week Reedy came by to thank me. "Holmes Alexander's column yesterday is the best thing that's ever been written about me," he said. "Hope you'll let me return the favor sometime."

"Don't you worry about that," I said. "I'm a favor-asker from way back."

In that hornets' nest around the White House and Democratic headquarters, it was comforting to have a loyal ally like Reedy. I have in mind, for example, my strained relations with James Rowe.* Though there was no personal resentment between us, I found myself at odds with Rowe on two or three issues. Our most serious disagreement arose from a memo he wrote to Lyndon suggesting some sort of accommodation with Bobby Kennedy.

While we were having dinner that evening, Lyndon handed me the memorandum, saying, "What do you think about this, Sam?"

I read it hurriedly, no doubt shaking my head at every paragraph. "I don't like the idea," I said. "I'll prepare my opposing brief tonight. You'll have it in the morning."

* Rowe was ostensibly LBJ's campaign manager.

THE McCARTHY-KENNEDY CHALLENGE

Rushing back to my room, I dictated a long memo into a tape recorder, attempting to put the whole Kennedy political structure into sharp focus but still hoping to remain objective. It was, I'll have to admit, a very negative picture. But I didn't feel like pussyfooting on such a crucial matter. The next morning I placed the memo under my brother's napkin before he got to the breakfast table. He read it between cups of coffee, pursing his lips tightly as his eyes raced down the four pages. Then, with a curious glance my way, he shoved it into a coat pocket and said, "Let's keep this between you and me, Sam Houston. I don't want it circulated."

Knowing that Lyndon considered me overly antagonistic against the Kennedys, I also told him about an article that had been written about them by Gore Vidal, who was indirectly related to Jackie Kennedy. (They had shared the same stepfather at different intervals.) In a piece entitled "The Holy Family," which appeared in the April, 1967 issue of *Esquire*, Vidal had expressed these opinions about the Kennedys:

> The cold-blooded jauntiness of the Kennedys in politics has a remarkable appeal for those who also want to rise and find annoying—to the extent they are aware of it at all—the moral sense. Also, the success of the three Kennedy brothers nicely makes hash of the old American belief that by working hard and being good, one will deserve (and if fortunate, receive) promotion. A mediocre Representative, an absentee Senator, through wealth and family connections, becomes the President while his youngest brother inherits the Senate seat. Now Bobby is about to become RFK because he is Bobby. It is as if the United States had suddenly reverted to the eighteenth century when the politics of many states were family affairs. . . .

Commenting on the heavy influence of their father, Ambassador Joseph P. Kennedy, Vidal quoted Francis Morrissey, an old family friend whom Teddy later nominated for Federal District Judge *against* the opposition of various bar associa-

235

tions. (He later withdrew that nomination.) In any event, here's what Morrissey said about the father:

> During the Lodge campaign, the Ambassador told Jack and me clearly that the campaign would be the toughest fight he could think of, but there was no question that Lodge would be beaten, and that if it should come to pass Jack would be nominated and elected President. . . . *In that clear and commanding voice of his he said to Jack, "I will work out the plans to elect you President. It will not be any more difficult for you to be elected President than it will be to win the Lodge fight . . . you will need to get about twenty key men in the country to get the nomination for it is these men who will control the convention."**

About the well-known mystique of the "holy family," Vidal said the following:

> . . . Kennedy dead has infinitely more force than Kennedy living. Though his administration was not a success, he himself has become a world touchstone of political excellence. *Part of this phenomenon is attributable to the race's need for heroes, even in deflationary times. But mostly the legend is the deliberate creation of the Kennedy family and its clients.**

> Wanting to regain power, it is now necessary to show that once upon a time there was indeed a Camelot beside the Potomac, a golden age forever lost unless a second Kennedy should become President. And so, to insure the restoration of that lovely time, the past must be transformed, dull facts transcended, and the dead hero extolled in films, through memorials, and in the pages of books.

Neither Gore Vidal, nor I—nor anyone else, for that matter—had to tell Lyndon about the Kennedys. He knew them well enough. Consequently, it was no surprise to anyone

---

* My italics.

when he ignored Rowe's advice to "seek an accommodation" with RFK.

Nevertheless, he was still not anxious to buck the Kennedy machine head-on. This was especially true during the early weeks of 1968, before Bobby announced his candidacy. Bearing in mind this hands-off attitude, I had to explain LBJ's refusal to enter the Massachusetts primary in those terms. State Chairman Hyman wanted Lyndon to run or to allow someone to stand in for him. "Otherwise," he told me, "Mc-Carthy will walk away with all the delegates."

"Well, he can't enter the Massachusetts primary," I said. "That will only antagonize the Kennedy people. In order to oppose McCarthy, my brother would have to fight him on the Vietnam issue. And since Bobby now agrees with Gene, he would also have to attack Bobby—in his own state."

And when I further reminded Hyman that as an LBJ delegate he might have to vote against Kennedy at the convention, he began to see the light my way. "We're just keeping you off the hook," I said. "We need your support as state chairman of Massachusetts, but you won't be chairman very long if you start opposing Kennedys in that state."

I had to take a somewhat different stance when I talked to John Burns, State Chairman of New York. He wanted us to order Congressman Joseph Resnick to stop his attacks on Bobby Kennedy. As a candidate for the U.S. Senate in the Democratic primary, Joe was strongly supporting the administration's policy in Vietnam. Paul O'Dwyer and Eugene Nickerson (Bobby's man) were opposed to our policy, and Resnick was getting at Nickerson by leveling his guns at RFK.

"I know this is embarrassing for you," I told Burns. "But you can't expect the President to gag a man who is one of his most loyal supporters. But I will tell you this, Mr. Burns —whoever wins this primary will get our support, even if it's O'Dwyer. We've always supported the Democratic nominee, no matter what. Lyndon stood behind Adlai Stevenson against

Ike in 1952 although he was a sure loser in Texas. He knew it might jeopardize his own reelection in 1954, but he stuck with Adlai, anyway."

In my subsequent off-the-record interview with Robert Novack, I mentioned my talks with Hyman and Burns, asking him not to quote me, but after Bobby Kennedy announced his candidacy, I told him he could quote me directly.

Kennedy's decision to run was certainly no surprise to me. Just after the Tet offensive I told Lyndon that Bobby would be his chief opponent.

"Bobby wants Gene to find out how cold the water is before he takes a plunge," I said.

However, despite the bad news from Vietnam, Lyndon didn't think that either McCarthy or Kennedy were serious threats. The New Hampshire primary election was a real shock, and I saw no point in denying it. As the final results started flashing across the TV screen, I dictated the following memorandum:

To: The President
From: Sam H. Johnson

There is no question but what we suffered a defeat in New Hampshire, and I do not think there is really anyone to place the blame on. The only thing that could have been salvaged was the way the delegates were chosen. It appeared that too many Johnson men wanted to get their foot in the door, but you can't really hold anything against them for wanting to be 100 percent for Johnson. Therefore, I think New Hampshire served us well, inasmuch as we can profit by the mistakes that were made.

Bobby, of course, sent his men up to help McCarthy and probably helped finance the campaign. McCarthy's people feel they won it without Bobby and don't want to give up any credit for what they did. Bobby has the image of an opportunist, and from here on out will only solidify that image throughout the nation. One of the dangers is that in the long run it will bolster McCarthy's image considerably when Bobby tries to take his delegates away from him.

Congressman Resnick of New York is waiting with a letter challenging Kennedy to a debate on Viet Nam the minute Bobby makes his decision, *which will be no later than next week.* I think they have bitten off more than they can chew. . . .

My prediction was right on the button. Four days after McCarthy's victory Bobby made a bashful admission of his urge to be President. He didn't even wait for Gene to holler, "Come on in—the water's fine!" He took a big noisy plunge that practically forced McCarthy out of the water. Poor old Gene was cheated out of his moment of triumph. The headlines were grabbed away from him by one of the most skillful grabbers in the business. Some of the liberal columnists started calling Bobby a ruthless opportunist, and McCarthy's loyal, idealistic kids called Bobby every dirty name they could possibly think of.

I frankly had a grudging admiration for him. He had always known that politics was an ugly game and he played it according to the rules. His sudden grab for power (after telling McCarthy he would stay out) was a pretty sneaky trick, but that's how he saw the game. His cold, practical instincts told him he had to act quickly to stop the McCarthy boom, no matter how unethical or ruthless he might appear to the amateurs.

As much as I disliked him, I had to admit he was a real pro—a tough operator who could play ball with Mayor Daley and still somehow convince a few naïve journalists that he was a saint.

In his recent book,* Jack Newfield quotes RFK, his hero, as saying: "Gene just isn't a nice person. In 1964 he was pulling all sorts of strings trying to get the Vice-Presidential nomination. Hubert Humphrey had been his friend for twenty

* *Robert Kennedy, A Memoir* (New York, E. P. Dutton & Co., Inc., 1968).

years, and he was trying to screw Hubert. At the same time, Bob McNamara twice turned down the Vice-Presidency because he felt I should get it. This is the difference between loyalty and egotism."

That's what always amazed me about Bobby: He could be so self-righteous about other people's morals.

I also admired his strong stand against egotism.

But, whatever his tactics, the threat posed by Kennedy had to be met. The day Bobby announced his willingness to save the country, Lyndon asked me to call some of the state chairmen to get their reaction. One of the people I talked with was the Louisiana chairman.

"How's my brother doing down there?" I asked.

"Not worth a damn," he said.

"Well, they're not backing Kennedy, are they?"

"Hell, no, we're not!" he replied, almost snorting. "You couldn't sell me that long-haired runt on a Bible. All he's got is a bunch of hippies backing him."

"Could it be McCarthy?" I asked, knowing it could not be.

"Now, you know damned well we can't take him."

"Then it's got to be Lyndon," I said, not wanting to mention George Wallace, his probable choice.

"Not as long as he keeps shilly-shallying on this war business. We're getting shoved around all over the damned Orient," he said. "Take this here *Pueblo* incident, for example. Those little Korean bastards grab our ship and we just twiddle our goddamned thumbs. We ought to serve notice on them to return the *Pueblo* immediately or get themselves blown off the map. That's what you ought to tell Lyndon."

"Now, just a moment," I said. "I know exactly how you feel about that. I had the same reaction at first, but when the President explained all the different ramifications and all the dangers of a third world war, I thought a little different."

I doubt that I changed his mind, but at least I got some notion of the dilemma Lyndon was facing on our Southeast Asian policy. The *Pueblo* incident was especially ticklish. I first heard about it while I was splashing around the White House pool, exercising the muscles that had gone flabby after my second accident. The physiotherapist came by and told me he had just heard about one of our ships getting kidnapped off the North Korean coast. Scrambling out of the water, I went back to my room to get the latest reports on TV, all of which made me angry as hell.

When I saw Lyndon that night, I told him exactly how I felt. "We ought to tell those bastards to give it back in twenty-four hours or we'll bomb their whole fleet. And that's just for starters."

"Now, just a minute, Sam," he said, touching my forearm. "Don't you start flying off the handle. There's a lot you don't know about this. And you may never know. My first impulse may have been the same as yours, but I can't go around giving in to the first impulse that hits me. I'm the President of this country and my responsibilities are to the whole world on something like this. I've got to hold back on a lot of things that could lead to a third world war—or maybe the last one. So I'm not going to let myself start shooting without giving the matter a lot of good hard thinking."*

Lyndon was right, of course. He couldn't afford to act impulsively, and that's the point I tried to get across in my conversation with the Louisiana State Chairman. I remember discussing his tough, gung-ho attitude with Glenn and Marie Wilson when they came to dinner that night. Lyndon and Lady Bird had left to spend the weekend at the ranch, and I had the "penitentiary" all to myself. Zephyr fixed us a spectacular meal, and I asked one of the servants to turn on every light in the White House to celebrate the occasion.

Had Lyndon seen his home shining in a blaze of glory with that shameful waste of electricity, he would have blown

* During his campaign Nixon was extremely critical of Lyndon's failure to get tough on the *Pueblo* incident—but once he became President he was equally cautious when the North Koreans shot down the EC-121 observation plane in April. Now that he's in the White House, Trigger Dick is less apt to shoot from the lip.

his stack. I'm sorry I didn't take a picture of it. Had he been disposed to poke fun at himself, it would have made a nice Christmas card.

The following week President Truman took a brief vacation in Key West, Florida, and I asked Dr. John Adams, one of the White House physicians, to stay with him and attend all his needs. In view of the squabbles inside the Democratic party, I felt it would strengthen our hand to have HST on our side. I therefore asked Dr. Adams to get a reading on Truman's political pulse, hoping he might make a public statement backing LBJ.

"Feel him out on this McCarthy-Kennedy situation," I said. "And if you can nudge him a little bit now and then, sort of prime him, then maybe we can get him to hold a press conference in support of Lyndon. But we've got to make sure he can handle himself."

The following memorandum, which I gave to Lyndon on March 20, indicates how successful the Adams mission was:

Dr. Adams has been assigned to President Truman during his visit to Key West. President and Mrs. Truman and Margaret and Cliff Daniels have talked with him all during the day. He has kept me informed as to President Truman's thinking with daily phone calls and detailed letters.

1. President Truman is behind you 100 percent and indicates to Dr. Adams that the bunch who are running against you are "a damned bunch of smart-alecks." That includes Republicans, too. President Truman states: "President Johnson dominates party leaders too much and does not consult them enough." My reply to Dr. Adams was, "I wish that my brother did dominate the party, because if he did the party wouldn't be in the fix that it is now. The fact is that President Truman has it in reverse. He is doing more consulting and less dictating."

2. President Truman suggests that you "get off your high

horse and be one of them [that is, the voters]." My reply was that you didn't know how you could do more than you were doing in view of your spending 95 percent of your time making the Truman Doctrine a reality by your stand in Vietnam.

Dr. Adams detects a little hard feeling on President Truman's part because he has not been consulted, particularly with reference to Israel, which, of course, became a state under his administration.

Dr. Adams told Mrs. Truman that he was my doctor and had occasion to talk to me frequently and that among the things I had told him was, "Lyndon says he never realized what President Truman had to go through until after he became President, and that even though he has not felt like calling on President Truman much because he didn't want to burden him with all the problems he has before him now, he feels like he is consulting with President Truman every day through one of the great men of our time—Clark Clifford."

3. Mrs. Truman consulted with Dr. Adams at length in regard to the former President's health, and it was Dr. Adams who made the decision that Truman could very easily hold the press conference. . .

Dr. Adams has been listening and not talking; but if called upon to express an opinion, he has been told to say that you are just carrying out what he started in the original Truman Doctrine. I believe that Truman now has his fighting clothes on and wants to and could be used in any way you see fit. . .

Summation: I don't think any harm could be done by calling Mr. Truman and paying respects to the grandfather, since you are a grandfather, too. You might also bring your grandson to visit his grandson when convenient.

Only Dr. Adams and I were aware of his special mission (not even LBJ knew about it till it was over), but I must have slipped up somewhere, causing the good doctor to write me a short note that said: "The moral is: 1) Damn you, Sam Houston, you are going to get me fired!; or 2) Loyalty with honor for my Commander in Chief."

The Adams episode was not the only time I acted without Lyndon's prior approval. There were many such occasions. I particularly remember a press conference I called for him, specifically against his orders. In 1955, at the tail end of his recuperation from a heart attack—on his birthday, August 27—I arranged for him to meet several reporters and television commentators although his doctors had told him he wasn't ready.

It had been commonly rumored that he was an invalid, that his political career was over, that his aides refused to tell the press the truth about his condition. I knew we had to act, or the public speculation would indeed ruin him. Knowing he might object, I didn't tell him about the conference until an hour before it was scheduled.

"You'd better get dressed and shaved," I told him. "The press will be here shortly."

"Who in the hell told them to come?" he snapped.

"I did, Lyndon."

"Well, goddammit, Sam Houston, you know the doctors won't let me."

"Screw the doctors," I said. "What the hell do they know about politics?"

"I won't see them," he said.

He knew damned well I had him locked in. He had to see them, or they would start some wild conjectures about his health. It was too late to call it off. He finally saw them and did a fine job of answering all their questions—as I knew he could. But he chewed me out afterward.

"You acted against my orders," he grumbled.

"I've done that a lot of times," I said. "And I'll do it again if I figure it's for your own good."

"Damn you, Sam Houston, I'm going to fire you one of these days."

"You can't," I said. "You can't fire your own blood."

In any event, the Truman statement was about the only happy event in the gloomy month of March. But it didn't do much good. Less than two weeks later, Lyndon announced that he would not seek reelection.

CHAPTER THIRTEEN

Neither Seek nor Accept

I didn't realize this would be Chapter 13 when I started this book, but I guess the number fits the subject matter pretty well.

On the afternoon of March 31 I rode over to Baltimore in a White House limousine to meet with some Democrats who wanted me to discuss my brother's plans for the approaching campaign. Although he had not announced his candidacy, it was generally assumed that he would run. Since Lyndon was scheduled to make a nationwide address on Vietnam that evening, I had asked for an early dinner so that we might all see and hear the speech on television. Rumors had been floating around Washington concerning a new development on the war, but I also had a hunch that he might spring a surprise on the political front.

A well-known California congressman had told me on March 30 that some of his friends were ready to oppose Jesse Unruh, the political boss who was heading Bobby Kennedy's group in that state. (He himself preferred to remain out of the picture.) I told him we would probably make our stand in California, and he had gone there to line up an anti-Unruh faction.

"They'll be coming to Washington to see you this weekend," he said. "To discuss their strategy."

"Why don't you tell them to hold off awhile," I said. "Let's hear what Lyndon has to say on Sunday night—then we'll decide what to do out there."

I had no idea what Lyndon might do or say, but I didn't want those people (or the congressman) to expose themselves prematurely and unnecessarily. If my brother should suddenly withdraw, they'd be out on a limb with no candidate and Unruh itching to cut them off. I was halfway hoping Lyndon wouldn't run—had dictated a memo to that effect early in February that I discreetly kept to myself—but I didn't really expect him to pull out that soon.

Consequently, I was just as surprised as everyone else by his abrupt announcement at the end of his speech on March 31. The main body of that memorable speech was a surprise in itself.

First of all, he set a ceiling of 549,000 American troops in Vietnam, clearly stating that the only new men would be support troops previously promised. Wheeler's request for an additional 200,000 men was flatly rejected. Secondly, we would accelerate our training and equipment of Vietnam forces so that they could take over major combat responsibilities previously assumed by us. Third—speaking directly to Hanoi—he said we would greatly restrict our bombing of the north as an inducement to an immediate commencement of peace negotiations. He had been strongly influenced by Clark Clifford's serious misgivings about the war. Clifford's tough skepticism had finally undermined the faltering in-and-out optimism of Robert McNamara. If Lyndon had gotten rid of McNamara in 1965, replacing him with a man like Clifford, the Vietnam War might have ended by 1966 or early 1967—and my brother would have been unbeatable in 1968.

My friends in Baltimore clearly hadn't expected this sudden change in our Vietnam policy, and they most certainly didn't expect the clincher at the end:

"With America's sons in the fields far away," Lyndon said. "With America's future under challenge right here at home, with our hopes and the world's hopes for peace in the balance every day, I do not believe that I should devote an hour or a day of my time to any personal partisan causes or to any duties other than the awesome duties of this office —the Presidency of your country.

"Accordingly, I shall not seek, and I will not accept, the nomination of my party for another term as your President."

Well, there it was. He had given up politics for peace. There were tears in my eyes when I heard it—and a smile on my lips. I was relieved to know that he wouldn't have to put up with all the abuse he was bound to receive during a long campaign, with thousands of demonstrators insulting him, cursing him, calling him a warmonger and murderer —not to mention the potential danger to his life. He was out of it, free to pursue peace without the nagging pressure of partisan politics.

The Maryland Democrats who were watching the speech with me couldn't believe he had withdrawn. An hour before Lyndon spoke, I had been mediating between Governor Tawes, Attorney General Birch, and other bigwigs—all of whom wanted to be the big cheese. In a joking manner, I had figuratively drawn and quartered Kennedy and McCarthy, giving them each a limb. Now the picture had drastically changed.

"Does he really mean it?" one of them asked me. "I mean, irrevocably?"

"You heard what he said," I answered. "Neither seek nor accept. That sounds pretty definite to me."

"Did you know it was coming?" someone else asked, staring at me suspiciously.

"Didn't have the slightest inkling," I said. "You don't think I would drive all the way to Baltimore to waste your time and my own if I knew he was pulling out? To tell you the God's truth, I don't think he decided this till the very last minute. He's been thinking about it—for some time probably—but I doubt that he'd made a hard and fast decision until this evening."

I won't go into the public reaction to Lyndon's withdrawal. It's all widely documented elsewhere. But I should mention Senator McCarthy's statement that he now believed Johnson was sincerely interested in ending the war. I conveyed my own personal reaction in a memo that was delivered to Lyndon's bedroom early the next morning. I didn't think I could tell him face-to-face how I felt; it would choke me up.

April 1, 1968
6:30 A.M.

To: The President
From: Sam Houston
Last night was the happiest moment of my life.

I was having dinner with Victor Frankel and family when I heard the announcement. I felt just the same way that I felt that afternoon when I was in your room on Dillman Street and you received the message that Justice Black had put your name on the ballot. I dictated a memo several weeks ago stating that I hoped you would not run in '68.

I discussed my feelings numerous times with Dr. Adams, and Saturday morning I sent my trunk with all my personal material that I have saved through the years to my chaplain friend, Captain Sales, who volunteered to help me organize my work in connection with your library.

The few who sought to destroy you have destroyed themselves. I do not care to have any more to do with any campaign at any time. I know exactly how you feel, and you have shown again the great love you have for your country. I am proud to be your brother.

249

When I saw him at breakfast that morning, he reached over and pressed my arm, a hint of tears in his eyes. "Sweetheart," he said, "that was a nice memo you sent me. I appreciated it."

He had never called me "sweetheart" before, but when he said it there wasn't the slightest lack of masculinity in his manner. It was simply a note of brotherly affection. He had often called me "sonny boy" or "Sam" or, when he was in a mean mood, "Sam Houston." Whenever he used my full name, I knew he was angry about something. The same thing held true for my two nieces. The minute he called them "Lynda Bird" or "Luci Baines," those girls would either squirm or stiffen a little, knowing their old man was on the warpath again.

Since he so frequently addressed me with a gruff "Sam Houston," it was rather pleasant and amusing to be called "sweetheart" by my brother. Then, carrying his brotherly mood one step further, he insisted that I accompany him to Chicago, where he was scheduled to make a luncheon speech before the annual convention of the National Broadcasters Association.

"When are we going?" I asked.

"Right away," he said.

"I'll have to pack, Lyndon."

"You don't have time, sonny boy. We've got to take off in a few minutes."

Without even bothering to get my hat and overcoat, I hobbled after him out to the helicopter pad on the White House lawn. In less than twenty minutes we were headed for Chicago on Air Force One.

Leaning toward me as the plane skimmed over the capitol, Lyndon asked, "What should I tell these broadcasting executives? I haven't decided what to talk about."

"This being the first of April," I said. "I think it's pretty obvious what you should tell them."

"What do you mean?"

"Just tell them, 'APRIL FOOL! I was only joking last night. I'm going to run for President, after all.' Then you turn around and walk off the platform without saying another word," I said. "That will really set them on their ears."

He laughed, of course. And as the idea caught hold, we both started laughing and nudging each other. "Wouldn't that be a bitch?" he said, rearing back in his seat with a huge guffaw. "April fool! I can just see their mouths hanging open."

"You ought to do it," I said. "You really should."

Later on, as he was being introduced, Lyndon looked in my direction and gave me a sly wink, a big grin momentarily crossing his face. For a fleeting moment I actually expected him to do what I'd suggested. I'm sorry he didn't. That would have been a great gag and a perfect occasion for it.

Though I would have preferred the April fool ploy, I thought his speech was forceful and effective, much more natural than the bland sterile crap his speech writers generally produced. He made an even more forceful impromptu talk to a few reporters who came back to Washington with us. Because of the suddenness of our trip, the arrangements for the press corps were inadequate and some of them had to sit in the Presidential section of the plane. Furthermore, the press bus had broken down on the way to the airport, causing a long delay that put Lyndon in a grouchy mood.

Surrounded by nine or ten correspondents, he let loose with a scorching sarcastic lecture that stunned them, some of them getting tears in their eyes—either in anger or shame.

"Well, you fellows won't have me to pick on anymore," he began, referring to his surprise withdrawal from the Presidential race. "You can find someone else to flog and insult. And I want to tell you here and now that this damned credibility gap you've been harping about is something you've all created yourselves. . . ."

It was a tough, bitter scolding that made me squirm as

251

if I were one of them. Knowing how he felt about many of the political reporters, I shouldn't have been too surprised, but I must frankly confess I was. When I noticed the grim expressions all around me, the tightened lips and hard-set eyes, I wondered whether he should have allowed himself to vent his long-simmering resentment. In retrospect, I imagine he would have wanted to apologize to them. But that's not his way. He couldn't bring himself to say "I am sorry."

He was still in a sullen frame of mind when he was informed that Bobby Kennedy had sent him a telegram (released to the press before it was received at the White House) asking for an immediate appointment and expressing his "admiration" of Lyndon's decision to withdraw from the race.

"I won't bother answering that grand-standing little runt," he told one of his aides. "From now on I shall refuse to answer or comment on any telegram that is given to the press before it gets to me. And that's a standing order."

In that same "ordering mood," he snapped a few instructions to people at the air base shortly after our arrival, and I suddenly noticed they weren't responding with their customary alertness and precision. There was a certain drag in their manner that made me feel they were already regarding my brother as a lame-duck President.

It pained me to realize that he himself was still unaware of their changed attitude. He was no longer the total boss. To them, he was just another leader on his way out. Knowing how difficult it would be for a proud man like Lyndon to accept the lesser status of a lame duck, I went up to my room and bawled like a little kid who has just found out his father can't lick everybody on the block.

The following morning my secretary came by with some memos and letters that needed my signature. One of them was a thank-you note to Frances Levine, a very lovely Associated Press correspondent who had interviewed me the previous week. The second paragraph of the letter, which I had dictated two days before Lyndon's withdrawal, said the following: "In the months ahead I hope you and millions of others will help me maintain my quarters, as I have a great respect for the third floor of the White House and would like to remain here for some time."

I scratched through that paragraph and scribbled an arrow to a "P.S." that said, "Evidently my brother thinks that all of us should vacate, but thanks—SHJ."

The person most likely to benefit from the sudden turn of events was, of course, Hubert Humphrey. Although Lyndon was "officially neutral," we all knew he would throw his weight behind his loyal Vice-President when it became necessary. The President always controls the machinery of his own party unless he's politically naïve or indifferent— and you certainly couldn't say that about Lyndon.

In view of his many obligations to LBJ, I felt that Hubert should make some outward gesture of loyalty to my brother, something dramatic that would ease the depression Lyndon would inevitably feel. With this thought in mind, I called Warren Spanneous, the state chairman of Minnesota, and asked him to advise Hubert to start a "demand movement" for LBJ.

"I'm sure it won't change my brother's mind," I said. "He's undoubtedly determined to step aside. But I think it would make him feel better to know that thousands of Americans were *demanding* that he run again. And it can't hurt Humphrey one way or another; he'll still be Vice-President if (by some miracle) the 'demand movement' works—or, what is far more probable, he'll get all the Johnson support for making a generous and loyal gesture."

He asked if Lyndon was aware of my idea, and I said, "Of course not! He would chew my ass if he knew I was promoting something like this. But I'm doing it, anyway. It's not the first time I've acted without his permission."

Spanneous, with whom I had been coordinating our unofficial efforts in Minnesota, thought it was a fine idea and promised to call Humphrey immediately. Hubert was in Mexico on March 31, and he seemed genuinely affected by my brother's decision—but he never made a move to follow my suggestion. Perhaps he thought it would queer his chances for the nomination or that Lyndon would get angry at him. Whatever the reasons, my little plan died on the vine.

Several weeks before they went to Mexico—prior to Lyndon's withdrawal—the Humphreys had come to dinner at the White House. Hubert seemed a bit nervous that evening, less talkative than usual. Perhaps he was worried about the poor showing we had made in the Midwest polls, no doubt expecting my brother to make a harsh comment about it. (Although he had not announced his candidacy for reelection, Lyndon's name had been included in the polls—and McCarthy was doing better than expected.) Sure enough, Lyndon did bring up the opinion polls, but in a roundabout way. As we were having our dessert, he looked at me with a mock-serious scowl. He said he had been meaning to ask me about the situation in the Midwest. I'd given him the idea that it was all tied up for him, he said, but the polls did not seem to bear that out.

"Now, just a moment," I started to say, knowing damned well he was really digging at Hubert—that I was a mere foil. The old LBJ technique: using me to get at someone else.

"Now don't you go making excuses," said Lyndon, shooting a glance at poor old Hubert. He went on to tell me that Spanneous and others had promised to wage a big campaign out there and that he had expected much better results. By now, there were tears in Hubert's eyes, and his lips were trembling a little. He knew—and so did his wife Muriel—that my brother was actually needling *him* for failing to influence the Midwestern polls by a larger margin for LBJ. After all, Minnesota was his home state, and a Vice-President is supposed to pull some weight, at least in the Midwest. Realizing that Lyndon might go on in that embarrassing vein for another half hour, I decided to cut him short by switching the subject.

Just after dinner Lyndon excused himself to attend to some personal correspondence in his room, and he asked me to accompany him. (Lady Bird stayed behind to chat with Muriel and Hubert.) When we got up to his room I realized that Lyndon merely wanted to get a massage before going to bed. "I thought we might talk a little while I'm getting my rubdown," he said.

"If you're thinking about Hubert," I said, "I want you to know I felt sorry for him, Lyndon. You were pretty hard on him."

"Hubert can take it," he said, stretching himself out on a rubbing table.

"I know he can—but it would be easier for him if Muriel weren't listening," I said. "As a matter of fact, I've been wanting to discuss some strategy with him, but not while she's with him."

"Call him in here," he said. "Lady Bird can stay with Muriel."

When Humphrey came into the room a few minutes later, Lyndon appeared to be dozing as Chief Mills (a Naval petty officer) massaged his back.

"Senator, I've been talking about the campaign with the President," I said. "And I've got a few ideas he thought you might want to hear."

Glancing uncertainly at Lyndon, who seemed half asleep, he said, "I'd be glad to hear anything you have to say."

Recalling the days when he had fought my brother on civil rights and certain labor legislation such as the Taft-Hartley Act, I expressed the conviction that he had a natural "in" with all the liberal elements of the Democratic party, that they owed him a special allegiance.

"Now, we're expecting Bobby Kennedy to get in this race right soon," I said. "And he's going to be relying on support from these very same people. But you've got a more natural right to it, Senator—except that you haven't exploited it enough. You've let some of these damned fuzzy-brained liberals put you on the defensive. But you can't let them. You've got to call in these liberal friends of yours and get them in line—tell them the facts of life. You're going to have to convince them you're still as liberal as they are— *without* pussyfooting on Vietnam. You can't abandon Lyndon Johnson on that issue. You've got to back him and still prove you're liberal. . . ."

Humphrey kept glancing now and then at Lyndon, who simply went on pretending he was asleep. But from my angle of vision I could see a flickering smile on his lips.

"You might point out," I continued, "that you would be President if my brother should die, that they would have a proven liberal in the White House. . . ."

I went on in that vein for about a half hour, putting it as strongly as I could, without a single interruption from Lyndon. If I had said anything he didn't like, I'm sure he would have broken in with a gruff order for us to leave the room. "You two are ruining my rest," he'd say. "Go talk somewhere else." His silence was approval of what I was saying, and Humphrey undoubtedly knew it.

He was doubly certain when Lyndon mumbled, "Good night, Hubert. See you, Sam," as we left the room.

I don't know what steps Humphrey took to win back the support of his former liberal allies, but I imagine it was easier for him after Lyndon bowed out of the race on March 31, even though he had to maintain an LBJ stance on Vietnam. Once in awhile he would falter, he would seem to hedge, and my brother would have to let him know—directly or indirectly—that he was unhappy with such shilly-shallying.

Humphrey was lucky in one respect: He didn't have to face McCarthy or Kennedy in any of the remaining primary elections in Nebraska, Indiana, Oregon, or California. He had entered the race too late to get involved in any of these contests. He could build his strength within the LBJ organization, and let Gene and Bobby tear each other to pieces.

Having no further personal interest in the final outcome, I was able to view that strange duel with a certain detachment. McCarthy reminded me of Adlai Stevenson in his aloof disdain of the ordinary voter. He quoted a lot of poetry and used fancy language no one could understand, obviously pandering to intellectual snobs like himself.

"Gene doesn't seem to realize there are more working people than college professors," said Lyndon one evening as we were having dinner. "I don't see how he ever got elected to the Senate."

Bobby, on the other hand, was a practical nose counter from way back. He knew where most of the votes were, and he went after them like a Boston ward heeler. Lower-income voters (who were leaning toward Governor Wallace) hated McCarthy because he was a snob but seemed to like Kennedy because he could talk their language. But there was something about Bobby that aroused deep passions —pro and con—that seemed to polarize one group against another. People could be neutral about McCarthy—but not about Kennedy.

The reactions of Kennedy and McCarthy to the assassination of Martin Luther King offer at least one clue to the distinct difference in their political styles and personalities. (I remember discussing this with Lyndon, and we both felt the same way.) Robert Kennedy immediately announced to the nation that he was sending the family airplane to Memphis to take King's body back home to Atlanta. He and the entire Kennedy entourage went to the funeral and stood alongside numerous other politicians. I later heard that certain black leaders expressed great resentment against the political exploitation of King's death. Senator McCarthy, whose wife is a long-time friend of Mrs. King, also attended the final rites; but he stayed very much in the background, no doubt feeling that his presence might be considered political.

Though he was deeply affected by King's death, my brother felt he should remain in Washington, where there was still a great deal of tension following several days of rioting that had been triggered by the assassination. He asked Hubert Humphrey to act as his official representative.

Shortly after the funeral, McCarthy and Kennedy resumed their campaigns in what appeared to be a standoff, each side sniping at the other with increased and desperate fury. RFK won in Indiana and Nebraska, then McCarthy came back with a surprising win in Oregon. Then it was California, the state that could finish the hopes of either man. With much more ample funds, Kennedy seemed to have the inside track on election eve. But his victory, despite all the subsequent claims of great triumph, was a narrow one.

It was enough, however, to encourage Bobby to tell one of his aides, "Find out where Hubert's going to be. I'm going to chase his ass wherever he goes"—or words to that effect.

A few minutes later he went down to the ballroom of the Ambassador Hotel in Los Angeles to make his victory statement. I had been watching the returns on television in my suite at the Watergate Hotel, having turned off the sound in order to dictate a memo to my secretary on the final outcome. When I saw the sudden frenzy on the screen, the look of horror on every face, I turned on the sound and heard what had happened.

I am not going to say that I was overwhelmed with grief, because that isn't true. But I was saddened by Bobby's death just as I am saddened by the death of any man—friend or foe. My first reaction, however, was stunned disbelief.

Grabbing the phone, I called Richard Brockman—he's the son of David Brockman, an old friend of Lyndon's—who was staying in the same hotel. "Can you drive me to the White House right away?" I asked.

He agreed instantly, and we were on our way in just a

few minutes. There were no lights on in the family quarters when we arrived, so I assumed Lyndon was still unaware of Kennedy's death. I was correct in that assumption: He had gone to bed an hour before it happened.

When he was finally awakened, not long after we got there, he stared at us with total disbelief in his eyes. "Oh, my God!" he said. "Not again. Don't tell me it's happened all over again."

The next few hours were a kind of controlled bedlam. Reporters, photographers, and politicians swarmed into the White House. The phones were ringing constantly, and people scurried back and forth with anxious looks on their faces. Lyndon stood in the center of all the frenzied activity, his mouth set tight, his eyes clouded with concern.

"We've got to protect Ted Kennedy," he said to one of his aides. "That family seems to be cursed. This may be a plot or just another madman like Oswald, but I'm not taking any chances. I want the Secret Service to provide protection for every candidate—including Teddy Kennedy."

"But he's not a candidate," someone reminded him.

"That doesn't make any difference," he said. "I want him protected, anyway."

"The laws may not permit it, Mr. President. They're pretty specific about such—"

"I don't care what the law says! I'm going to have him protected if I have to issue a special executive order to do it. So you call the Secret Service right away."

As usually happened in such cases, he got his way without any undue fuss from the legal people.

Like everyone else, I thought the funeral was a very dramatic and stirring event. In some respects it was more spectacular than President Kennedy's funeral, especially the scenes that took place along the route to Washington. There was, however, a certain lack of privacy at times. I don't think they should have permitted the cameras to probe into the private grief of Mrs. Kennedy when she came into the church alone far past midnight. No matter how touching it was, I felt like an eavesdropper when the TV cameras focused on her, as if it were recording a scene for a Hollywood movie. Perhaps I'm squeamish and old-fashioned, but I feel there are some moments—even in the lives of prominent figures—that should be personal and free of public scrutiny.

Lyndon has often said that he wants a quiet funeral, without the usual fanfare, and that he prefers to be buried in the family graveyard at the ranch. I hope he gets his wish.

After this second interruption, the Democratic primary campaign was resumed under a cloud of unease and despair. The two assassinations and the President's sudden withdrawal from politics, all within a space of a few short weeks, had unsettled the party. The Democratic convention in Chicago, with its threat of violence by student radicals and adult demonstrators against the war, would prove to be even more unsettling.

Assuming he would stick to his guns on the crucial Vietnam issue, Humphrey had the nomination locked up before the convention started. Any attempt by him to back away from our commitments in Southeast Asia would automatically work against him. We all knew he was being tempted but nevertheless felt he would ultimately stay with LBJ. He knew, as did all the news media, that my brother still controlled the party machinery and that he was not about to accept the adoption of an anti-Vietnam platform or the nomination of a candidate who opposed his views. John Criswell would be handling the sound apparatus that's always so crucial in a convention. He could turn off or turn on the microphones on the floor, effectively squelching any moves by vocal dissidents to disrupt the proceedings. Congressman Carl Albert would be the permanent chairman—not quite as commanding as Sam Rayburn but certainly a capable parliamentarian.

Still undecided as to whether he would appear at the Stockyard Stadium for the big birthday party Mayor Daley had planned for him, Lyndon and a small group of staff members and friends flew down to Texas to follow the convention activities on television.

Our conversation was casual and lighthearted, but there was an edge of tough determination in Lyndon's manner. "I'm not going to let those smart-alecks take over that convention," he said, as we were nearing the air base at Austin. "I haven't worked all my life just to have my own party repudiate me at the last minute."

There had been some talk of his storming the convention (with Harry Truman at his side) if things should start to break apart—a sort of melodramatic last stand by LBJ supporters. I was frankly opposed to any such action, so I conveniently decided to stay in Austin with my sister and brother-in-law, Rebekah and Oscar Bobbitt.

"If they should suddenly decide to pull a stunt like that," I told them, "I don't want to be around to either lend my support or to throw a wet blanket on everything."

No one in the Johnson family wanted Lyndon to go to Chicago, especially after we saw the televised scenes of angry mobs milling in the streets around the major hotels. Mayor Daley had surrounded the convention hall with barbed wire and the police were prohibiting demonstrators from the surrounding area, and he had also planned for Lyndon to fly into the stadium compound by helicopter—but such security measures weren't reassuring enough for me. One quiet little maniac sifting through that maze, perhaps sneaking a badge from one of the delegates, could end my brother's life in a split second. The hurly-burly confusion of any political gathering offers a perfect cover for an assassin.

But aside from my natural concern for his safety, I had a vague fear that he might decide to let the convention nominate him if Hubert should suddenly falter. In that strange year of political upheaval, nothing would have surprised me. I was especially fearful of such a development when I heard Governor Connally hinting that he might nominate LBJ.

He was, of course, merely "keeping Hubert honest" on the Vietnam question; but in the heat and emotion of a Democratic convention anything can get out of hand. (Incidentally, it was during this period that I interviewed Aunt Jessie and heard her sharp no-nonsense advice to Lyndon: "You tell him to stay right there at the ranch, Sam Houston. He's got no business up there in Chicago. If he lets them talk him into running again, he'll get beat as sure as God made green apples.")

Realizing her feelings might be more widespread than we cared to admit, I shuddered at the notion of his waging a difficult, exhausting, and dangerous campaign and then finally losing. What could be more humiliating than losing to Richard Milhous Nixon?

With the tension beginning to build at Chicago, there were certain discomforting signs of an incipient revolt that could easily lead Lyndon to drastic action. Mayor Daley, whom the Kennedys had always courted despite the hatred he aroused among the most fervent Kennedyites, let it be known that he wanted Teddy to run. And Senator McCarthy offered to go along. To add fuel to the fire, the California, New York, and Wisconsin delegations were trying to stampede the convention into an abrupt recess.

Fearing a sudden turn, I repeatedly called our people at the ranch and kept hearing their reassurances that Criswell and Albert had everything under control. With their expert hands on the sound-system controls, they could cut off any rambunctious rebels from the Kennedy-McCarthy states. Sometime during those hectic sessions, I got a long-distance call from Senator Mark Hatfield, the Oregon Republican whom I would support for President against any Democrat except (possibly) my brother.

"What's happening out there, Sam?" he wanted to know. "Are those people a serious threat?"

"I don't think so, Senator," I said. "But you know us Democrats. We're like a bunch of damned crabs in a barrel."

The so-called "Teddy threat," which was blown up to major proportions by TV, never materialized. Early this year Ted Kennedy told a *Look* reporter that he never considered running. If that was so, why did he bother to set up a special command post under the skillful management of his brother-in-law, Steve Smith? I seriously doubt that they were merely testing their machine for 1972. I also doubt that an old pro like Mayor Daley would go out on a limb without some indication that Teddy might openly declare his candidacy. But, of course, they were practical enough to see that Lyndon's people had firm control of everything; that they had enough votes to give Humphrey the nomination on the first ballot.

As we all know, Hubert Humphrey got the nomination with votes to spare, and he accepted his victory with that familiar happy smile most people can't resist.

Lyndon stayed away. He didn't go to his birthday party.

Although he tried to mask his feelings, I knew how bitter he felt inside. He had hoped to make a graceful triumphant exit from public life—he had certainly earned it—but we all knew that wouldn't be possible in the hostile atmosphere that hung over Chicago.

Aside from the angry demonstrators battling the police downtown, there were a lot of diehard LBJ foes inside the convention hall itself. Democrats have always hollered and clawed at each other, but there was a certain meanness in this crowd I'd never seen before. Their mood affected everyone, even the supposedly cool, objective TV commentators.

In full view of millions of ABC spectators, Gore Vidal called William Buckley a crypto-Nazi, and Buckley called Vidal a "damned queer" and further threatened to bash his face. And out on the floor of the Stockyard Stadium, with all three networks focused on them, Mayor Daley and Senator Abe Ribicoff exchanged insults that went beyond the usual political muck. Not being a lip-reader (you couldn't actually hear him because the Illinois delegation's microphone was off), I don't know exactly what Daley said, but I'm sure it wasn't complimentary.

There was a mean, nasty climate inside and outside the stadium.

I was glad Lyndon stayed home.

With the convention out of the way, I resumed my visits and interviews with older members of the Johnson clan, tape-recording personal memoirs for the archives of the projected LBJ library at the University of Texas.

Lyndon's personal secretary, Juanita Roberts, had started keeping the "LBJ Archives" long before there was any talk about a memorial library. With the help of Dorothy Territo, an expert from the Library of Congress, Juanita had first organized his files for posterity back in 1957, and she was sometimes amusingly overprotective about the records that she stored in the Old Senate Office Building.

George Reedy, whose press office was at the Capitol, once asked her to send over Lyndon's high-school graduation picture for a background story he was preparing. Without a trace of humor, Juanita asked if Reedy had an air-conditioned vault in which to keep it! Flabbergasted at first, Reedy's assistant (Marie Wilson) started to say No, then suddenly remembered the office refrigerator.

"Sure," she said. "We've got a perfect place to store it."

When the picture was delivered a half hour later, Marie elaborately placed it on a plastic tray and set it on the second shelf next to a bottle of gin. "Any visitor can view it," she said, "if they've got the proper credentials."

I took a peek at it three or four times in one day—and poured myself a drink each time.

Juanita's compulsiveness about those archives became somewhat of a legend among us. An ordinary wire service item with a passing mention of Lyndon would be sealed in plastic and stamped as something of "archival value" with her accompanying initials, "MJDR," short for Mary Juanita Dugan Roberts. (Incidentally, those initials gave the Johnson staff its own personal "four-letter word.") In any event, we talked a lot about "archivality," a word that was coined by Bill Bramer, a staff member who was told by Juanita that she regretted to report that most of his letters to constituents—all signed by LBJ, mind you—would not be retained because they had no archival value.

Later on Bill wrote *The Gay Place*, a novel that won the Houghton Mifflin Literary Fellowship Award in 1961. Others who have won this award are Phillip Roth, Eugene Burdick, and Robert Penn Warren. But despite the literary talent he devoted to Lyndon's letters, good old Bill got MJRD'd right out of the archives.

Some of the staff may have been annoyed or amused by Juanita's single-mindedness, but we all realized she was intensely loyal and a fine secretary.

I wish now that she had been put in charge of preserving my daddy's watch. Shortly after his death, we were all gathered in the living room of the old family home in Johnson City. As we were deciding what to do with some of his personal belongings, Lyndon reached for his beautiful old watch, and my sister Lucia held his hand back.

"No," she said. "You can't have the watch. That belongs to Sam Houston now. Daddy wanted him to have it. We all know that."

It was an embarrassing moment for Lyndon, and I felt sorry for him. As a matter of fact, I wanted him to have it, because he was the older brother—but I didn't press the point for fear of antagonizing my sisters.

But as the years went by I would occasionally misplace Daddy's watch (it had also been my grandfather's watch), and the thought of ultimately losing it bothered me a great deal. Later on I was given a further burden of responsibility: Grace Tulley, FDR's secretary, gave me a silver cross that she had gotten from Roosevelt.

Finally, after a very practical evaluation of my life-long tendency to lose things, I decided to free myself of both bur-

265

dens. On Christmas morning, 1958, I wrapped the watch and silver cross in pretty red paper and gave them to Lyndon.

"I want you to have the watch," I said. "Daddy really wanted you to have it. Anyway, I'm liable to leave it somewhere."

He accepted it with a kind of sad smile; but when my sisters heard what I had done, they raised Cain with me.

"What's wrong with you," said Rebekah. "Why are you always kowtowing to Lyndon? Are you afraid of him or something?"

Well, they fussed on for awhile, but I finally made them see it my way. But, now, here's the damned irony of the whole story: The watch has apparently disappeared. When we started preparing the family section of the library, we couldn't find a single trace of it anywhere.

I found it difficult to tell my sisters about it, knowing how they would react. They are sometimes apt to be overcritical of Lyndon, but I guess most successful men have to expect a certain degree of petty criticism within the family.

However, such minor matters were of no consequence when you consider the really onerous troubles Lyndon had to face in his public life. Not even his lame-duck status could save him from the nagging tensions of the Presidency.

The Abe Fortas matter, for example, was still pending when Nixon won the election in early November. I won't bother to comment on his victory—too much has been written about that—but I will say that Lyndon was not exactly overjoyed.

When it became apparent that Nixon would be the Republican nominee for President, Chief Justice Warren had sent my brother a letter announcing his intention to retire from the Supreme Court, but there was an unusual hitch to his plan: He stipulated that his retirement become effective upon the confirmation of a new chief justice. Realizing that Warren had never liked Nixon, the Republicans denounced the "contingent retirement" as a transparent move to deprive Nixon of the chance to name Warren's successor.

To no one's surprise, Lyndon had nominated his good friend and adviser, Justice Abe Fortas, to replace Warren; but his choice of Homer Thornberry to replace Fortas was somewhat unexpected. Fortas' judicial qualifications were known to everyone, but Homer Thornberry's were somewhat less apparent.

He was one of Lyndon's oldest friends, whom I especially remember because he would always start laughing at my brother's jokes even before Lyndon got to the punch line. Aside from this rather amazing ability to sense what LBJ was going to say, I had no personal notion of his legal capacities. Having heard of the dual choice before it was announced, I immediately drafted a memo suggesting a procedure that might facilitate Senate confirmation of both men.

I urged, for example, that he submit only one name at a time. First of all, he should request Fortas' elevation to chief justice, simultaneously asking his old Southern friends on the Senate Judiciary Committee to give him some suggestions on the man to replace Fortas. Because of Fortas' liberal reputation, those Southerners might wish to oppose him—but they would go along with Lyndon if he gave them some indication that they could name (or approve) his successor. If they knew he had already picked Thornberry, *without* consulting them, they would naturally be resentful and hostile toward both men. He couldn't afford not to ask their advice.

Then, after he had gotten Fortas confirmed, he could pretend to give full consideration to their various suggestions —and finally reach the conclusion that Thornberry was the best compromise choice. I personally felt Judge Jim Coleman, former governor of Mississippi, would be a better choice.

I was, in other words, merely setting forth a familiar LBJ formula, and I had expected him to follow some variation of that formula. But, before I had a chance to give him the memorandum, Lyndon violated his own time-tested procedure and announced his dual nomination to the press.

The reaction was predictable. The powerful Southerners on the Judiciary Committee—old Senate collegues who had backed him on many other occasions or who had offered only token resistance on others—now felt they had been ignored and consequently balked. So did a number of senators outside the committee. Both nominations, which could have been confirmed if submitted in the aforementioned manner, went down the drain.

During a very pleasant trip to Nassau last summer, I struck up a warm friendship with Senator Mark Hatfield, who I hoped would become the Republican Vice-Presidential nominee. While discussing the Fortas-Thornberry nominations, he told me he would back LBJ on both nominations. Quite aside from his enlightened political views, he was extremely kind, frequently helping me in and out of my wheelchair. His wife Antoinette is also a wonderful person. Later on, in spite of strong pressure from the GOP high brass, he stuck to his promise and voted to confirm Fortas. You have to admire someone like that. I hope he becomes President someday.

Lyndon, of course, was bitter and a bit mystified by the Fortas-Thornberry affair. He simply couldn't get used to the fact that he was being treated like a lame-duck President who no longer had the power to pressure Congress into accepting his suggestions.

Perhaps it was just as well that he didn't succeed in elevating Abe Fortas to the position of Chief Justice. The subsequent controversy concerning Abe's dubious connection with the Wolfson Foundation (which forced his resignation) would have been doubly embarrassing for everyone, including my brother. I am sure Lyndon was totally unaware of the Fortas-Wolfson relationship, and it undoubtedly hurt him deeply to be deceived by an old and trusted friend.

The sudden eclipse of Abe Fortas' brilliant career was just

another reminder of the precarious status of any public figure: Even the high and the mighty are vulnerable. As I am finishing the last few pages of this book, we have witnessed the sudden fall from grace of Senator Edward Kennedy. Despite the family mystique and its great influence with the press, that tragic incident at Chappaquiddick incurred the disfavor and suspicion of the national press media. Even the circumspect *New York Times*, especially James Reston, was critical of the senator's belated explanation.

I have no personal comments to make about that sad episode, except to observe that the Democrats have been deprived of a leading contender for the Presidency in 1972. Senator Edmund Muskie now seems to have the inside track, but he could be challenged by Hubert Humphrey or Senator George McGovern—or perhaps a relatively unknown person who could come on strong at the last minute like Wendell Willkie did. Whomever the Democrats choose, you can rest assured that Lyndon will have his say.

He has been very quiet during the first four months of what the newspapers call his "exile" at the ranch. Wishing to give his successor a fair chance to launch his own programs, he has wisely refrained from any public comments on the Nixon administration. But when the customary honeymoon is over, probably in the early part of 1970, I would expect my brother Lyndon to come out of hibernation with a number of strong statements on domestic and foreign affairs.

No one knows more about the government of these United States than Lyndon Johnson, no one has a deeper concern for his country. And since he is not a naturally reticent man, it would be most uncharacteristic for him to remain silent.

We haven't heard the last of LBJ.

Index

INDEX